PRAISE FOR
THE GLITTER IN THE GREEN

"Fantastically informative.... *The Glitter in the Green* braids the cultural history and daunting needs and feats of these wondrous birds with vivid accounts of the author's sometimes hazardous, far-flung mountain, forest, and island expeditions.... Exceedingly well-researched and packed with fascinating lore, it should appeal to avid birders and general readers alike."

—*Wall Street Journal*

"Dunn combines an intense emotional response to the radiant appearance of each transfixing bird with a pervasive anxiety that many of the birds he witnesses are on the verge of extinction."

—*New York Review of Books*

"Dunn's vast love letter is as gleaming and mesmeric as its tiny subject. His travels to observe the often-elusive family Trochilidae take him from the smoky air of an Alaska besieged by wildfire, to coastal Santa Marta, Colombia. The book is packed with tidbits and anecdotes— Ian Fleming named his famous MI6 character after an ornithologist called James Bond; there was a nineteenth-century fraud of 'manufacturing' Frankensteined bird specimens to sell to collectors—and is as much an ode to our world writ large as it is to one of its most captivating birds."

—*Vanity Fair*

"Natural history writer, photographer, and hummingbird obsessive (within the first hundred pages he crosses both a bear and a puma in pursuit of this tiny, glimmering bird) Jon Dunn has written a book that is both an ode to hummingbirds and a remarkable piece of travel literature."

—*BookPage*

"Hummingbirds must be among the most beautiful organisms on Earth. Yet for anyone who has never seen one in the flesh, it is difficult to convey the psychological effects of a first encounter.... A good place to begin to understand the birds' dramatic pleasures is with this entertaining book. One of Jon Dunn's real achievements is his ability to conjure the plastic form and astonishing chromatic architecture of many hummingbird species."

—Spectator

"Full of natural history, quotes from early explorers, local history, and adventure, Dunn's chronicle of his hummingbird quests will make readers just as obsessed with these small, quick birds dipped in rainbows."

—Booklist (starred review)

"A natural history writer and photographer, Dunn travels up and down the full range of these tiny birds, which now live only in the Americas, from near the Arctic Circle to the tip of South America. He writes not only about how they live and are faring, but about their history as a subject of fascination and exploitation."

—Associated Press

"A worldwide travelogue examining some of the world's most charismatic and mysterious migrators."

—Revelator

"*The Glitter in the Green* contains astonishing photographs and stories about these rare and beautiful birds."

—Herald (Scotland)

"At times a thriller, the history of hummingbirds in art, religion, and superstition—past and present—is fascinating, enlightening, and entertainingly informative to those of us who are smitten with them."

—Bird Watcher's Digest

"In this book, British natural history writer, photographer, and wildlife tour leader Jon Dunn takes readers on a journey throughout the range of hummingbirds: from near the Arctic Circle to near-Antarctic islands. He encounters birders, scientists, and others as he unravels the story of one of Earth's most charismatic bird families. The birds, revered by humans, exist on a knife-edge, fighting for survival in boreal woodlands, dripping cloud forests, and subpolar islands."

—*Bird Watching Magazine*

"Natural history writer Dunn takes readers on a wondrous globe-trotting pilgrimage to seek out hummingbirds as their populations are threatened.... Dunn's vivid prose, balanced with just the right amount of detail, will captivate birders and non-birders alike."

—*Publishers Weekly* (starred review)

"Dunn chronicles his travels from his home in the Shetland Islands to the Americas in search of this alluring bird.... A mesmerizing, wonder-filled nature study that also serves as a cautionary tale about wildlife conservation."

—*Kirkus* (starred review)

"An engaging history of the species.... This inviting narrative describes the author's search for the rare Mangrove Hummingbird in Costa Rica, as well as others threatened with habitat loss in Cuba and Mexico.... Notably, the author takes care to consider the place of hummingbirds in the history, literature, and cultures of their locales. Dunn writes passionately."

—*Library Journal*

"Jon Dunn's book is an adventure-filled, continent-spanning travelogue. It is also meticulously researched. By carefully peeling back layers of history to find shimmering hummingbirds hidden within, Dunn has created essential reading to understand human obsession— past and present—with these remarkable creatures."

—Jonathan C. Slaght, author of
*Owls of the Eastern Ice: A Quest to Find and
Save the World's Largest Owl*

"Glittering gems of the Americas and nowhere else on Earth, hummingbirds lure Jon Dunn from Alaska to Chile in this whizzing travelogue of hummer natural history. In an adventure replete with pop culture and literary references, Dunn treks deserts and jungles, investigates a slaughter of hummingbirds for love potions, unmasks the real James Bond, and in Colombia sees an otherworldly hummer, 'like some enameled god fallen to earth.' The book is that exquisite."

—Dan Flores, author of the *New York Times* bestseller
Coyote America: A Natural and Supernatural History

"More than just an observant birdwatcher, Jon Dunn is a talented traveler and writer, capturing just the right details of people and place to make his hummingbird odyssey come alive. *The Glitter in the Green* is a vivid exploration of a dazzling subject."

—Thor Hanson, author of *Buzz:
The Nature and Necessity of Bees*

"This is more than a bird book, but still, it is. It combines one person's adventure with arguably the most spectacular group of birds in the world: hummingbirds! The immensely talented writer Jon Dunn follows these highly diverse jewels from Alaska, down the Americas to Tierra del Fuego, and weaves an environmental and cultural dialogue around these hummers and the human-dominated world they live in."

—Joel Cracraft, curator in charge, ornithology,
American Museum of Natural History

"Jon Dunn's wide-ranging journey underlines how hummingbirds' famous beauty has often blinded us to the deeper wonders of their daring, passionate lives."

—Jonathan Meiburg, author of
A Most Remarkable Creature

THE GLITTER
IN THE GREEN

Also by Jon Dunn

Orchid Summer
Britain's Mammals
Britain's Sea Mammals

JON DUNN

THE GLITTER

IN THE GREEN

IN SEARCH OF
HUMMINGBIRDS

BASIC BOOKS

New York

Para mi musa de los colibríes—sigue tu corazón, y disfruta el viaje

---

Basic Books
Hachette Book Group
1290 Avenue of the Americas, New York, NY 10104
www.basicbooks.com

Printed in the United States of America

Originally published in hardcover and ebook by Basic Books in April 2021.
First Trade Paperback Edition: May 2022

Published by Basic Books, an imprint of Perseus Books, LLC, a subsidiary of
Hachette Book Group, Inc. The Basic Books name and logo is a trademark of the
Hachette Book Group.

The Hachette Speakers Bureau provides a wide range of authors for speaking events.
To find out more, go to www.hachettespeakersbureau.com or call (866) 376-6591.

The publisher is not responsible for websites (or their content) that are not owned by
the publisher.

Print book interior design by Amy Quinn

The Library of Congress has cataloged the hardcover edition as follows:
Names: Dunn, Jon (Conservationist), author.
Title: The glitter in the green : in search of hummingbirds / Jon Dunn.
Description: First edition. | New York : Basic Books, 2021. | Includes index.
Identifiers: LCCN 2020038844 | ISBN 9781541618190 (hardcover) |
  ISBN 9781541618183 (ebook)
Subjects: LCSH: Hummingbirds.
Classification: LCC QL696.A558 D86 2021 | DDC 598.7/64—dc23
LC record available at https://lccn.loc.gov/2020038844

ISBNs: 9781541618190 (hardcover), 9781541618183 (ebook),
        9781541601413 (paperback)

LSC-C

Printing 1, 2022

CONTENTS

INTRODUCTION

THIS STORY BEGINS IN A MORE INNOCENT TIME, A TIME WHEN, whilst we maybe worried a little about pollution and saving the whale, most of us still had no inkling that our appetite for consumption and an easy life might have profound and far-reaching consequences for the well-being of the very planet upon which we lived. That era was the early 1980s, a time of unfortunate hairstyles, recording mixtapes from the Sunday chart show on Radio 1, and a day trip to London with my mother on a Trathens coach.

This, in itself, was a notable event. We rarely, if ever, left the boundaries of southwest England. Other families took themselves further afield, but we only ever went west, back to my grandmother's house in Cornwall. London was unthinkably foreign and had, in my mind, assumed a dangerous presence of Dickensian proportions. My curiosity was reserved entirely for the natural world and was not piqued by the lure of red buses or black cabs, Buckingham Palace or the Changing of the Guard. All of these, to a greater or lesser extent, figured during our day out in the capital, but it was the London Dungeons and the Tower of London that I, a boy who was happiest when outside in the open countryside, found to be the most depressing places of all, the very fabric of which reeked of despair. Black rats, kept to illustrate the story of the Black Death plague, scurried ceaselessly behind a glass screen inside a too-small vivarium in a dimly lit room. I knew how they felt. I wanted to escape into the open air as soon as I possibly could.

I was stopped in my tracks, however, by the Crown Jewels. In that dark, soulless place they were excruciatingly brilliant and intense, emanating stabbing shafts of white, blue, red, and yellow light. I found them mesmerising, and their memory lingered and danced on the back of my eyes like sunspots. I was drawn to colour like a moth to a flame, and so, when we entered the entrance hall of the Natural History Museum in the late afternoon, I gave the suspended diplodocus skeleton above my head barely a second glance. This was the one place in London I'd been looking forward to visiting. I didn't know what to expect, but in the event one exhibit above all others proved irresistible. Like the Crown Jewels before them, a large glass case filled with hundreds of hummingbirds impaled me with colour. Here was something otherworldly, something quite extraordinary.

I was used to seeing British birds in our garden and in the Somerset countryside that surrounded our village home. Some of those birds, the Blue Tits and the Goldfinches, wore gaudy plumage that set them apart from the subtle sparrows and the drab warblers. These hummingbirds though—they were dipped in rainbows, with plumage that sparkled and shone, that changed colour depending on the angle from which one looked at them. With my nose pressed against the glass of their display cabinet, I refused to be drawn away from them.

That they were long-dead, shot many decades ago by forgotten men with fowling pieces loaded with dust-fine shot, and prepared for awkward display by a dexterous taxidermist who had never seen them in real life and had no idea of what poses they might naturally strike . . . none of this mattered to me at the time. While I was dispassionately aware that these birds were shapes and sizes quite unlike those of the birds with which I was familiar, I was swiftly lost in the spectrum of their gorgets, their mantles, their wings, and their tails.

The history of this display was, of course, completely wasted on me at the time. It was only in later years—when the craving to see my first, exuberantly animate hummingbirds where they belonged in the wild had grown to the extent that I was devouring every scintilla of information I could find about them—that I learned some of the colourful story of the contents of the Natural History Museum's hummingbird cabinet.

Their very genesis is uncertain. They may, or may not, have been amassed in the early nineteenth century by William Bullock, curator of museums in Liverpool and London. Bullock's career was as rich and varied as a hummingbird's plumage. Benjamin Haydon, an artist and contemporary of Bullock's, recalled he "loved the game of ruin or success—Westminster Abbey or Victory."

Bullock began his working life as a goldsmith and jeweller in the industrial surroundings of Birmingham, and clearly had a keen eye for the beautiful and unusual—by 1809 he had moved to London, where he set about amassing a large collection of works of art, armoury, natural history specimens, and other assorted curiosities. These were sourced from all around the world, with some items provided by members of James Cook's fateful expeditions to the Pacific Ocean. Bullock was an acquisitive collector, and a determined one. He visited Orkney, in the north of Scotland, in an attempt to obtain one of the few remaining Great Auks—despite coming close to catching one of the, by then, almost-extinct flightless birds in a hired *sixareen*, or six-oared boat, he had to settle for purchasing the doomed bird's carcass the following year from another, more successful hunter.

Money was no object when it came to acquiring the perfect specimen for display, and neither was taste, nor morality—Bullock sought advice as to whether it would be possible to exhibit "the Head of Oliver Cromwell still intire with the flesh on" and fixed upon a pike. He did, however, show some rare restraint in 1810, when he refused the advances of one Alexander Dunlop, an army surgeon who proposed that Bullock should add Sara Baartman, a woman from the nomadic Khoikhoi people of southern Africa, to his collection as a living exhibit. Dunlop had brought the unfortunate Baartman to England and, in the absence of investment from Bullock, proceeded to exploit her himself as the so-called Hottentot Venus, the most extreme example imaginable of the fetishisation of the "exotic" that exploded in Europe at the time.

If Bullock showed decency and restraint in that instance, he was unabashed in his acquisitiveness elsewhere and, by the time he sold his entire collection, it numbered some thirty-two thousand items, including a number of highly prized stuffed hummingbirds. In time, Bullock went on to travel extensively in Mexico and the United States, where his urge to collect cultural artefacts and natural history specimens was only matched by his ambition to found a utopian community on the banks of the Ohio River—the latter initiative was a dismal failure, but Bullock's new collection, exhibited in London, was well received and popular at the time.

Despite having sold off his initial grand collection in 1819, it was the hummingbirds that rekindled his collecting zeal. In 1823, stopping in Jamaica whilst travelling to Mexico, he both saw his first live hummingbird and started to collect them once more. He wrote, "In Jamaica I procured the smallest known, which is considerably less than some of the bees; and in Mexico many new species, whose splendid colours glow with a brilliancy and a lustre not surpassed by any with which we were previously acquainted."

We know that Bullock had a jeweller's eye for a pretty object as well as one that would attract paying viewers, and we know that he considered hummingbirds to be the epitome of natural beauty.

"There is not," he said in 1824, "it may be safely asserted, in all the varied works of nature in her zoological productions, any family that can bear a comparison, for singularity of form, splendour of colour, or number and variety of species, with this the smallest of the feathered creation."

The catalogues of his collections bear testimony to a mounting obsession with hummingbirds. In 1805 he displayed a case containing

"24 species with their Nests" in the Liverpool Museum. By 1810, this had been upgraded to a grander cabinet altogether, now containing seventy hummingbirds and, just two years later, Bullock was proudly boasting that he now had almost one hundred assorted hummingbirds, said to be the finest collection in Europe. Some were so small, he asserted, that, "A cockchafer [beetle] would destroy them by collision in mid-air."

His hyperbole was reminiscent of the greatest showman, P. T. Barnum and, like Barnum, he was well aware of the power words could exert over the paying public. Applying the same acquisitive fervour he displayed for hummingbirds to his marketing spiel, he borrowed extensively from the writings of the late French naturalist and aristocrat Georges-Louis Leclerc, the Comte du Buffon, for his museum catalogue: "The precious stones polished by art, cannot be compared to this jewel of nature. The emerald, the ruby, and the topaz, sparkle in its plumage, which is never soiled by the dust of the ground."

These fine words were matched by the manner in which he displayed his burgeoning hummingbird collection. In the Liverpool Museum, they were shown within a bell glass mounted upon "an elegant bronzed Egyptian tripod." Years later, whilst in Mexico, he conceived of a plan to transport them as living exhibits back to England and, by offering locals a reward, he soon had almost seventy birds incarcerated in small, glass-fronted cages. These sorry prisoners were all doomed to die within a matter of days or weeks, well before they could be subjected to the ordeal of a transatlantic crossing. Oblivious to their suffering, Bullock dispassionately observed that, "In a space barely sufficient for them to move their wings [they hovered] apparently motionless, for hours together."

Back in the late spring of 1819, the sale of Bullock's grandest collection took place in an auction that spanned an epic twenty-six days. The proceeds would go towards funding his later explorations of Mexico and the United States. On the nineteenth day of the sale, Lot 92 came under the hammer. This was Bullock's hummingbird cabinet, containing "upwards of One Hundred specimens absolutely unrivalled in any cabinet that exists."

This grand claim was borne out by one of the buyers that day. George Loddiges, a nurseryman from Hackney, was a dedicated collector of hummingbird specimens. Whilst importing orchids from the Americas to sell to the equally obsessed collectors of the time who were infected with orchidelerium, Loddiges instructed his overseas staff to send him hummingbird skins. His personal collection grew to contain over two hundred species of hummingbird, and he was both keen to buy some of Bullock's collection and well-placed to judge the quality of it. Of the day in question, Loddiges recorded in his notebook, "This Collection of Hummingbirds is unique; as a whole it greatly exceeds in beauty, [and] variety of number, the celebrated Collection in the Royal Museum in Paris."

Perhaps Bullock's hyperbole was not wholly misplaced. Lot 92 was, against Bullock's express wishes, not sold as one entire lot, but was broken down into smaller parcels. Given the febrile atmosphere that surrounded the sale, this was probably a commercially astute decision by the auctioneer. Earlier in the auction, on the sixth day, a buyer for the University of Edinburgh, allowing himself to become carried away, lamented, "Today I have perhaps [bought] too many monkeys . . ."

The genesis of the hummingbird cabinet now on display in the Natural History Museum in London is unclear, but there are almost certainly some of Bullock's specimens in its collection, for we know that Loddiges' hummingbird collection eventually ended up in the museum's hands and, back in 1819, he successfully bid for some of the offerings from Lot 92.

I began to realise that these charismatic birds had a host of stories fluttering in their wake every bit as colourful as the birds themselves. Men and women had, for centuries, fallen under their spell. Some of the greatest explorers, naturalists, and figures from history had been touched by hummingbirds, sometimes literally. Not only that— hummingbirds were to be found exclusively along the length and breadth of the Americas and nowhere else on Earth, from Alaska in the far north to the very southernmost tip of South America, on the shores of the Beagle Channel in Tierra del Fuego. They lived at the feet of glaciers and in baking hot deserts; in lush, humid rainforests and above the treeline high up in some of the world's most dramatic mountain ranges. They were small, but they had a strength that belied their diminutive stature.

I had to see them for myself. Stuffed historical specimens had sown a seed that had, in time, flourished into a consuming hunger. Photographs and glimpses of footage on television wildlife documentaries only served to pour fuel on the fire. It wasn't until my mid-thirties that I finally saw my first hummingbirds in the wild. In the resinous surroundings of Madera Canyon in Arizona, nestling in the Santa Rita Mountains with the city of Green Valley inching, like a melanoma, across the skin of the Sonoran Desert below me, my first hummingbird was magnificent.

Indeed, it was magnificent in every sense—Magnificent Hummingbird was an eponymous species, a large and dramatic hummingbird with plumage worthy of the name. I use the past tense—in the years since that first encounter, Magnificent Hummingbird has been "split" by taxonomists into two different species. The bird I saw in Arizona is now known as Rivoli's Hummingbird, whilst a small population of the former Magnificent Hummingbird found in the highlands of Costa Rica and western Panama now revels in the title of Talamanca Hummingbird. This is a fine example of the taxonomic flux that are hummingbirds—the more we study them, the more we realise that there is more to them than first meets the eye.

Back then, in Madera Canyon, it was impossible to look beyond the consuming beauty of what I found before me. Sooty black underparts provided the perfect counterpoint to a glittering, emerald-green throat, an amethyst-purple crown, and a tail of burnished bronze. The air buzzed as he hovered just a few metres from where I stood, a suspended crucifix, his wings a blur, but his body impossibly still. I was close enough to be able to see myself and the surrounding trees and blue sky reflected, in miniature, in the black of his eye. I found myself holding my breath as this apparition, as if from nowhere, fed busily and then vanished as quickly as he had come. In an instant the name *hummingbird* made sense—the sound of those wings, beating many dozens of times every second, blurred into a constant hum, like a sonorous, deep bumblebee.

My first hummingbird. The entire encounter was over in less than a minute, but the rush of adrenaline it provided was utterly intoxicating. I realised, in an instant, that the hummingbirds I had seen all those years ago in the Natural History Museum were a dusty, faded, inanimate shadow, an apology for the real thing; what naturalist W. H. Hudson had described in 1917 as a "science of dead animals—a *necrology*." I had yearned, for some twenty years, to see a live hummingbird for myself. Now, nothing else would do but to see more of his kind, in every distant corner of the Americas.

No other family of birds could come close to them—their otherworldly, metallic, and jewel-like plumage was without compare, and they came in a bewildering rainbow array of colours, shapes, and sizes. Beneath those psychedelic feathers were a host of adaptations to a nectar-fuelled, hovering life that I found irresistible. A quarter of a hummingbird's bodyweight was accounted for by the pectoral muscles that drove its wings. Those wings could beat between fifty and two hundred times per second, reduced to a mere blur to the human eye. Sustaining such flight required a hummingbird to consume copious energy-rich nectar, powering a heart that beats around twelve hundred times per minute. These bald, startling statistics raised my human heart rate above the average eighty beats per minute. Now that I had experienced the hummingbird drug for myself, I accepted, gladly, that I would need to feed my addiction. I wanted to immerse myself in the hummingbirds' world.

I planned a journey to find them across their global range. My travels would take me from Alaska to the southern tip of Argentina. I would search for them in the most extreme habitats in which they were found. I would look for the most beautiful and dramatic examples of their kind. I would meet people as lost to the allure of hummingbirds as I had become, and I would learn the stories of the lives of the birds and the places in which they were found. And, of course, as a birder I wanted to find the very rarest species of all, the ones that precious few people had ever laid eyes upon.

I knew I could not possibly see them all—there are over three hundred species in total, and it is the work of a lifetime to lay eyes upon every one. Some are found in politically unstable and dangerous areas it would be imprudent to visit. Besides, my interest in them lay much deeper than simply completing a list. I wanted to explore their world, to see for myself the habitats and forces that shaped and formed them over millennia, and to understand how they were responding to newer, more urgent pressures and changes in their worlds.

Beyond simply appreciating them in their own aesthetic right, I was also aware that they had evolved so much, stretching the boundaries of what was biologically feasible to such extremes. I wondered if we were the ones who were now moving too fast—in the face of accelerating climate change and human demand for the land in which they were found, could hummingbirds possibly keep up with us? I hoped that, by the end of my hummingbird odyssey, I would at least have a better understanding of the questions we are asking of them in the twenty-first century. I had a fear that hummingbirds might prove to be the most colourful canary in the coalmine, prophets of change that did not bode well for them or us alike. Selfishly, I knew that in addition to bearing witness to the pressures they faced, I also wanted to see some of them before they were gone altogether. The decline of some species was already well known, and the clock of extinction is ticking loudly for them.

My challenge, then, would be to witness them in their varied habitats in addition to bearing witness to their disparate shapes, sizes, colours, and behaviours. Some of this journey would be relatively easily accomplished—in some parts of North, Central, and South America there are well-established feeding stations in gardens and at lodges that bring the hummingbirds to their admirers. Hummingbird feeders, plastic containers filled with sugar water, have small apertures that mimic flowers, enticing some hummingbird species to abandon their innate caution and become accustomed to feeding in close proximity to their spellbound audience.

Other hummingbirds, however, are not as readily seen or found. Some eschew the offer of a free meal and remain denizens of the thickest, deepest forests. Some are found only on remote mountainsides or on distant offshore islands—seeing Juan Fernández Firecrowns would, for example, mean taking myself some four hundred miles out into the Pacific Ocean and following in the footsteps of Alexander Selkirk, the eighteenth-century inspiration for Daniel Defoe's Robinson Crusoe, marooning myself on a small volcanic Chilean island for as long as it took to see the birds I craved. These firecrowns are one of the more endangered species—BirdLife, the international organisation that keeps track of such data, estimates there are a mere one thousand individuals of this hummingbird remaining on Isla Robinson Crusoe. Other species I would encounter would be more common, but all would be wonderful and new to me.

My journey would take place over a number of years, but here, trapped within the comfortable confines of a narrative, it unfolds geographically, exploring the hummingbirds' world from northern to southern extremities.

CHAPTER ONE

MIGRATION

~

USA, Alaska. 60° N

*A*LASKA IS BURNING. A WHITE SHEEN OF SMOKE RENDERS A glassy, still blue sea and snow-marbled glaciated mountainsides opaque. It's like viewing the world through an apocalyptic cataract. Almost one hundred thousand acres of pristine Alaskan wilderness have been consumed in the past month by the Swan Lake wildfire and, when I arrive in Anchorage, it continues to rage silently over the horizon, undamped by any rain during this longest, hottest Alaskan summer on record.

Riding a train that slowly traverses the length of the Turnagain Arm, a long, tidal finger of the Cook Inlet that reaches deep inland from the Gulf of Alaska, it occurs to me that the fire—appearing to have started by natural causes, a lightning strike somewhere in the vicinity of Swan Lake—is not really the point. Climate change is acting like a bored child with a magnifying glass on a long, hot summer's day, wreaking havoc where it ought not to be. A wildfire that covers an area a quarter the size of London, on the doorstep of the Arctic Circle? As I leave Anchorage and head towards the port of Whittier to catch a ferry to the remote small township of Cordova, with the faint and deceptively pleasant tang of wood smoke in the air, I am aware that this is far from normal.

My journey had begun, but already I was not making it easy for myself. I could see a Rufous Hummingbird easily in the lower United States—but if I wanted to see the most northerly humming-birds in the world, I would need to see my Rufous Hummingbirds in Alaska. This is why I came to find myself on a train out of Anchorage bound for Whittier, heading to catch a ferry that would carry me, for seven hours, through Prince William Sound to Cordova, officially a city but with a resident population only twice that of Whalsay, the small Shetland island on which I have lived for the past twenty or so years. Some 2,500 people call Cordova home, but it was one person in particular I was heading to Cordova to meet— Kate McLaughlin is a hummingbird researcher and champion, who, on June 28, 2010, caught a Rufous Hummingbird in Alaska that, some five months earlier, had been caught and ringed by another hummingbird researcher in Tallahassee, Florida, some 3,500 miles away and, to this day, represents the longest known migration ever recorded by a hummingbird.

I was looking forward to meeting Kate and, as the *Aurora* pulled away from Whittier, I sat on the upper deck in the unseasonably hot sunshine, daydreaming about Rufous Hummingbirds, and worrying that I might not be fortunate enough to see one in the short time I had in Cordova. Kate had written to me the previous week, warning me that the male birds had already departed, and that their mates and offspring were on the move too. Early July marks the end of the breeding season for these tenacious birds, and I would perhaps miss them altogether.

The first hummingbirds to return to Alaska from their winter-ing grounds are the males, who arrive at a time when there are limited sources of nectar to sustain them. All hummingbirds live on a precarious nutritional knife-edge, needing to take on board sufficient nectar daily to sustain their fast metabolisms. A hungry hummingbird is, in a very short period of time indeed, a moribund hummingbird. The male Rufous Hummingbirds, back on their breeding grounds early to stake a good territory before the female birds arrive, must find sustenance in a landscape that is only just feeling winter's hold loosening, ever so slightly—a landscape that has yet to bloom. These pioneering male birds must resort to subterfuge and outright larceny if they are to survive. To do so, they must find the local sapsuckers.

Sapsuckers are small woodpeckers and, as their name suggests, they extract the sap from trees as their primary food source. Each bird drills rows of small holes in a tree's bark, creating small wells that will, in time, begin to ooze and fill with sap. The sapsucker returns, time and again, to harvest the fruits of its labours. The male Rufous Hummingbirds have learned to be opportunistic sneak thieves, darting into the sapsucker's larder, hovering in front of those carefully excavated wells, and feeding from them as if they were nectar-bearing flowers. Rufous Hummingbirds are nothing if not fearless, particularly if they are hungry.

While I was lost in my thoughts, keeping half an eye on the sea around me, hoping for a sighting of Pacific seabirds during our passage to Cordova, a young man in his early thirties approached me where I sat in one corner of the upper deck. I had my camera beside me, ready to seize the moment if it presented itself.

"Hey. That's a big camera."

I looked up, realising for the first time that I had company. Daniel, a Yup'ik man from Hooper Bay with a pleasant, crooked smile, was travelling with a small party of other Yup'ik to Cordova to work for the next few weeks in the salmon-processing factories that handled the salmon catch upon which the town's fishermen and their families depended. Wearing an arresting acid pink T-shirt, ripped jeans, and a pair of Crocs the same cerulean blue as the glassy sea we were crossing, Daniel cut a striking figure amongst the other passengers on deck. Perhaps I did too—I was the only one with a camera and a pair of binoculars. We chatted for a while about Cordova and the work that awaited Daniel and his fellow Yup'ik. He laughed, "Yeah, the others, they think they're going to be out fishing. I think they're in for a surprise. Me, I know what to expect. I'll earn good money and, when it's over, the company will buy me a ticket back to Hooper Bay. My wife, she's there now with our kids. She looks after the money."

He asked me what I was heading to Cordova for. I explained about the Rufous Hummingbirds, and how I wanted to see them at the most northerly outpost in which hummingbirds bred. Daniel became more animated.

"Yeah, I know them! They're cool. They're the only birds in the world that can fly backwards, right? Like helicopters?"

I was pleased to see his enthusiastic reaction. To meet an Alaskan Native, in his thirties, from one of the most remote towns in Alaska, and to find that hummingbirds elicited such an engaged and interested response was encouraging to say the least. I had wondered, before setting off on this quest, if it was just me and a cadre of birders that found these birds so compelling.

Daniel asked me where I'd come from, so I told him about my home in Shetland.

"I live on an island in Shetland. There's about one hundred islands up there, at 60° north, the same latitude as here, but less than a dozen have people living on them. I live on Whalsay—there's around a thousand people on there. It's pretty far north, but in some ways it's not like here. We don't have many trees there, for starters. And no glaciers, either."

We were passing by the gnarled snout of the Billings Glacier, nosing down on our left-hand side towards Prince William Sound. Behind us, Whittier was dwindling in the distance, smudges of trees visible darkly around it. Daniel looked thoughtful.

"No trees? Huh. That's like Hooper Bay. It's mostly, what would you call it, tundra there?"

We were finding common ground. Daniel continued, "And only a thousand people on the island you live on? Yeah. That's like, the same as back home . . ."

He paused. "You got bears on your island?"

The question caught me slightly off guard, and my amused denial of any bear presence in Shetland made Daniel grow more serious.

"We've got bears here," he told me gravely. "Where you're going, there's bears. You've not seen a bear before? You need to take care, man. They're big. And fast too. Yeah. Watch out for bears if you're hiking in the woods looking for birds."

One of Daniel's friends, David, a younger Yup'ik man in his early twenties, had joined us, and he nodded gravely in agreement. "Yeah, you gotta watch out for bears. My dad, he was a hunter. Had a team of dogs, he used to mush the hell out of them. He always told us to watch out for bears. You're best carrying a gun. I don't suppose you've got a gun? No? Get yourself some bear spray, man."

David told me more about his family's former life as hunters. On his way to spend a few short weeks processing salmon, he sounded wistful for a lost way of life. Our conversation was, in time, interrupted by the ferry's PA system announcing a pod of Killer Whales seen from the side of the boat. My new Yup'ik friends were unmoved by the news.

"They're *really* bad news, my dad always said," David told me. "He didn't like them at all. You can't trust them."

I said goodbye to Daniel and David for now, and made my way to join the small crowd of passengers looking east towards the distant shore. Every now and again the Killer Whales' black dorsal fins broke the surface as they passed us quickly by, heading in the opposite direction to the *Aurora*. It felt a little like being at home—in the summer, Shetland is visited by Killer Whales too.

The parallels between this area of Alaska and Shetland ran deeper, however, than a shared line of latitude or cetaceans. Both maritime communities had, in the recent past, been touched, in the worst way possible, by the vicissitudes of fate and the oil industry.

On March 24, 1989, the *Exxon Valdez* oil tanker ran aground on the Bligh Reef in Prince William Sound, spilling almost eleven million gallons of crude oil into the pristine marine environment upon which so many Alaskan communities depended for their livelihood. The resulting environmental catastrophe was unimaginable. Just a handful of years later, on January 5, 1993, a similar horror was unleashed upon Shetland when the *Braer* ran aground at Garths Ness, spilling twenty-five million gallons of oil into the sea.

Both communities had, in time, recovered—and it was their shared history that was to provide me with a home in Cordova while I met Kate McLaughlin and looked for a Rufous Hummingbird of my own. A Shetland friend, Dr. Jonathan Wills, a reporter in Shetland at the time of the *Braer* disaster, had subsequently investigated the causes of the tragedy that unfolded on our shores. As a result of this he had met David Lynn Grimes, his counterpart in Alaska. Jonathan had affectionately described David to me as "crazy like a horse," and spoke warmly of him. He told me, "He's an ornithologist, wildlife guide, singer-songwriter, and troubadour, famous for his barefoot glacier excursions and Copper River raft adventures. Back in 1990 he was involved in the Oil Pollution Act campaign with Rick Steiner, then the marine conservation professor at the University of Alaska—they swam the Potomac to board a vessel where an oil company PR event was being held, having been refused admission shore-side. He's one of the best guys around."

Jonathan had put us in touch with one another, and David had immediately offered me a place to stay at the Eyak Lake Compound, a little way outside of Cordova itself. It was David who met me off the ferry when we arrived in Cordova late in the evening, our arrival heralded by swirling clouds of clamorous Glaucous-winged Gulls that rose frothily from the still water of the harbour. David had told me to look out for a big, sand-coloured van and, in the empty car park at the quayside, the vehicle was readily found. I was unprepared for what I discovered inside the van, for here David's artistic spirit had run, gloriously, amok in an interior that looked like the lovechild of an old canal boat and a hippy camper van. Lined with varnished wood, the walls and even the ceiling sported artwork, while strings of feathers swayed around us. A carved and painted American Kestrel stood proudly on the dashboard alongside a jam jar of fireweed and other wildflowers.

David immediately proved an affable and friendly host, conversation spilling from him as varied as the seashells that formed some of the van's internal decoration. Within five minutes he'd spoken of the universe, fate, karma, and had described us all as mere "human molecules," an echo of theoretical physicist Richard Feynman, who described himself as both a universe of atoms and an atom in the universe as a whole. I liked him immediately. As we drove through the few streets of Cordova and along the shore of Lake Eyak, it was hard to pay attention to my surroundings whilst I concentrated on the first of many hummingbird stories he had to share.

"Forty years ago, me and some other young naturalists first came to Cordova, and a remarkable birder, Pete Isleib, took us under his wing. Roger Tory Peterson thought Pete the best birder on the Pacific Coast of North America—he described him as 'peerless and indefatigable'."

If Roger Tory Peterson, arguably the father of birding in the twentieth-century United States, had thought highly of Pete Isleib, I knew he would have been an extraordinary ornithologist. Meanwhile, I privately wondered what had brought David to Alaska in the 1970s. Perhaps it had, unwittingly, been another oil spill that was the genesis of the journey that brought him there. The Santa Barbara oil spill in 1969 fouled the Californian coast with some one hundred thousand barrels of crude oil, and it was witnessing this that led Wisconsin senator Gaylord Nelson to found the first Earth Day. It was a time when the Vietnam War still raged far overseas, and students nationwide overwhelmingly opposed it. Inspired by the student anti-war movement, Nelson hoped that the fledgling public awareness of air and water pollution could be channelled with similar vigour, and force environmental protection onto the national political agenda.

On April 22, 1970, the first Earth Day, some twenty million Americans took to the streets across the United States in the first national act of solidarity that unified disparate voices with environmental concerns. By the end of 1970, the United States Environmental Protection Agency (EPA) had been formed, and the Clean Air, Clean Water, and Endangered Species Acts had made significant progress. Nelson recalled, "It was a gamble, but it worked."

Earth Day also sparked a back-to-the-land movement that saw many young, disaffected men and women heading for the countryside and the promise of a better, cleaner, and simpler life. For some that meant hippy communes in California, but others cast their eyes to the north where, in Alaska, the federal government continued to offer free land in a state renowned for encouraging a pioneer spirit.

I was travelling light to Alaska with just my camera bag and what little I could squeeze in around my camera gear itself but, beside toiletries and a waterproof, I carried with me a copy of T. C. Boyle's *Drop City*, a fictionalized account of a group of idealistic hippies who had travelled from California to Alaska to form a community in the wilds there. Their new life disintegrated spectacularly, but for others in the real world the move to Alaska offered genuine opportunity and moments of quiet revelation.

David continued, "It was Pete who introduced me and friends to commercial salmon and herring fishing in Prince William Sound and the Copper River Delta, and helped stoke our interest in the local flora and fauna. In the early eighties a number of us were having dinner at Pete's, and afterwards he asked us if any of us had seen a hummingbird up close, and held out his hand with a docile little beastie motionless within.

"Now, over the subsequent years I've rescued the odd hummer from cobwebs up in the rafters of houses, and of course held them when assisting Kate McLaughlin with her captures."

In another happy moment of serendipity, it transpired that David and Kate were firm friends.

"But at the time, in answer to Pete's question, we all answered no. He then carefully placed the utterly calm bird onto my palm, and I felt a trembling sense of wonder at the miracle of it all.

"A week later, I finally thought to ask Pete just how he captured the bird—with Pete, one might have believed he had simply thrust his hand in the air and snagged one in flight. Pete waited a moment, and then, with a little twinkle in his eye, he said, 'A little alcohol in the sugar water slows them down for a while . . .'"

We arrived at the Eyak Lake Compound, a large and magnificent wooden cabin built overlooking the lake itself. A hummingbird feeder, filled with sugar water, was hanging over the lakeside veranda. I assumed it probably did not contain any alcohol, and I would need to rely on sharp eyes and good fortune rather than a slyly administered sedative to see my first Alaskan Rufous Hummingbird. Meanwhile, David casually told me that the cabin, some years ago, had almost been swept away by a winter avalanche that stopped mere feet from it.

"It blew all the windows out, and tore apart everything else between us and the mountain," he confided. "You can see the path of it up there on the mountainside."

Sure enough, looming above us was the mountain. While on a warm summer evening it was hard to imagine the land covered in deep snow, the absence of trees in a wide swathe of the mountainside leading directly towards the Eyak Lake Compound spoke eloquently of the risks inherent in living there. While I was instinctively drawn to the wild, I wondered if I would be able to live somewhere with such an omnipotent, looming risk for a neighbour.

As he showed me around, David encouraged me to try the salmonberries that grew prolifically all around the cabin.

"They're delicious right now," he said. "Better still if you can find a blueberry to pop inside one."

Salmonberries, I discovered, were like multicoloured raspberries, available in everything from citrine yellow to garnet red. Many were bright orange, and all, as David had promised, were delicious.

"Bears love them too," he confided, and then looked thoughtful. "If you're thinking of hiking in the woods, you should get some bear spray. This time of year, when the moose calves are getting too fast for the bears to catch, they're eating salmonberries until the salmon start to run up the rivers."

I had seen a mother moose and her calf running across a meadow, spooked by the train that had carried me from Anchorage to Whittier. They had been moving extremely quickly, and were now a chastening reminder of just how fast a hungry bear might be able to move if it put its mind to it.

The following morning I went to meet Kate McLaughlin. When she's not studying hummingbirds, Kate works in the offices of the Chugach National Forest. If she was surprised to see me—and, having exchanged some emails in the preceding weeks, I got the impression Kate did not quite believe I would travel all the way to Alaska to see Rufous Hummingbirds—she hid it well, and welcomed me warmly to Cordova. Her enthusiasm for the hummingbirds she had devoted years to studying was infectious.

"I'm one of just a handful of certified hummingbird master class banders in the USA," she proudly told me, going on to share the full story of the epic recovery of H82779, the female Rufous Hummingbird who bore the tiny metal ring on her leg that Florida hummingbird ringer Fred Dietrich placed upon her in Tallahassee on January 13, 2010. Five months later, on June 28, H82779 found herself in the careful hands of Kate in Chenega Bay, Alaska, some 3,500 miles from where human eyes had last set sight of her. By any avian standards, a 3,500-mile migration is an epic undertaking— but for a bird that weighs at best 3.5 grams, less than a penny coin, it's nothing short of miraculous.

Birds have migrated for millennia, swapping clement winter quarters for seasonally suitable homes in which to breed in the months of summer. It is only in the past century that we have been able to chart these immense journeys with any sort of precision, and it is bird ringers who have provided a window into the private lives of these nomadic creatures. On May 6, 1911 John Masefield, a sixty-one-year-old solicitor living in Cheshire in northwest England, ringed a swallow chick in her nest in the porch of his Cheadle home. Her light aluminium ring bore the engraved number B830—and it was this ring that identified the swallow when she was discovered on December 23, 1912 by farmer J. Mayer, trapped inside a barn on his farm near Utrecht in the former province of Natal, South Africa. She was some 6,000 miles from her birthplace, revealing an unthinkable act of migration to the ornithologists of the day—nobody knew that birds travelled so far. Ringing has subsequently revealed the longest migration of all bird species—Arctic Terns travel annually between the Arctic and Antarctic, swapping one summer for that of another a hemisphere away.

Yet these are all tough birds. Swallows and terns are powerful fliers, masters of the skies and oceans. A hummingbird, on the other hand, is a mite largely dependant on sugar for fuel. To a hummingbird, 3,500 miles must feel at least as long as the journeys those swallows and terns make. Longer, even.

If I was to see one of the local Rufous Hummingbirds for myself, I would need to cover some miles too. I had hoped to see Kate ringing hummingbirds, but she told me that the ringing season was over.

"The birds are out migrating now. The hummingbird season was very poor this year, and the males have already pulled out. That said, find the right blooming lilac bush, fresh-filled feeder or a patch of columbine by a stream, and you may see females or young birds."

Kate recommended some local trails that might prove fruitful, but seasoned her advice with a now familiar warning.

"Watch out for bears. They're pretty cranky right now—the salmon has only just started to come into the creeks to spawn, so the bears have been eating berries, and they're hungry. You've got some bear spray, right?"

I didn't want to look like a greenhorn in front of Kate.

"Oh yes. I've got bear spray."

Having seen a woman picking salmonberries at the side of the road into Cordova earlier in the morning, wearing a handgun on her belt, I began to appreciate the respect the locals afforded their ursine neighbours. As soon as I left Kate's office, I resolved to buy some bear spray before I set off to spend the remainder of the day hiking the length of the Heney Ridge Trail.

Cordova is a small town, so it was just a short walk to the general store. I asked a store assistant for bear spray, and she led me to a shelf laden with insect repellent. Perhaps it was my English accent that was causing the confusion. I repeated myself, with a little mime thrown in for good measure.

"Bear spray? Grr!"

I raised my hands above my head in an approximation of the angry, hungry bear I had no wish to meet. Understanding dawned on the young assistant's face.

"Oh, you mean *bear* spray? No, we don't stock that. You need the Whiskey Ridge cycle store for bear spray."

While a cycle shop was not perhaps the most obvious place in which to buy bear deterrent, nor did I expect to find it stocked with quite such an extensive range of hunting paraphernalia. Rifles hung from the wall behind the counter, while boxes of ammunition lined the shelves beneath. Cycling was, apparently, as fraught with danger as berry picking. I asked the friendly, bearded man behind the counter for bear spray, and he pointed me towards a display of large blue and yellow canisters on the end of the counter. I blanched slightly at the price—$50—and had one last moment of indecision about whether I really needed bear spray.

"Have you had much bother with bears lately?" I asked. His reply settled the matter once and for all.

"Yeah, when they're hungry they come into the town and get in folks' yards and make trouble. We shot twenty right here in town last summer."

My purchase made, he showed me how to use my bear spray should the occasion arise.

"You wear it on your belt. Make sure the safety catch is pulled out before you try to use it. And make sure you point it at the bear, and not your face. You don't want to blind yourself when you've got a pissed bear charging at you."

I could think of little worse than spraying concentrated chilli pepper extract into my eyes before being mauled by a bear I could no longer see. I paid close attention to his advice and, suitably equipped, drove out of town to the head of the Heney Ridge Trail. By now it was early afternoon and the temperature was rising. I had not expected Alaska to be so hot. The deep shade of the trees that overhung the trail as it followed the contours at the side of Hartney Bay and the shimmering creek that fed into it was welcome. I grazed on the abundant salmonberries that lined the lower reaches of the path I was following, and self-consciously followed the other bear-related advice I had been given—clapping my hands periodically, particularly at blind summits and corners. While this might warn a bear of my approach, allowing it time to amble away, I also felt certain I would not see many birds of any kind. I was used to moving as unobtrusively as possible through the landscape, so this noisy behaviour felt deeply counterintuitive.

My musings were interrupted by a large pile of dung at my feet in the middle of the path. It was larger than a football and packed with small berry seeds, so I had my suspicions what sort of animal was responsible for it. I looked nervously around me, and clapped my hands some more for good measure. Nothing moved in the moss-festooned trees that shrouded the narrow trail. I knelt to take a photo of the pile with my phone and, as I moved nearer to it, I could feel the heat radiating from the droppings. They were fresh.

Very fresh.

It was at this point that I became aware of splashing sounds coming from the creek below me. My heart began racing as I tried to see through the veil of trees to the water. There, hanging in the clear creek, were the dark-grey torpedoes of salmon facing upstream. Periodically one would break the surface and thrash the water loudly.

At the very moment I told myself that this was what I had heard, the distinctive sound of something large wading in the water filtered through the trees. Silhouetted by hemlock branches, the obscured but unmistakeable dark form of a bear was making its way across the creek away from me.

I froze. The bear melted from sight as quickly as it had come, leaving me pulsing with adrenaline in its wake. I had not expected to come this close to a bear, let alone this quickly. I began questioning whether it was entirely prudent to continue along the trail looking for hummingbirds. Eventually I concluded that I was equally likely to encounter another bear on my way back to my car as I was continuing out of the woods and into the boggy muskeg areas beyond, and resolved to continue, more cautiously—and loudly—than hitherto.

I saw no more signs of bears, but neither could I find any hummingbirds, despite finding abundant stands of orange-flowered columbines, a favoured wild nectar source. Biologists studying the many species of columbine, or *Aquilegia*, native to North America have discovered that red- and orange-flowered species are mainly pollinated by hummingbirds, while the white- and yellow-flowered species are generally pollinated by hawkmoths.

This intimate relationship has transformed the shape of hummingbirds and flowers alike over the course of countless millennia. At some point in the Cretaceous period flowers started to evolve colours and scents to signal the presence of pollen to insects. These insects, visiting many flowers, would inadvertently pollinate them. In time, flowers added nectar to the mix, giving insects an additional inducement to visit them—and simultaneously, these insects evolved the equipment necessary to first find the flowers, and then to extract pollen and nectar alike. These coevolutionary interactions inadvertently provided the fuel for a much larger organism, the ancestors of today's hummingbirds, to evolve in their own right to exploit this rich food source. To extract nectar from flowers, hummingbirds evolved to hover, like a hawkmoth, in front of the flowers—a biomechanical innovation previously unthinkable amongst vertebrates, achieved by rotating their wings in flight, giving uplift on both the upstroke as well as the downstroke of each wingbeat. The flowers, meanwhile, continued to evolve in their own right. While the shape and form of a columbine flower is fundamentally the same between species—all have a long spur containing nectar that excludes all but the longest-tongued pollinators from drinking it—their flower colours evolved to attract specific pollinators. Red, to all species of hummingbird, signals a potential food source. White and yellow are, to insects that can see light in the ultraviolet range, a powerful promise of nectar and pollen.

There is even an expression to describe the process by which one event can, in a chain of causal consequences, lead to a seemingly unrelated innovation, like the process by which the sexual reproduction strategies of plants led to the extraordinary evolutionary design of hummingbirds. Coined by author Steven Johnson, it is known as the Hummingbird Effect. The same process applies to many technological advances we take for granted today. The example Johnson gives to introduce the concept is that of the invention of the printing press by Johannes Gutenberg. This led to increased demand for reading glasses in Europe as the new practice of reading made the literate aware that they were, generally, long-sighted. A burgeoning market for reading glasses spurred research in the design and production of lenses. This experimentation led to the invention of the microscope and, subsequently, our discovery that our body comprised many microscopic cells. The invention of the printing press had opened our eyes to perceive the world at a cellular level—not an immediately obvious vehicle of change, but a perceptible one. A similar story unfolded with the evolution of pollen and the marvel of hummingbird flight, an unanticipated biomechanical change precipitated by a seemingly unrelated innovation.

Back in the spongy, mossy muskeg bogs, there were other botanical treasures to distract me—I risked wet knees to examine closely the ruby red, glistening Round-leaved Sundews and the delicate violet flowers of Common Butterworts, both of which appeared to be the same species as those I was familiar with in my Shetland home. I found the crisp spires of green and white orchids, Slender and White Bog Orchids, respectively, and, while these new species for me thrilled my latent orchid-hunting spirit, they did little to assuage my frustration and fear that I was too late to see a Rufous Hummingbird at this northerly latitude.

My time in Cordova was prescribed by the timetable of the ferry that serves the community. I had only a day remaining to me before I needed to leave for Whittier and my onward journey to Anchorage. This would be time enough to hike another, longer trail, but nevertheless it was a despondent naturalist who returned to the Eyak Lake Compound. There I found I now had company—Pete and Tim, two fishermen in their fifties from the lower states, newly arrived after a week at sea harvesting salmon for one of the smaller canneries in Cordova. They were in exuberant form, celebrating a successful week's work with a steady stream of tequila mixed with grapefruit. Tim recounted a past fishing trip on which a bush pilot brought a new deckhand and cases of beer to join the crew.

"We were sitting on the beach when Captain Fancypants brought his Piper Cub down to join us," he recalled. These small light aircraft were ubiquitous on Lake Eyak, sitting on floats in sheltered harbours along the shore. Tim continued, "We were more excited to see the beer than the new guy. We'd been dropping acid. It was a trip."

It felt like I had stepped straight into the counterculture pages of *Drop City*. I had only a day of Alaskan experience to draw upon for a story of my own, so could only counter with my ursine close encounter whilst looking for hummingbirds. Tim looked thoughtful.

"You were on the Heney Ridge Trail? That's the place where a bear fucked up Thea real bad the other year. Life-changing injuries, man."

The following morning I had arranged to hike up Mount Eyak, a brooding presence that loomed over the cabin from the opposite shore of the lake, with Mitch Kochanski, a young American traveller I had met on the ferry from Whittier. After my near miss the previous day, and with Tim's stories ringing in my ears, I felt more comfortable looking for hummingbirds in Alaska in company rather than on my own, particularly as Mitch's rucksack sported a bearbell—a small, metal device like a modest cowbell—that loudly announced our presence with every step we made.

In the end, I need not have worried, for a hummingbird found me before we left the Eyak Lake Compound. Standing in the kitchen with a mug of coffee in hand, looking out across the lake at the cloud-shrouded mountain, it took me a moment to realise what was hovering at eye level before me—a female Rufous Hummingbird, dipping her bill into the hummingbird feeder David had hung from the cabin's eaves over the veranda. We looked one another in the eye and then she was gone, in an instant. I had barely time to register her presence before she had vanished, leaving the merest impression of her sombre buff, green, and white plumage in my mind. Male Rufous Hummingbirds are a simmering confection of cinnamon and burnt-orange plumage as fiery as their famously pugnacious tempers, but female birds have a more subtle character altogether.

My camera lay, useless, on the table behind me, yet this did not seem to matter in that moment. She had felt like a messenger, acknowledging that this, in the furthest reaches of her kind's range, marked the start of my hummingbird odyssey. I wanted to believe that she was a relative of H82779, fanciful though that notion was.

The brevity of her visit was typical of her kind. Hummingbirds often feed in short, intense bursts of activity, interspersed with time spent perched, preening or simply resting. The mechanics of their feeding have only recently been understood fully. For over 150 years after it was first proposed in 1833, scientists believed hummingbirds fed by capillary action. Their thin tongues—so long that, when retracted, they coil inside the birds' heads around their skulls and eyes—fork into two at the tip, each edge curving inwards to form a thin tube that runs parallel to the other. These were the tubes that scientists believed drew nectar passively into themselves. However, nectar is thick, syrupy stuff. Hummingbirds can flick their tongues into a flower eighteen times per second. Capillary action simply should not have time to work, if that was what was happening.

It was only recently when Margaret Rubega, a professor at the University of Connecticut, convinced that the mechanics of this were fundamentally impossible, commissioned research using high-speed cameras that recorded 1,200 frames per second and artificial flowers with transparent sides, that the truth was revealed. The humming-birds' forked tongues open when they are immersed in liquid, and the edge of each fork unfurls to reveal a row of minute flaps. The tongue, like the plants the hummingbird visits, blooms. When the tongue is retracted, the fork and flaps close, trapping nectar within. When the tongue is next extended, the trapped nectar is forced backwards into the throat. The entire process is passive—all the hummingbird need do is flick its tongue in and out. While I knew this—I had read the research just before my visit to Alaska—it served not only as a wonderful insight into the hummingbirds' world, but also as a reminder that, even now, we know so little about how they work, and what they need from the world in order to prosper.

Kate had told me that Rufous Hummingbirds were, on the whole, in decline. Their traditional wintering grounds in Mexico are under stress, with drought a particular problem. More, like H82779, are wintering in Florida instead—where once no Rufous Humming-birds were to be found in winter months, the species is now a regular sight. Kate hypothesised that this was due to the proliferation of open land and flower-rich suburban gardens where once hardwood and pine forests stood and, in some of those gardens, well-stocked hummingbird feeders like the one at which I had just seen my fleeting Rufous female.

However, if the conditions in their former Mexican wintering grounds were changing, perhaps fuelled by climate change, so too were the conditions in their summer range. Kate told me that another hummingbird species, Anna's Hummingbird, was also changing its patterns of distribution. She explained that this hardy, high-altitude species has traditionally been considered to be rare in south central Alaska—before the 1930s, they were known to breed only in Baja, California, yet now they are expanding their range into the North Gulf of Alaska and the vicinity of Prince William Sound.

"I banded an adult female and an immature male bird here in October one year. That's a good indication of a breeding population of Anna's Hummingbirds in south central Alaska. Most are likely migrating to the Lower 48 in the fall like the Rufous hummers do, but with their cold tolerance, a few may be choosing to stay in the milder coastal areas throughout the winter.

"I've even seen one here in mid-January, coming to a feeder. Hummingbirds in the snow—who'd have believed it?"

As my ferry pulled away from Cordova into Prince William Sound, early in the morning of my last full day in Alaska, I found myself dwelling on signs, both real and imagined, proven and yet to be fully understood. I had visited Alaska at the end of a spring and summer of unprecedented, abnormal heat. In March temperatures across Alaska averaged 11° Celsius above normal; in the Arctic, on March 30, this deviation was even more extreme, with thermometers registering 22° Celsius above normal. The severity and extent of the Swan Lake wildfire was a visible, omnipresent reminder of how tinder-dry Alaska had become, but other changes were less visible, yet more pernicious still.

The waters of the Gulf of Alaska were 1.5° Celsius warmer than usual by late May. That may not sound like much, but it speaks of an entire ecosystem heating up. The energy required to warm such an enormous mass of cold water is unthinkable. Rob Campbell, a biological oceanographer at the Prince William Sound Science Center, warned that sustained warming of this scale would have cascading effects, the consequences of which we might not appreciate until years later.

The transformation of Anna's Hummingbirds from rare vagrant to apparent breeding Alaskan resident may seem like a benign consequence of this new, warmer north. What could be less threatening than a hummingbird? I was reminded, however, of David Lynn Grimes' words recalling the terrible events of 1989. David told me, "The Exxon spill was an extraordinary crisis at a time of great change in the world. The wall came down in Berlin and the Soviet Union was tearing itself asunder. Tiananmen Square transpired in China; apartheid was falling apart in South Africa and Nelson Mandela was soon to be set free. And, in the global symbol of remnant Eden, all the wild animals died for our sins in the oil of Alaska."

The invocation of Exxon, three decades after the *Valdez* oil spill felt particularly meaningful that morning as the ferry pulsed slowly across the glassy still waters of Prince William Sound towards the hazy, smoke-filled skies in the north. The immediate effects of the 1989 spill were all too apparent, with countless thousands of animals perishing in the smothering oil. Who could say, at this stage, what the long-term consequences of global warming would be here in Alaska? I feared that most, if not all of them, would not be good for this beautiful land.

There may be a handful of beneficiaries, species that expand their range north into newly warmer habitats—but what will be lost will surely be irreplaceable, subarctic species and habitat that has nowhere left to go and, once gone, will be gone for good. The principles of Steven Johnson's Hummingbird Effect echoed in my mind—while that concerned the incremental, unforeseen effects of innovation, I wondered if the Hummingbird Effect might also be used to describe the revelation of the first, unanticipated effects of a profound change in an ecosystem. After all, hummingbirds, being so highly evolved, might well be one of the first species to react to altered circumstances we may not yet comprehend or discern. Changing migratory patterns of Rufous Hummingbirds, expanding breeding ranges of Anna's Hummingbirds—none of these events took place overnight, and we were only now beginning to recognize and understand them, at much the same time as we awoke to the realisation that our climate was changing at a global scale.

However, it seems as if some of us, at least, knew about those changing circumstances long before they became public knowledge and widely accepted as scientific fact. In recent years documentary information has come to light that suggests Exxon knew about the possibility of anthropogenic climate change as early as the late 1970s. By the time the *Exxon Valdez* ran aground in 1989, the company, publicly at least, remained convinced the science that underpinned climate change was controversial. Yet by 1989 Exxon had helped to found the now-discredited Global Climate Coalition, a lobby group created specifically to question the scientific basis for concern about climate change. The fossil fuel industry's legacy, in one form or another, was unfolding in Alaska to this day. The oil spill might be a fading memory, but the changing seasons and their effect on Alaska's wildlife were very real and present.

Some hours later, I stood in line for check-in at the airport in Anchorage, behind an ebullient party of friends who had come to Alaska from Europe for a fishing holiday. Helmut, a hotelier from Switzerland, told me this was his second vacation in Alaska.

"This time the weather is much, much better!" he exclaimed happily, a sunburned red nose bearing testament to the fact. "There were not so many salmon in the rivers, but we have some to take home with us."

The trolley in front of him was piled high with waxy cardboard boxes, presumably packed with fish. Water dripped slowly from one corner of the lowest box. Helmut asked what had brought me to this remote place, and was surprised to learn it was a desire to see the most northerly hummingbirds in the world.

"I have never seen one," he told me. "They are not here! Here there are salmon, moose, bears . . ."

"Have you seen a bear?" I asked. Helmut's friends responded before he could.

"Tell him about the bear!" they chorused. Helmut lowered his voice conspiratorially.

"The last time we were here, we were fishing on a river. And there was a bear in the water. The others, they kept their distance. But I came too close to him, and he ran to attack me. I sprayed him in the face, *pffft!*"

Here Helmut's moustache bristled with emotion. "With my bear spray. And that stopped him. Long enough for us to pack up and leave."

In Alaska, it seemed, hummingbirds were hard to find, but everybody had a bear story.

CHAPTER TWO

WILD AMERICA

~

USA, Arizona. 31° N

As a young boy, I wanted very badly to be Gerald Durrell. My godmother gave me a copy of *My Family and Other Animals*, a book that I read obsessively time and again. The Somerset countryside was a poor substitute for the sun-drenched Corfu of the great conservationist's childhood, and I found myself yearning to swap what his elder brother, novelist Lawrence Durrell, dismissed scathingly as "Pudding Island" for more exotic, overseas places in which to look for wildlife. If the islands of Greece seemed an unlikely place for my unadventurous family to visit, North America was an unattainable dream altogether. I had my godmother to thank for planting that seed too, for she had given me a second book, one very different from Durrell's golden account of childhood.

It took me a while to read *Wild America*. At first glance, this hardback book was not as inviting as the slim Durrell paperback. It was thick and weighty, clad in a dark-green dustjacket that depicted two white egrets in flight over a gloomy, swampy pond on the edge of which lurked an alligator. In time, however, I allowed myself to give it a try. Written by Roger Tory Peterson and James Fisher, *Wild America* was an account of their journey around North America over the course of one hundred days in 1953—a marathon journey during which Peterson introduced Fisher, an English ornithologist, to the birds and other wildlife of his American homeland. He promised Fisher an odyssey that would start in Newfoundland and continue, clockwise, around the continent, to Alaska by way of Mexico. Fisher would hope to see more of wild America than almost any living North American, let alone an Englishman.

What followed was the story of their epic journey, by the end of which they had seen over six hundred species of birds, and had further cemented their friendship. As a young, rather solitary boy with no friends who shared my interest in the natural world, I wished I too had a friend with whom to explore pastures new and, better yet, to share with me the wildlife of his or her home country somewhere far away from the English southwest.

My initial reticence to dive into *Wild America* was, once I started reading the friends' account of their adventures, soon a thing of the past. I returned to the book shortly before setting off to look for hummingbirds in the USA. While my affection for the story remained undimmed, I instinctively knew that what I would find in America would be very different. The passage of the intervening sixty years would not have been kind to much of the countryside through which Peterson and Fisher had travelled. Fisher's concluding thoughts, at the end of his time there, were at once elegiac and naively optimistic—he marvelled at the countryside he had passed through, and the birds and other wildlife he had encountered, and warmly praised what he perceived to be a benign footprint of mankind in its midst.

Yet he would, surely, have been aware of the damage already wrought upon the avifauna the first European settlers had found when they began their inexorable spread from east to west across the American interior. My time in Alaska had been all too brief, but plenty long enough to fall helplessly in love with the untrammelled wilderness I found there. It reminded me, profoundly, of the character and spirit of my adopted Shetland home. However, the cautionary tale of the insults visited upon it by the industry of man provided the counterpoint to my blind love. Fisher's rose-tinted impressions had, evidently, not been borne out by the passage of time.

Only forty years before Fisher joined Peterson for their grand tour, a pigeon died in captivity in Cincinnati Zoo. Her name was Martha, and she died alone, the last of her kind. That she was named after Martha Washington, the first First Lady of the United States, would have been scant consolation to her had she known. When Martha Washington was alive in the eighteenth century, her pigeon namesake's kind blackened the skies above the American plains. Martha was a Passenger Pigeon, a migratory pigeon species believed to be the most numerous bird in North America at the time Europeans began to colonise the continent, with a population estimated to number between three and five billion strong.

While it seems inconceivable that mankind could wipe out a bird this commonplace, that is exactly what happened. Indigenous American tribes had always hunted them for food, but European settlers commercialised the practice in the nineteenth century and compounded the hunting pressure with widespread deforestation, depriving the pigeons of their breeding habitat. The native Choctaw name for them was *putchee nashoba*, or lost dove—a name that was to prove bleakly ironic when Martha breathed her last on September 1, 1914, four years after her mate had passed away, a lonely old pigeon who had become a minor celebrity in her final years. The offer of a $1,000 reward for anyone who could supply a male pigeon to be her companion and, perhaps, father some new Passenger Pigeons had failed to find a bird, but had brought further publicity and paying visitors to the zoo.

Martha's death marked the extinction of the Passenger Pigeon. Extinction is never glamorous, but so famous was Martha that she suffered further indignities in death—she was hastily transferred to the Cincinnati Ice Company's premises where, held by her feet, she was summarily frozen inside a 140 kilogram block of ice. In this state of suspended animation she was then sent by express train to the Smithsonian Institution in Washington, DC, and there, once defrosted, she was butchered. Her innards were dissected, to be retained by the National Museum of Natural History, and her skin was mounted, to be displayed on a small branch alongside a male Passenger Pigeon that had been shot and stuffed in Minnesota in 1873. She had, in death, at last found a companion.

Fisher would undoubtedly have been aware of the story of the extermination of the Passenger Pigeon. Perhaps he also knew the tale of the Carolina Parakeet, one of only two parrot species native to the United States. Just like the Passenger Pigeon, it was once abundant and widespread. By the middle of the nineteenth century it was rare, victim of habitat loss and hunting—it was considered a pest by cereal growers. The parakeets' last stronghold was in the swamps of central Florida, habitat they shared with Ivory-billed Woodpeckers, another doomed bird. The coincidences mount up alarmingly in the tale of the demise of the parakeets, for the last of their kind, a lonely parakeet called Incas, died in captivity in the Cincinnati zoo in 1918, just four years after the loss of Martha. In a final hollow note of pathos, the cage that housed Incas to the bitter end was the very same cage in which Martha had been incarcerated.

Fisher certainly knew only too well the decline of the immense Ivory-billed Woodpecker, a bird that Peterson described as both archaic and the rarest bird in the world. Peterson inferred they were from another time and, when birdwatcher Whitney Eastman had discovered Ivory-billed Woodpeckers in Florida's Chipola swamp in 1950, he described the moment as the greatest thrill of his birdwatching life. To this day, American birdwatchers know them as the grail bird, so mythical have they become. Having searched and failed to find them with Fisher in the moss-festooned cypresses of the Chipola swamp in 1953, Peterson wondered whether they had, perhaps, joined the spectral company of the Carolina Parakeet and the Passenger Pigeon.

He was, probably, correct.

In the decades that followed, sporadic sightings of Ivory-billed Woodpeckers were reported, even as recently as the early years of the current century, yet none of these reports ever culminated in unequivocal proof that the bird had, somehow, clung on. If their continued existence remains a subject of conjecture, the reasons for their decline do not, and were all too evident by the middle of the twentieth century. Ivory-billed Woodpeckers required vast territories of virgin timber, expanses of ancient woodland that harboured enough dead and dying trees to support the grubs upon which the woodpeckers fed. The felling of these great trees began in the eighteenth century and accelerated in the century that followed, feeding a seemingly insatiable lumber industry, but starving out the beleaguered birds.

The engines that drove the decline and loss of these three iconic North American birds—hunting and habitat loss—were well known by the time Peterson and Fisher embarked on their birdwatching tour de force. Yet they chose, Fisher in particular, to gloss over them. Returning to the pages of *Wild America* before embarking on my hummingbird quest, I wondered at their motives for this, whether knowing or subconscious. Their book was inspiring, but with hindsight I felt it was slightly disingenuous. I ought, I felt, to tell the truth of what I found in my journey through the Americas, for good and ill alike.

Amongst the 601 species of bird the two friends found on their travels were a handful of hummingbirds. Their appearances were only fleeting, coming and going in their account as quickly as the birds themselves. They saw their Rufous Hummingbird on Destruction Island, off the coast of Washington State, a long way south of the Alaskan outpost my hardy female bird called her summer home. They had better luck in Arizona, where the United States begins to bleed into the outskirts of Central America. Hummingbirds live a precarious, seasonal existence on the knife-edge frontier that is Alaska. Further south, in warmer and more clement surroundings, theirs is an easier existence, and it was there I would find more diversity of their kind.

Hummingbirds had fascinated American birdwatchers from the very outset. Over a century before James Fisher admiringly described the American countryside as a garden, naturalist and artist John James Audubon described mango hummingbirds as "the greatest ornaments of the gardens and forests," and Ruby-throated Hummingbirds as "curious florists." Audubon, it seems, could not resist flowery language to describe them—he referred to them as a "glittering fragment of the rainbow" and, of the Rufous Hummingbird, he wrote in *Birds of America* that it "seemed like a breathing gem, or magic carbuncle of glowing fire . . . as if to emulate the sun itself in splendour."

Audubon's weakness for purple prose drew opprobrium from his contemporary, ornithologist George Ord, who scathingly dismissed him as "a back-country upstart who romanticized his subject matter."

History appeared to vindicate Audubon, as he is now firmly established in the pantheon of American naturalists. George Ord, on the other hand, has faded into some obscurity.

Long before Audubon, the very first European settlers had fallen under the spell of these otherworldly birds, so very different from the muted birds they had left behind an ocean away in the Old World. I wondered at the nature of those early, largely undocumented encounters. Did the Pilgrim Fathers first notice hummingbirds in the wild outside the boundaries of their New England settlement? Contemporary accounts certainly record the hummingbirds coming to their gardens, as bold and innocent then as they remain to this day. William Wood, writing in *New England's Prospect* in 1634, introduced prospective settlers to these curious birds, so unlike any found in Britain:

> The Humbird is one of the wonders of the Countrey, being no bigger than a Hornet, yet hath all the demensions of a Bird, as bill, and wings,

with quills, spider-like legges, small clawes: For colour, she is as glorious as the Raine-bow; as she flies, she makes a little humming noise like a Humble-bee: wherefore shee is called the Hum-bird.

The early European settlers were said to have encountered Native Americans wearing hummingbird earrings—Nehemiah Grew, in 1693, wrote, "An *Indian Saggamore* is not in his full Pomp and Bravery without one of these Birds in his Ear for a Pendant."

That story is perhaps as apocryphal as the tall tales about hummingbirds that flew east in the years that followed, to be recounted with wonder in the coffeehouses of northern Europe. Hummingbirds, apparently, migrated tucked inside the feathers of geese, or impaled themselves by their bills in the trunks of trees in the autumn, dying there during the winter—only to revive with the coming of spring.

The former story echoed similar beliefs about the smallest migratory birds in Europe—for example, the contemporaneous tale that Goldcrests hitched a ride on the backs of Eurasian Woodcock, a larger forest-dwelling member of the shorebird family. The latter story, that of hummingbirds impaling themselves on trees, was surely borne of an early European settler in America seeing a hummingbird feeding from a sapsucker well in a tree trunk early one spring. Hummingbirds have always caught our eye, wherever and whenever our paths cross—they are an irresistible glitter in the green.

Those that followed the Pilgrim Fathers across the Atlantic certainly paid attention to the birds they encountered. Writing from Boston in 1670, Francis Willoughby, "a Gentleman," reported to the Royal Society of London:

I send you withal a little Box, with a Curiosity, which will perhaps be counted a trifle, yet 'tis rarely to be met with even here. It is the curiosly contrived Nest of a Humming-Bird, so called from the humming noise it maketh whil'st it flies.

'Tis an exceedingly little Bird, and only seen in Summer, and mostly in Gardens, flying from flower to flower, sucking Honey out of the flowers as a Bee doth; as it flieth not lighting on the flower, but hovering over it, sucking with its long Bill a sweet substance.

There are in the same Nest two of the Birds Eggs. I never saw but one of those Nests before; and that was sent over formerly, with some other Rarities, but the Vessel miscarrying you received them not.

Willoughby might be excused for taking hummingbird nests containing eggs on the grounds of novelty at the time; however, in the years that followed, the hummingbirds' innocence and beauty continued to be poorly served by our forebears. Writing to the Royal Society of London from Boston in 1697, Benjamin Bullivant related:

The Hum-bird I have shot with Sand, and had one some Weeks in my keeping. I put a Straw for a Perch into a Venice Glass Tumbler, ty'd over the Mouth with a Paper, in which I cut Holes for the Bird's Bill (about as long and as small as a Taylor's Needle), and laying the Glass on one Side, set a Drachm of Honey by it, which it soon scented, and with its long Tongue put forth beyond its Bill, fed daily; it muted the Honey pure, and was a Prospect to many Comers; it flew away at last.

It is unclear whether the bird Bullivant shot was one and the same with that he kept in captivity until it flew away, but he certainly appears to have pioneered an early hummingbird feeder, and generally seems curious rather than ill-disposed towards the birds. Settlers in Pennsylvania during the eighteenth century, however, were known to press hummingbirds, like wildflowers, within the pages of heavy books before mailing the dried, iridescent husks back to their families in Ireland and Scotland, colourful souvenirs from the wild American frontier.

The following century, Henry David Thoreau noticed hummingbirds in the Massachusetts countryside around Walden. In his journal for May 16, 1858, he recalls,

A hummingbird yesterday came into the next house and was caught. Flew about our parlor to-day and tasted Sophia's flowers. In some lights you saw none of the colors of its throat. In others, in the shade the throat was clear bright scarlet, but in the sun it glowed with splendid metallic, fiery reflections about the neck and throat.

Where Audubon reserved his most florid descriptions for the hummingbirds themselves, in *Walden* Thoreau was more reserved in his descriptions of the birds and preferred to eulogise the places in which they are found:

White Pond and Walden are great crystals on the surface of the earth, Lakes of Light. If they were permanently congealed, and small enough to be clutched, they would, perchance, be carried off by slaves, like precious stones, to adorn the heads of emperors.

[White Pond] has rarely been profaned by a boat, for there is little in it to tempt a fisherman. Instead of the white lily, which requires mud, or the common sweet flag, the blue flag *(Iris versicolor)* grows thinly in the pure water, rising from the stony bottom all around the shore, where it is visited by hummingbirds in June.

This fleeting mention, however, was enough to inspire the makers of the Walden computer game who, in 2017, allowed players in their immersive, open-world simulation of Walden to stand beside those blue irises and watch the hummingbirds hovering and feeding from them.

Walden provided real-life inspiration to a latter-day naturalist, who, in the early 1960s, decided to abandon the trappings of an increasingly complicated and overcrowded United States and live somewhere closer to nature. Anne LaBastille was, by any measure of a life, a remarkable woman. Ferociously intelligent, an ecologist by training, daughter of a professor and a concert pianist, she retreated to a remote fastness on the banks of Twitchell Lake in New York's Adirondack Mountains and there, in 1964, hand-built a log cabin in which to live without electricity or running water. Henry Thoreau spent just two Spartan years in relative isolation in his cabin at Walden, with his mother taking care of his laundry; Anne LaBastille was still living, at least part-time, in her cabin as recently as 2007, with sixteen books, two dozen scientific papers, and over 150 magazine articles to her name, her location thinly disguised as "Black Bear Lake."

She witnessed change in the intervening four decades. Before we better understood the forces driving global warming, LaBastille noted that the ice that once thickly sealed the lake between November and February every year was becoming thinner, making winter snowshoe journeys across the lake a more dangerous and unpredictable prospect. This was the consequence of warmer winters and more rainfall in the late winter period—what we would now describe as man-made climate change. She also documented the pollution that contaminated the lake by which she made her home—while she had largely removed herself from the modern world, the pervasive effects of mankind's passage through the twentieth century reached her, unbidden and unwanted. They may even have contributed to her death, for she developed terminal Alzheimer's in later life—in her earlier writing, she noted presciently that the dangerously high levels of mercury and other metals she found in the drinking water she drew from her lake could lead to health problems.

LaBastille chronicled her life in the Adirondacks over the course of four books; the fifth volume of the *Woodswoman* series was unpublished, her writing cut short by her illness and untimely death. Describing her life at her cabin in those earlier, more untroubled days, she recounted how her time writing was interrupted only by the occasional visit of the mail boat, feeding the stove, or admiring the hummingbirds. Whilst she was alone in the woods, surrounded by nature she never considered herself really alone.

I felt a kinship with Anne LaBastille, for I too had taken myself from the bustle and whirl of modern life to live somewhere more remote and, perhaps, to enjoy a more simple and uncomplicated way of life. I too had seen change in the course of the years I had lived in Shetland—birds that, at one time, were common breeding species in the summer were now in decline or absent altogether. More than that kinship, I also felt that LaBastille's life was a cautionary tale for us all. No matter where we run and hide, no matter how well we individually try to live our lives, the excesses of humanity are inescapable and will come to find us.

Hummingbirds remain inspiring to the present day, and they count amongst their American admirers some more unlikely devotees than birdwatchers and ecologists. Spencer Pratt, a larger-than-life reality TV personality, is better known for his appearances on *The Hills* and *I'm a Celebrity . . . Get Me Out of Here!* than for his love of hummingbirds yet, pinned to the top of his Twitter feed, he has posted a video of himself wearing a pair of sunglasses on the lenses of which are attached red and yellow plastic hummingbird feeder flowers. A hovering hummingbird darts back and forth, drinking sugar water from the flowers, almost touching Pratt's impassive face with her wingtips. The video has been viewed over eight hundred thousand times, and his Instagram account, amongst idyllic photos of his picture-perfect family life, features many more short videos of feeding hummingbirds. The grounds of his Los Angeles home are planted with nectar-bearing plants and bedecked with hummingbird feeders. Dozens of hummingbirds visit the property daily. Pratt describes an Anna's Hummingbird he has named Tiki as one of his best friends in the world, including humans. He seems addicted to fame and hummingbirds in equal measure.

Their pop culture appeal flew further afield for a while, providing eponymous inspiration for Australian indie music band The Hummingbirds. The latter were said to have stated their ambition was to be the ultimate pop band and, in his obituary of founding member, lead singer, and guitar player Simon Holmes, music journalist and birder Andrew Stafford recalled, "The Hummingbirds' career was true to their name and their sound: a blur. They were here and they were gone, leaving just two albums and a clutch of glorious singles behind."

I could understand that an indie band, even one half a world away from the Americas in which hummingbirds were exclusively found, might want to name themselves after these feisty, beautiful birds that lived fast and died young. Many hummingbirds will die in their first year. Those that survive the trials of early life can expect an average lifespan of just three to four frenetic years. They seemed like the perfect metaphor for the rock and roll lifestyle.

Yet beyond their appeal to reality TV stars and hard-living musicians, hummingbirds touch something within people no less remarkable but rather less famous. In Las Vegas, for a few years, an investigator called Marion Brady-Hamilton worked around a crime scene investigation (CSI) career in the United States' most hedonistic city to devote herself to caring for injured hummingbirds.

Brady-Hamilton found herself under the hummingbird spell by accident rather than design. With more than twenty years of working for the North Las Vegas Police Department under her belt, Brady-Hamilton was also volunteering at a local, nonprofit nature sanctuary during 2008, when a hatchling hummingbird was brought in for care. A young hummingbird needs to be fed several times an hour and, just like an adult hummingbird, it needs more than simply natural nectar or homemade sugar water—hummingbirds need protein too. Adult birds find this by fly-catching for small insects—but providing protein for a young hummingbird in captivity is a more complicated business for its human foster parent. Until she discovered a protein powder suitable to mix into sugar water for her young charge, Brady-Hamilton resorted to pulverising mealworms she sourced from a local pet shop. She later ruefully recalled that it was easier to mix the birds a proprietary protein shake than to squeeze the guts from a mealworm.

Due to the frequency with which a young hummingbird needs to be fed, Brady-Hamilton was entrusted to take the bird in question home with her. A rolled up sock in a birdcage in her home gym was pressed into service as a nest, and the young bird thrived. In due course he was released into her garden, and went on to rear a brood of his own in the wild there. Her fame as a hummingbird carer spread by word of mouth and, in the years that followed, she successfully rehabilitated dozens more birds—sometimes even taking the youngest, neediest birds to work with her, innocent witnesses to Las Vegas crime scenes.

In California, meanwhile, a teacher named Terry Masear was taking hummingbird advocacy to another level entirely. Over the course of a decade at the start of the century, Masear and a network of hummingbird rehabilitators took in excess of forty thousand telephone calls from members of the public concerned about the well-being of hummingbirds. Some five thousand birds have been taken into care; and the majority of these, having been looked after and their needs seen to, have been released back into the wild.

From Brooklyn, New York, Courtney Gillette shared with me a more personal account of what hummingbirds had meant to her family: "When my sober, septic worker father retired to Arizona, he got a hummingbird feeder for his apartment patio. He introduced me to the hummingbirds when I first visited. 'That one's Flash,' he said. 'And that one's Bubba.' I think about this a lot."

The more I heard how individuals felt touched by these charismatic birds, the more questions I found myself asking. What was it about hummingbirds that struck such a chord with people who had, hitherto, not considered themselves birders as such? The connection people felt was clearly more than a simple aesthetic attraction. Time and again I heard similar stories to Courtney's, of a friend or family member who had found a hummingbird visiting their garden, either to attend a dedicated feeding station or nectar-bearing flowers, and had duly given the bird a name.

Hummingbirds seemed to elicit a personal response that other colourful North American bird species simply did not. I wondered if the attraction stemmed from the hummingbirds' apparently fearless nature, and willingness to approach us closely, right up to the boundaries that separated our homes from the wild. We are used to wild things treating us with caution. Historically, we have given them ample cause to do so. Hummingbirds, perhaps, touch some deep ancestral place within us, reminding us of innocence lost. Maybe they seem to confirm what we want to believe we are, benign and friendly apes that wild creatures can approach without fear. The reality, often, may be more prosaic.

"When we bought our house, we were thrilled to find that hummingbirds would hover outside our window," Adrianne Covino recounted to me from Connecticut. "We told a neighbour, and were told the hummingbirds were doing that because the previous owners had a feeder there. We were being harassed for food and didn't realize. Of course, we bought one!"

For all we may subconsciously choose to anthropomorphise hummingbirds, giving them human names and attributing emotional agency to them, there is no getting away from the fact that they are still truly wild animals. Indeed, they are infamously pugnacious, possessed of a ferocity to their own kind that defies all odds and makes a mockery of the collective noun sometimes applied to them—a bouquet of hummingbirds, for anyone who has spared them more than a passing glance, is cloyingly and inaccurately saccharine.

Jonathan Franzen, author of *The Corrections* and a keen birder, shared his experience of putting a hummingbird feeder up in the garden of his Californian home:

> I find hummingbirds gorgeous, amazing, terrible, and therefore somewhat comic. For a while, I was putting out a feeder for them, but it was just too depressing, and ridiculous, to see a single male Anna's Hummingbird park himself on a branch above it, not particularly to feed, just to drive away other Anna's and try to murder the Allen's Hummingbirds.
>
> It put me in mind of something John Irving [author of *The Cider House Rules*] once told me about wrestlers—the heavyweights are nice enough, the guys you have to watch out for are the little ones. This was in the context of US Congressional politics—I was comparing Dennis Hastert's affability to Tom DeLay's nastiness. Hastert (a former wrestler) was about

six feet four and weighed about 280 pounds; DeLay was wiry and even shorter than the 5'7" at which he was listed. DeLay was the hummer.

The power of feeders to draw hummingbirds, like moths to a candle flame, into a domestic garden is remarkable. It is also addictive, for many householders soon find themselves adding further feeders to their garden's repertoire, enhancing the reputation of their home amongst the burgeoning numbers of hummingbirds that visit and, if word gets around, amongst birdwatchers too. Often, the addition of a second feeder comes as a response to the vehemence with which one hummingbird will defend the first feeder against all comers, but in no time more feeders proliferate as the hummingbird bug bites deeper.

Some gardens have become nationally renowned as places at which to see hummingbirds, none more so than that of the late Wally and Marion Paton's house in Patagonia, Arizona. The Patons began to invite birders into their garden shortly after moving to Patagonia in the early 1970s. Wally had formerly worked in Boston at an aerospace company that made parts for the Apollo Moon Program—an industry that knew a thing or two about feats of precision flight. Little did Wally know when he moved his family to Arizona that their future would be indelibly bound with the greatest of all nature's fliers.

Their home itself was a modest, single-storey white clapboard house with a blue tin roof. Their garden was modest too, but as soon as they began to put feeders out for the birds, they realised they lived somewhere special. Patagonia is a small town, to this day with fewer than one thousand residents, sitting in the Sonoran Desert near the border with Mexico. In its heyday the town was at the heart of the Hollywood western moviemaking industry, the surrounding desert landscapes providing evocative settings for movies like *Hondo* and *The Outlaw Josey Wales*.

If the Sonoran Desert once proved attractive to actors like John Wayne and Clint Eastwood, the green, lush areas of Patagonia act like magnets for birds; and feeding stations in those green spaces exert an even more potent force. The Patons found themselves inundated with birds of all kinds, both resident species and migrants passing back and forth from Mexico.

Amongst this plethora of birds was a particular hummingbird that, in turn, attracted birdwatchers. At first there were one or two birders, but soon, as word got around, many more were to follow. Violet-crowned Hummingbird was a species at best scarce in the United States, and certainly hard to see—but not at the Patons' home, where it was encountered regularly, an elegant bird with snow-white underparts and a glittering violet headpiece like a shard of amethyst. It was to prove a potent lure for a nation's birders. Linda Stitt, a friend of Marion Paton, recalled lines of people gathering in the street to peer into their yard through the fence.

Happily for all concerned, the Patons did not mind the attention their humble garden was beginning to receive. In fact, they welcomed it, and for years were warm and generous hosts to birdwatchers from all around the world. If you were lucky, Marion might even bring you some freshly baked cookies to enjoy while you sat watching the many hummingbird feeders that hung from the eaves of the house. The Patons provided benches for their visitors, offered the use of field guides for those who were unfamiliar with the birds before them, and set up a blackboard for their visitors to record their sightings. A sun-faded sign on the perimeter gate left no doubt one had found the right place—"Birdwatchers are welcome"—and a tin can nearby for donations to "the sugar fund" indicated that this was a place where hummingbirds took front and centre stage.

In the early years of the current century the Patons passed away, but their legacy endures to this day. When their daughter, Bonnie Paton Moon, put their former home on the market in 2012, the forthcoming sale came to the attention of Ann Cullen Smith—a remarkable woman in her own right who, at the age of 104, was still both a keen birder and a redoubtable champion of all things environmental. She contacted Victor Emanuel, a prominent and passionate American birdwatcher, and he, in turn, spearheaded a fundraising campaign with the American Bird Conservancy (ABC) and the Tucson Audubon Society (TAS).

A nation's birders rallied to the cause—so many of them had seen their first Violet-crowned Hummingbird there, amongst shifting, buzzing drifts of other, commoner hummingbirds that were gathered at Wally and Marion's feeders. Acclaimed American bird artist David Sibley painted a gouache Violet-crowned Hummingbird for auction towards the fundraising effort, recalling the pleasure he had found sitting and birding in the Patons' yard. This alone raised $1,660.

In late 2014 ownership of the now rebranded Paton Center was formally passed to TAS, to be maintained for birders in perpetuity—a place intended to inspire people to take an interest in birds in particular and conservation in general.

I met David Sibley in Boston in February 2001, on one of those uniquely Bostonian winter days, when the air burned in your lungs and your bones ached with the force of the cold. Hummingbirds could not have been further from my mind, and while I was aware of the reputation of Wally and Marion Paton's home, I did not appreciate their New England roots. David signed my copy of his new, groundbreaking field guide and, years later, it was with this book in hand that I stepped through the gates of the Patons' former home, on a pilgrimage to visit somewhere that held a special place in many birders' hearts. I would soon come to appreciate why that reputation was so well-deserved.

Perhaps a dozen hummingbird feeders hung along the length of the house. It was early April and, while that still felt like winter in my Shetland home, here in Arizona a cold desert night had melted into a warm spring day. The garden itself was compact. Sitting on one of the famous benches, one could see all the feeders set out before you. I joined a small group of other birdwatchers, all American but for me. One couple were relatively local, having travelled down from Tucson; but others had come from further afield, from

New York and Oregon. Introductions made, we sat in companionable silence watching Rufous Hummingbirds dominating the feeders. Occasionally a male Broad-billed Hummingbird would chance a visit—a confection of countless shades of blue and green rippling behind a lance-like black and red bill. The Rufous Hummingbirds, furious darts of flame, would not tolerate him for long and were quick to drive him back into the trees that framed the garden boundary, the air ringing with their angry, scolding chatter.

In the trees lurked something more unusual still, and it was this hummingbird that I longed to see more than any other whilst I was in Arizona. This was, of course, the species that fixed the Patons' home as one of the brightest stars in the American hummingbird firmament—the Violet-crowned Hummingbird. The blackboard that recorded all the latest sightings promised a male bird had been seen the previous afternoon. While the Rufous Hummingbirds squabbled and jousted around the feeders, tension was mounting amongst their human audience.

"Maybe it's moved on?" said one of the New York birders, gloomily. "It should be showing by now if it's here."

His pessimism was just the challenge Fate needed, for shortly after this pronouncement the star of the show deigned to take to the stage. Compared to the vivid colours of the main cast of Rufous Hummingbirds and their Broad-billed understudy, the plumage of the male Violet-crowned Hummingbird that hovered, painfully briefly, before us was an exercise in restraint and subtlety—a hummingbird of two halves, pale mink above and snow white below. It was only when he perched high in the branches of an overhanging tree after he had fed, fastidiously wiping his bill clean on the branch at his feet, that the eponymous violet crown announced itself in the low, golden sunlight—piercing flashes of amethyst purple glancing off him as he twisted his head to and fro, like sparks rising from a stirred fire.

A low gasp came, spontaneously, from the small audience around me. I may even have joined them—in that moment, there was simultaneously a sense of release and pure appreciation of the beauty of the bird before us. The rarity of the species in the United States only served to gild the lily still further, at least for my American counterparts for whom this bird was a new bird, a so-called life bird—a new bird for their life lists.

I am unusual amongst birdwatchers in not keeping many lists. For many, those lists are fundamental. A life list keeps an overall tally of how many different bird species one has encountered in a lifetime. Then there are national lists—British, United States, and so forth. Drill down a little further, and there are county or state lists; patch lists of birds found around a birder's home area; a house list of birds seen from one's home . . . and then there are lists delineated by periods of time—with a year list being a common self-imposed time limit within which to see as many species as possible in a given geographical boundary.

One of the best-known examples of a compulsive list-keeper must be American birder Sandy Komito. Played as Kenny Bostick with slapstick gusto by Owen Wilson in the movie *The Big Year*, Komito's portrayal of himself in real life is every bit as hyperbolic and colourful. While *The Big Year* movie was based upon the book of the same title by Mark Obmascik, Komito himself wrote a personal account of his record-breaking year list in *I Came, I Saw, I Counted*—a sequel to his earlier *Birding's Indiana Jones*. If the titles give a clue to the nature of the birder, the contents are more revealing still. While Komito clearly loves seeing birds, particularly species that are new to him, appreciation of aesthetics or simple wonder, while present, take a backseat to the main task at hand—building a big list, and beating his year-listing rivals. Recounting a trip to Arizona in 1987, Komito visited Madera Canyon, some fifteen miles northwest of Patagonia, to look for a Berylline Hummingbird, a Mexican species rarely seen north of the border. After several hours of fruitless waiting, he eventually caught sight of the bird and, after taking a handful of photos to document his sighting, he got straight back into his car and set off for Cave Creek, many miles away across the state, looking for more new hummingbirds for his year list—Calliope and Violet-crowned.

The entire encounter with the Berylline Hummingbird was over in a matter of minutes, reduced to a few hasty photos and a number on a list. Berylline Hummingbird is just one more component of a final total of some 725 species Komito would personally see in the course of the year, a truly epic undertaking on his part and, personal satisfaction aside, all for the perceived kudos attached to having recorded the biggest year list ever amassed to date in the United States. The commitment of time and money would have been considerable, and way beyond the means or inclination of many—but, as many birders' families would ruefully attest, even at a local level the birder in their life will commit countless hours to adding to a patch list, a county list, a year list, or their life list. Birders *love* lists.

Me? Not so much.

Before I moved to my Shetland home, I was as compulsive a list-keeper as the best of them. Something changed though once I found my own Walden or Black Bear Lake—the only list that mattered to me then was my house list. My focus turned in upon itself, and I began to appreciate birds in their own right rather than as numerical abstracts. I became more interested in other aspects of the natural world—insects, wildflowers, mammals, molluscs, lichens—and more concerned about the habitats and environments upon which they all depended.

While I don't keep lists, and could not readily tell you how many species of anything I've seen in any given place or time, what I do know is what I haven't seen before, and, just like the keenest list-keeping birder, I love to see new birds. This male Violet-capped Hummingbird in the Patons' garden was a new bird for me—that alone always makes my spirits soar. If the bird in question is a hummingbird, the experience is elevated to something purer, more transcendental. We all have our favourites, if we only care to admit them.

If the Patons' garden was a place of specific pilgrimage, a bird-watcher's Mecca, the state of Arizona as a whole was like the Holy

Land in general, redolent with birding history. All of the United States' most respected birders had, at one time or another or, indeed, repeatedly come to pay their respects. It goes without saying that during their *Wild America* travels Peterson and Fisher found hummingbirds in Arizona, but as the latter half of the twentieth century unfolded and birding increased in popularity, others followed in their footsteps.

In 1973 a young birder dropped out of high school in Kansas and hit the road, hitchhiking his way around America, searching for birds and trying to set a new United States year list record. Kenn Kaufman was just sixteen years old, and had little more in the world than the clothes he stood up in and his binoculars. Hitchhiking was a decision made of economic necessity, and meant that at times his progress was painfully slow. His penurious state drove other, more extreme measures to be taken in his pursuit of birds—he subsisted at times on pet food, rationing a box of Little Friskies dry cat food to last him days, and sold his blood plasma twice a week for $5 a pint to raise critical working capital.

Kaufman spent a lot of time in Arizona that year, searching for lost Mexican hummingbirds in Ramsey Canyon, and finding a White-eared Hummingbird in the Chiricahua Mountains. On the subject of bird-listing, he was thoughtful.

"Any bird-listing attempt limited by time was like a reminder of mortality. The day ends, the year will end, everything will end. *Time is short*, reads the underlying message. *Make the most of it.*"

This was a sentiment I could relate to. While my hummingbird quest was not about seeing every single species—in other words, keeping a list—there was certainly a sense of the finite driving me. I was aware that some hummingbirds teetered on the brink of extinction; and that many others existed in habitat that was threatened and could, all too quickly, be gone forever. Where my hummingbirds were concerned, I did not want them all—but I certainly wanted to see some of them before they were gone for good.

Stuart Winter, a friend of mine, went a step further. In 1995, a year before the author of *Wild America* passed away, he took afternoon tea with Roger Tory Peterson. Stuart recalled:

I was sitting face to face with Roger Tory Peterson, childhood hero, living legend, and the giant upon whose shoulders generations of bird-watchers had been awakened. I had been granted the equivalent of a papal audience or royal investiture with the right to interview Dr. Peterson at his idyllic home. To say I was simply star-struck would have been diluting such an awesome moment.

As we drank our tea and spoke about Dr. Peterson's memories of England and his wartime experiences, my eye was drawn to a flicker outside. More conversation. More flickering. Outside a sprite seemed to be dancing on zephyrs, all speed and vim without shape or form. One second casting a shadow on the studio windows, the next a vanished apparition on the mind's eye. By now I was struggling to convert Dr. Peterson's hushed tones into contemporaneous notes. The more my eyes detected movement, the greater the effort to pay attention. Only when I was invited to go for a birdwatching walk with my hero could I assuage my curiosity.

Outside the studio, Dr. Peterson was in his element, detecting the faintest bird call or flash of wings and delivering an immediate identification. In minutes we had seen a handful of warblers, flycatchers, and vireos amid the tangles of lush vegetation. From nowhere, another bird materialised, the source of my earlier distraction. It hovered by a flower with the upright posture of a feisty barroom brawler, upright and with wings beating in a blur. In deference to the great ornithologist, the hummer rested on the flimsiest of sprigs and looked our way, spreading its gorget in the afternoon sunlight as if it was a poker-player fanning a crimson-hued hand of diamonds and hearts. Dr. Peterson smiled. He sensed I was on to a lifer.

My audience with the great man soon came to an end. Yet there was still time for one more moment's example of his generosity of spirit. Shaking hands and thanking him for his time and hospitality,

he handed me a signed copy of his field guide. 'To Stuart, Good Birding! Roger Tory Peterson,' read the inscription written in his distinctive
handwriting with ink the colour of our Ruby-throated Hummingbird's
bejewelled throat. For me, it had truly been a red letter day.

I was too late to meet Roger Tory Peterson, one of my childhood
heroes, but if I was to go looking for hummingbirds anywhere in the
lower states, it had to be following in his and a succession of other notable American birders' footsteps, in Arizona. My visit to the Patons'
house was the start of several days spent exploring the famous sites on
the birders' Arizona circuit—delving into the various canyons in the
sky islands that rise from the otherwise flat Sonoran Desert, looking
for newly arrived migrant hummingbirds heading north from their
wintering grounds in Mexico for the breeding season to come.

Many were, like the Rufous Hummingbirds, relatively common
in the United States—though not as common as once they were before intensive agriculture changed the face of much of the country.
In 1895 Major Charles Emil Bendire recorded seeing Rufous Hummingbirds at a scarcely credible density of "a-thousand-to-the-acre"
in Oregon near Fort Klamath.

However, I also wanted to see if I could find for myself a vagrant
hummingbird or two, something that had drifted north of the Mexican border. Arizona is justly famous as a place in which to find all
manner of lost Central American birds, hummingbirds included. I
had now seen a Violet-crowned Hummingbird, but I longed to find
a Berylline or a Lucifer Hummingbird for myself.

I joined Teresa deKoker, a naturalist living in Green Valley, for a
few days exploring the Arizona hinterlands along the Mexican border. I soon realised I was, perhaps, a little early for the main thrust
of migration, as we were seeing for the most part resident birds with
just a few migratory species in small numbers, the vanguard of the
main force that was massing south of the border.

This was my first experience of birding so close to the Mexican border, and it was a mixed one. On the one hand, the desert

surroundings were so completely alien and new to me that the sheer novelty of being in the landscape was both thrilling and profound. We wandered amongst immense, corrugated Saguaro Cacti, startling noisy Gila Woodpeckers that nested in cavities excavated within the prickly, armed giants, and searched for Phainopepla, a shiny black silky flycatcher with a punk's Mohican crest and a taste for the pearlescent crimson berries of Desert Mistletoe. In damper areas we found Vermillion Flycatchers, their inky black and blood-red plumage advertising their presence from a distance.

On the other hand, while I was hoping to find migratory birds in the depths of Sycamore Canyon in the heart of the Pajarita Wilderness that runs along the Mexican border, the most abundant evidence was of migration of a different, human kind. Litter abounded here, caught up in the undergrowth—empty food packets and tins, all of Mexican origin; soiled nappies; discarded pieces of faded clothing—dropped by what appeared to be a steady trickle of immigrants who had crossed the barbed-wire border further down the remote canyon and headed north into Arizona, hoping for opportunities and a chance of a new life. If the trash weren't evidence enough, the footprints we found in the damp ground alongside the small pools and seeps that marked the passage of a stream running south through the canyon were more compelling still. All pointed north into the United States.

We had parked Teresa's venerable Volkswagen campervan at the head of the canyon, the only other vehicle there a pickup truck in the green and white livery of the Border Patrol, the armed federal police force that exists to secure the United States' borders, particularly that with Mexico, against illegal ingress. Under a cloudless blue sky a chocolate brown and white Arizona Woodpecker was noisily scrambling around the branches of the trees above us, but Teresa had eyes only for the pickup. There was no sign of life in the vehicle.

"They'll probably be down in the canyon, sitting hidden someplace and waiting to catch anyone heading north," she said sourly.

We were not sure whether to be reassured or perturbed by the presence of Border Patrol. Our encounters with them in the past days had left me with little love for their officers—they had been uniformly barely civil, finding my British passport suspiciously alien and my explanations of looking for hummingbirds scarcely credible.

Contrary to the anti-immigrant rhetoric that emanated from Donald Trump, many Arizona residents feel compassion for those desperate enough to risk all crossing the border and the uncompromising Sonoran Desert with little more than the clothes on their backs. Teresa told me how some rural householders regularly leave food on their porches at night for anyone passing by in the darkness. I was reminded of the folklore tales back home where, centuries ago, Shetland people were said to have left offerings of food for the trows, supernatural beings who dwelt in the surrounding hills. I wondered if the legend of the trows owed itself to the desperate remnants of the Picts, displaced from their homes by the invading Vikings. Pushed out onto the Shetland moors to a life on the margins of society, did they come back at night to see what they could forage from those who felt compassionately towards the circumstances in which they found themselves?

Our passage down the canyon was slow, following the meandering path that took us beside the creek bed and towards the border with Mexico. The sound of Canyon Wrens echoed from the bluffs above us, a sweet descending song that ended with two harsh, rasping notes. Another discordant bird call was more arresting still. *Wahk-wahk-wahk* . . . Something was croaking in the dense undergrowth that scrambled from the creek up towards the cliffs above us. Movement resolved itself into a bird—not a hummingbird, but something rare nonetheless. A male Elegant Trogon fell silent and eyed us suspiciously. Trogons are found in tropical forests around the world, with the American Neotropical region particularly blessed with species diversity. Their most northerly representative, Elegant Trogon, is irregularly seen north of Mexico. This was a significant personal discovery, and a colourful one too.

I greedily drank in the bird's lime-green upperparts and raspberry-red belly, the snow-white pectoral band and banana-yellow bill. It is no wonder that itinerant Elegant Trogons have long been recognised as being of considerable importance to Arizona. In the 1970s the Cornell Lab of Ornithology, a leading conservation organisation and global centre for the study of birds and biodiversity, viewed the presence of Elegant Trogons in Arizona as an important socioeconomic factor in the state. It has been estimated that as many as twenty-five thousand American birders annually visit Cave Creek Canyon, a site the birds favour in the Chiricahua Mountains, hoping to catch sight of one. Here, unscheduled and unexpectedly, Teresa and I had stumbled across not one, but two birds—for even as we watched, a female flew to an adjacent tree a little higher up the slope. They seemed to confer, briefly, before flying back into deep cover and were lost from sight.

My eyes were drawn upwards by their flight and, above us, at the base of the cliffs, I could see a number of cave entrances. The young boy within me could not possibly resist the opportunity to explore.

"I won't be long. I'm just going to have a quick look inside them," I reassured Teresa. She was visibly unimpressed.

"I don't think you should go up there. There could be people hiding up there during the day. They might not be pleased to see you."

High on trogons, I dismissed this innate caution out of hand. It was a fine sunny day, I was an obviously unthreatening British birder; I could speak Spanish; and, besides, there was a Border Patrol officer or two somewhere here in the depths of the canyon with us. How bad could things possibly be? I left Teresa on the path beside the creek and climbed up the steep rocky slope to the cliff base.

Despite Teresa's reservations, I found nobody hiding in the caves once I reached them. There were, however, signs that these caves were indeed used by people travelling north in search of a new life—circular firepits neatly ringed with large, soot-blackened stones, a scatter of empty, Spanish-labelled tin cans, and discarded blankets piled here and there. A recess at the back of the largest cave led darkly into the heart of the canyon wall. Exploring that would mean going on my hands and knees into the darkness, and somehow that didn't seem like such a good idea for all my earlier bravado. Teresa was calling me from the canyon base, so I headed back down the slope to her. She didn't seem entirely happy with my little solo excursion.

"Come on, I want to get moving. It feels like somebody's watching me," she said. I have never been a great believer in the idea of innately knowing when one's being watched—logically, I cannot conceive how it works. Now did not seem like an opportune time to explore this, as Teresa was clearly agitated. I tried to calm things down.

"It's probably just the Border Patrol guys waiting for someone to show up. Let's keep going and see if we can find any hummers, or maybe refind those trogons."

We made our way further down the canyon. Our passage was becoming increasingly difficult, with the path wending through thick scrub and between some large boulders. Eventually, we could go no further—the path ended at the edge of a deep pool in the creek, bordered by sheer sides of rock. We would either have to go chest-deep through it, or climb up the canyon sides and try to circumvent it. Neither was an appealing option—we had been out for a few hours, and wanted to make sure we got back to the trail head in daylight. While we had not found any migrant hummingbirds, in the Arizona Woodpecker and the Elegant Trogons I had seen two impressive new species, and I had ample cause to feel satisfied with the day's work. We turned around, and started to walk back into the thick bushes we had just pushed our way through a minute or two earlier.

The shock of almost treading on a Puma is hard to convey in words. Suffice to say, when it exploded from the undergrowth at my feet and ran up the sloping canyon sides to the cliff base, I was at first merely surprised, the sort of surprise you get when you accidentally flush an unseen grouse from at your feet. Startled, certainly. In the few seconds it was visible as it fled away from us, I registered that this animal was large and long, tawny brown, and seemed to almost flow effortlessly uphill. It moved unbelievably fast . . . And then the realisation of precisely what we were seeing kicked in. This was my first wild Puma, and I had almost been close enough to touch it. Wildlife encounters with large mammals rarely come as intimate as this, and my heart was racing.

It had no sooner reached the cliff base and vanished from view than a chorus of screeching, caterwauling screams began to echo off the rocks around us. This was a territorial big cat making absolutely certain we knew just whose territory we were on. Teresa swiftly quashed my plans to head up the slope to see if I could get some photos.

"You are absolutely *not* going up there. That's one unhappy kitty. You don't mess with a cornered cat."

Feeling a strange mixture of elation and chagrin, we walked—perhaps a little more quickly than when we had come down the path—back up it. There, in the mud amongst our footprints and those of the previous day's Mexican immigrants, were the paw prints of the Puma. It had stalked us down the trail. Those large paw prints began where we had earlier been watching the Elegant Trogons, in the place where Teresa had complained that it felt like someone was watching her. The elation gave way to something else. It is profoundly humbling to have been stalked, perhaps considered as prey, by a large carnivore.

The following day we crossed the border into Mexico at Nogales. The town straddles the border, the Arizona side an anonymous small American conurbation, the Mexican side a considerably larger, bustling hive of activity. Mexican Nogales also has good, affordable dentists, and it was one of these that Teresa wanted to visit. I was along for the ride and wandered the streets of the town while Teresa was otherwise occupied.

In the larger general stores I recognised some of the brand names I had seen on discarded packaging in Sycamore Canyon the previous day. I guessed many migrants would stop in Nogales, briefly, to stock up on whatever provisions they needed and could afford before striking out of the town along the border to find a place where they could melt into the United States unobserved.

In the backstreets, I found smaller shops selling a more diverse range of fresh produce and goods. Their shop fronts were brightly painted, as colourful as an Elegant Trogon, and just as enticing. I wandered in and out of them aimlessly, killing time. I was finally stopped in my tracks in one of them that had, on the outside, promised *plantas medicinales*, or medicinal plants. As a biologist, I was curious to see what I might find inside.

Behind the counter I discovered the very last thing I expected. A hand-painted sign, depicting hummingbirds in flight, advertised *chuparosas*. A shallow, compartmentalised wooden tray beneath the sign contained small plastic bags. It was hard to see what was inside them. The shopkeeper, a friendly woman I judged to be in her early sixties, saw I was interested in the chuparosas and helpfully told me about them, clearly hoping for a sale. She put the tray on the counter between us and held one of the small plastic bags up for my inspection.

"They are chuparosas, for love, you understand? Inside here is la chuparosa, and a prayer. It will bring you good fortune in love. Do you have a girlfriend?"

I could understand most of this, but was not familiar with the term *chuparosa*. Perhaps she could tell from the blank expression on my face.

"You know, la chuparosa? The little bird . . ."

She moved her hand in short, staccato bursts in midair in front of my face as she spoke, the plastic bag snapping against her hand each time it stopped. The meaning of the hovering hand pantomime was suddenly clear.

"You mean a *colibrí*?" I asked. "A hummingbird?"

"Si!" she smiled broadly, delighted that we were overcoming the language barrier so easily. "Look, I will show you!"

She carefully opened the bag, and tipped the contents onto the counter.

"Here, this is the prayer. And this . . ." She paused, untying a tassled length of black cord that bound a red cloth bundle, "this is la chuparosa. It's very powerful!"

She looked at me expectantly. This was clearly the close, the big reveal that would seal the deal. Long ago I had worked as a salesman, and I recognised the pregnant silence for what it was.

Set before me, on a shiny scrap of crimson satin, was a tragically small corpse. Death rendered the bird even tinier than it appeared in life. Wings tightly against its body, bill sticking out in front of it, it looked a little like a plump dart. I could not be sure, but it appeared to be either a Rufous or an Allen's Hummingbird, judging by the rich rufous tones of the feathers. I felt a little queasy. This was the first time I had encountered wildlife commercialised and rendered as a mere commodity. I tore my eyes away from it. I knew I should feel angry, should perhaps challenge the shopkeeper, but that was not what happened. The hummingbirds were just one product in a shop containing hundreds of remedies drawn from nature. There was no personal judgment to be drawn upon the shopkeeper—this was, apparently, an instance of the law of supply and demand, a demand that I had not hitherto realised existed. I found myself, instead, thanking her politely and making my excuses before leaving the shop. Nonetheless, I felt embarrassed and ashamed of myself as I walked back to meet Teresa for lunch.

Later, back at her parents' home in Green Valley, we sat outside and drank margaritas that numbed our faces in the warm early evening air. I could hear a hummingbird calling at the feeder that hung from their neighbour's porch. I still felt thrown by the chance encounter in Nogales, and the faint chattering of the unseen hummingbird sounded reproachful. Now I too was ascribing human emotions to a hummingbird.

Milton Oldman, a photographer in Quebec, told me how curious Ruby-throated Hummingbirds regularly came to investigate him at his family lakeside retreat.

"Hanging a yellow, orange, or red life-jacket to dry under the eaves of my shack's porch attracts them. They'll fly right at the jacket, hover in puzzlement six inches away for a few seconds, then zoom off.

"Similar things regularly happen when I'm sitting on the porch reading a book, with a Manhattan or a clear glass of Campari-and-anything on the folding table right near the front edge. The little buggers will hover a bit closer over a drink, almost as if they're contemplating perching on the rim of the glass. They always zoom off, though—I've never had one decide to take a sip."

Sitting in the gathering Arizona dusk, I wished the unseen hummingbird next door would come and investigate my margarita. On the whole, I felt I probably did not deserve that blessing, for I had done its kind no favours with my complicit silence earlier.

CHAPTER THREE

LA CHUPAROSA

~

Mexico, Mexico City & Jalisco. 19°–20° N

*T*HOSE CHUPAROSAS THAT SO UNSETTLED ME IN THE INTER-
stice between the United States and Mexico had their dark origins well south of those hinterlands, and many centuries in the
past. North of what would, in later years, become that hard border, hummingbirds featured in the rich oral traditions of the native
tribes. Hummingbirds were noted for their beauty, and often served
as messengers or bridges between the living and those in the spirit
world. A Cherokee story tells of a healer who transforms himself
into a hummingbird in order to search for and harvest a valuable lost
plant. An Apache legend speaks of a warrior who, killed tragically
young, returned to the world in the form of a hummingbird to visit
the woman he loved. His arrival heralded the end of winter and the
return of clement weather.

Hummingbirds were perceived as benign envoys in the north.
Further south, they had a very different and more central role in the

mythology and religion of the Aztecs. The pantheon of Aztec deities was every bit as complicated, fervid, and bloody as that of ancient Greece—and was populated by myriad gods and goddesses, many of whom displayed a penchant for warfare to one extent or another. That, almost certainly, was a reflection of a principal aspect of the earthly society of the Aztecs. Yet in a region that abounded with predatory fauna, from eagles in the sky overhead to Jaguars in the jungles on earth, it is intriguing that the principal god of war in ancient Mexico should be associated most closely with hummingbirds.

The precise meaning of Huitzilopochtli's name remains a source of contention to this day, but we can be certain that the Nahua word *huitzilin* or hummingbird forms the basis of it. The Nahua were a native people, who, in time, came to be subsumed within the broader Aztec identity. During the fifteenth century Tlacaelel the Elder, son of Emperor Huitzilihuitl and Queen Cacamacihuatl, held the office of *cihuacoatl*, or senior adviser to the emperor, for decades—decades during which the Aztecs consolidated their position as the dominant regional power.

Tlacaelel played a pivotal role during this time of increased militarism, and it is telling that he chose to elevate Huitzilopochtli to a position of preeminence amongst the Aztec pantheon. Here was a god of war who surpassed all others—not only was he the Aztec god of war, but also of the sun and human sacrifice, and the patron of the city of Tenochtitlan. Tenochtitlan sits in the heart of latter-day Mexico City and, back then, it was the capital of the expanding Aztec empire.

It is not entirely surprising to learn that human sacrifice was said to have increased in prevalence under the supervision of Tlacaelel, presumably to both please Huitzilopochtli and to wield as a powerful tool of state control—a visceral and ritualised slaughter that simultaneously was divine deterrent and earthly inspiration. Aztec legend had it that Huitzilopochtli required human blood to provide him with strength. War, conveniently Huitzilopochtli's particular specialty, provided the god—and his supporters—with a steady flow of the necessary human and material tribute.

When one has seen how pugnacious hummingbirds can be with one another, and even towards other birds and animals much larger than themselves should the occasion warrant, the choice of a hummingbird god for the Aztec's supreme god of warfare makes perfect sense. Hummingbirds are fast, belligerent, and utterly fearless in defence of what is theirs. For an empire that placed great emphasis on physical aesthetics, hummingbirds would have been even more compelling for their outward beauty too. Small wonder the Aztecs believed dead warriors would be reincarnated as hummingbirds.

Legend had it that Huitzilopochtli was born after his mother, Coatlicue, was struck and impregnated by a falling ball of fine feathers whilst she was sweeping a temple floor. She was the goddess who also begat the moon and the stars, but Huitzilopochtli was different from the very beginning. He was said to have sprung from her fully grown, armed with an eagle feather shield and extravagant plumes on his headpiece.

The inclusion of feathers in the legend is telling. At the time in Mexico and the surrounding countries that make up the pre-Columbian Mesoamerican region, feathers were considered of equal value to precious stones like jade and turquoise. They were perceived as symbols of fertility, but also of power generally. Only the rich could afford them, and some feathers were intimately associated with divine powers. Fine and colourful featherwork clad kings and emperors, priests and holy idols, and bedecked the ceremonial clothing of warriors and their generals.

When, in 1519, the Aztec emperor Moctezuma II sent emissaries to the powerful neighbouring Purépecha Empire to ask for their help against the invading Spanish, he sent, amongst other gifts designed to beseech and compel their assistance, the feathers of quetzals—extravagant members of the trogon family. The Purépecha themselves had a history of sending green feathers to would-be allies, the feathers of Resplendent Quetzals being particularly sought-after. Before battle, their foes were customarily shown feather-clad shields in an act of defiance that was said to predestine Purépecha victory. Unfortunately for Moctezuma, his feathery entreaties were not well received—the Purépecha summarily slaughtered the Aztec emissaries.

The Aztecs had, over the years, attempted on more than one occasion to conquer the Purépecha, but the Purépecha repelled them every time. Indeed, the Purépecha had not tasted military defeat until the arrival of the Spanish in the 1520s, but their collapse was swift in the face of the uncompromising conquistadors—their capital, Tzintzuntzan, or *Place of the Hummingbirds*, was governed by Tangaxuan II until the arrival of Nuno de Guzman in 1529. De Guzman summarily had Tangaxuan burned at the stake. The Purépecha's feathers had proven ineffectual after all.

One of the conquistadors, Bernal Diaz del Castillo, wrote an account of what the Spanish found upon arrival in the Aztec Empire. He described "enchanted scenes" reminiscent of the *Amadís de Gaula*, a chivalric romance popular in Spain at the time: "To many of us it appeared doubtful whether we were asleep or awake . . . it must be considered that never yet did man see, hear, or dream of anything equal to the spectacle that greeted us."

His commander, Hernán Cortés, writing to Emperor Charles V in 1520, marvelled at the extent of trade in fine goods across Mexico. Describing the city of Tlaxcala, he said, "There is in this city a market where, every day, more than thirty thousand people come to buy and sell . . . In this market there is everything they might need or wish to trade. There is jewellery of gold and silver and precious stones and other ornaments of featherwork, and all as well-presented as in any square or marketplace in the world."

Cortés had already seen for himself the value the Aztecs placed in the feathers of hummingbirds and other colourful birds. Before he met Moctezuma, the emperor sent ambassadors to the conquistador leader, bearing gifts. Bernal Diaz del Castillo recalled, "At this time four of the principal nobility of Mexico arrived, with a rich present. It consisted of gold to the value of ten thousand crowns, and ten bales of the finest mantles of feathers. Having saluted Cortés with the profoundest respect, the ambassadors delivered the message of their monarch."

Here were feathers being accorded a similar importance to gold. Feathers were sourced from, and traded across, the entire Mesoamerican region, valued not only for their beauty and symbolic power but also for their portability as a commodity. Back in the Aztec capital, Tenochtitlan, an entire district was given over to artisans who received these feathers and turned them into the fine works of art, clothing, and religious iconography that the Aztec empire demanded. The Amantla neighbourhood gave rise to the name for the artisans who worked with the feathers—they became known as *amanteca*, and the value of their work was reflected in the unusual esteem with which they as craftsmen and women were held. None of them was expected to pay tribute to the Aztec state, nor were they expected to perform any public service.

Needless to say, this much demand for colourful feathers came at a cost to the birds themselves. Resplendent Quetzals were reputed to die in captivity, so instead were trapped and plucked of their long, iridescent green tail feathers before being released back into the wild to grow new feathers. That, at least, was the theory, as history does not record how those quetzals prospered with their denuded, bald rears.

Other birds were less amenable, and hummingbirds certainly were way too small and delicate to lend themselves to a harvest of their tiny metallic feathers that was anything but terminal. The Spanish missionary priest and Franciscan friar Bernardino de Sahagun, visiting the region in the early sixteenth century, made a list of the many species he saw involved in the thriving feather trade—amongst them, inevitably, were hummingbirds.

The arrival of the Spanish in Mexico boded just as ill for the Aztec Empire as the demand for their feathers had for Mexican and other

Central American birds. If the Aztecs wanted colourful feathers, the Spanish wanted far more besides. New Spain was a cornucopia of valuable things they desired, offering a seemingly endless resource to be plundered and developed.

Initially, however, the Aztecs evidently had no idea of the scale of their visitors' colonial ambitions. When the Aztec emperor Moctezuma showered Hernán Cortés with gifts, he did not realise he was fuelling the subjugation of his people and the end of his imperial power. In 1519 Cortés sent a consignment of assorted treasures and wonders back to Spain. Writing of the combined gold, silver, jewels, and feathered shields and head adornments, he concluded, "They are so marvellous that, considering their novelty and otherworldliness, they are priceless."

A further shipment, sent in 1522, was seized by French pirates off the Azores. This shipment was said to have been grander still. One wonders what the pirates made of the feathery components of their treasure—presumably the gold and silver elements would have been more obviously valuable and disposable commodities and, once any jewels had been removed from feathered headdresses or shields, the colourful but apparently monetarily worthless featherwork would have been thrown overboard or burned. The birds whose lives were lost in the making of the amanteca's art had had their deaths diminished still further.

However, if the Aztec culture of feathers as ceremonial wear and currency died out with the rapid obliteration of their empire by the Spanish, the demand for feathers did not succumb with it. While initially the Spanish sought to suppress the work of the amantecas, seeing it as part of the Aztec religion they wanted to replace with Catholicism, they quickly came to value those creative skills for the production of iconography destined for the Catholic Church back home in Europe.

Christian-themed feather mosaics, comprising many minute fragments of feathers glued to a paper base, began to be created for export shortly after the arrival of the conquistadors. The feathers of tropical birds, including the intensely coloured plumage of hummingbirds, provided the artists with a palette of metallic and iridescent colours that mere paint simply could not match. The sixteenth-century Italian naturalist Ulisse Aldrovandi described feather mosaics as the "threshold between art and science."

Most of these Christian feather mosaics featured prominent figures in the Christian canon, from the Virgin Mary and Jesus down through a variety of patron saints. One such piece, *The Mass of St. Gregory*, was presented in 1539 to Pope Paul III by Diego Huanitzin, the nephew and son-in-law of Moctezuma. The beauty and value of this gift notwithstanding, the very making of it shows how rapidly the Spanish evangelists had subsumed the Aztec people.

The papacy were greatly taken by these new representations of the great and good of the church—in 1599, Ulisse Aldrovandi reported that Pope Sixtus V insisted upon touching a feather mosaic depicting Saint Francis of Assisi, so convinced was he that it was painted and not comprising slivers of artfully combined feathers. Naturally, these pieces being rare and expensive, they became sought-after not only by the church but also by kings and nobles in Europe. They were ostentatious examples of wealth and power as well as piety.

In the late sixteenth century, Juan Bautista Cuiris created one of the most famous feather mosaics of all—a portrait of Christ made of hummingbird and parrot feathers. Now in the Kunsthistorisches Museum in Vienna, Christ's cobalt-blue robes and the aquamarine background have, over four hundred years since the mosaic was created, retained a startling metallic intensity.

As Catholicism spread in the New World, the incorporation of hummingbird feathers in religious artwork took a further turn as European and Latin American artistic traditions fused in the creation of liturgical objects. The Los Angeles County Museum of Arts holds a chalice, donated to the museum in 1948 by the newspaper magnate and inspiration for the title character of *Citizen Kane*, William Randolph Hearst, which was made by an unknown Mexican craftsman in the late sixteenth century. It is a richly ornamented confection of silver gilt, carved boxwood, rock crystal, and brilliant turquoise hummingbird feathers—the latter used as the background to the intricate carvings on the stem and base of the chalice. More everyday pieces, destined for the use of bishops in Europe, included feathered mitres and chasubles.

However, by the end of the eighteenth century the creation of these jewel-like icons and vestments had more or less died out, the skills of the old amanteca masters gradually being lost in the intervening years. That said, when the great Prussian naturalist Alexander von Humboldt visited Mexico in 1803, he acquired a feather image of *Our Lady of Health*—her face and hands were rendered in oil paint, but the remainder of the icon comprised hummingbird feathers, a combination of old and new world artistic techniques that had become increasingly commonplace during the eighteenth century—perhaps not only an artistic fusion, but also borne of necessity as some of the more unusual feathers may well have grown harder to come by as the species to which they were attached in life had become much scarcer as a consequence of centuries of harvest.

Although the creation of these grand religious pieces was a dying industry, the contemporaneous manufacture of smaller amulets incorporating richly coloured feathers continued and was, I assumed, the genesis of the chuparosas I had stumbled across in a backstreet Mexican shop. Hummingbirds had enjoyed a brief flirtation with the Catholic Church, but had turned in time to perform a more secular role in Mexican culture. Once reserved for the cloaks of Aztec emperors, and then the collections of kings and popes, they now accompanied Mexican migrants heading north into the United States hoping to find economic opportunities and, perhaps, love too.

If I had been shocked to find dead hummingbirds offered for sale as love charms in a Mexican backstreet border town botanica, I was not alone. Some ten years ago agents with the US Fish and Wildlife Service (FWS) intercepted the first of many parcels containing dozens of dead hummingbirds, sent in the post from Mexico to the

United States. At first, the agents were baffled—what possible use could someone have for commercial quantities of dead hummingbirds? They were not, on the face of it, obvious examples of wildlife crime the likes of poached elephant ivory or endangered orchids torn from the wild.

The FWS enlisted the help of Pepper Trail at their forensic laboratory in Ashland, Oregon. Besides bearing the most marvellous name for a forensic ornithologist involved in helping to solve complex wildlife crimes, Trail was ideally qualified to help shed light on the mystery of the dead hummingbirds—he was said to be one of only two people in the world who could identify the victims of crime when the victim is a bird.

Trail may be a feather detective, but he is a birder and a poet too. While he admits to keeping a "death list" of over eight hundred bird species he has identified in the course of some twenty years working as a forensic ornithologist—a blackly humorous twist on the conventional birder's life list—Trail is clearly a sensitive soul. His Twitter account features beautiful haikus he has written, and hummingbirds have particular resonance for him. He has described them as powerful animals and has observed how humans respond to their beauty, energy, and vivacity. Echoing how I felt in the wake of my first chuparosa encounter, he found the revelation of their exploitation particularly sad.

One of the parcels intercepted by FWS agents appeared in his laboratory in 2013—within it were dozens of small red paper tubes, bound with satin tassels and, inside each tube, a dead hummingbird and a Spanish language prayer or *oracion*:

> *¡Oh, chuparosa divina!,*
> *tú que das y quitas el néctar de las flores,*
> *tú que das e inculcas a la mujer el amor,*
> *yo me acojo a tí como a tus poderes fluidos*
> *para que me protejas y me des las facultades*

de querer cuanta mujer(hombre) yo quiera,
ya sea doncella(o), casada(o) o viuda(o).

Pues te juro
por todos los espíritus de los Santos Apóstoles,
no dejar ni un solo momento de adorarte
en tu relicario sacrosanto,
para que me concedas lo que yo te pido,
mi chuparrosa hermosa.

The birds were chuparosas, a word which translates as rose suckers—a beautiful Spanish word for an ugly tradition. The prayer was an intriguing blend of pagan entreaty and Christian orthodoxy. The bearer of the chuparosa promises, by all the spirits of the Holy Apostles, to ceaselessly worship the mummified hummingbird they wear in a locket on a necklace. Then, and only then, will their entreaty for the love of the woman or man "either maiden, married or widowed" be fulfilled.

Closer examination of these first birds, and hundreds of subsequent hummingbirds seized by FWS agents in subsequent years and sent to Trail in Oregon, revealed that a third of them had been killed with shotguns loaded with fine lead shot little bigger than a poppy seed; the remainder had either been netted or caught with bird lime, a sticky substance applied to branches upon which the birds alight so they are subsequently unable to fly away. Alarmingly, the trade in chuparosas appears to be increasingly organised—Trail relates that each oracion is uniformly printed on paper, and the chuparosas' packages are marked with a "Made in Mexico" stamp or sticker.

To date, Trail has identified at least eighteen hummingbird species that have met this grisly end. Two-thirds of those species have legal protection under the terms of the US Migratory Bird Treaty Act, but all hummingbirds have international legal protection under the auspices of the Convention on International Trade in Endangered

Species, or CITES. Species covered by the latter treaty require permits and paperwork in order to be taken or sent across international borders, dead or alive. Inevitably, none of the chuparosas seized have any such sanction—the trade is wholly illegal.

Sometime after stumbling across chuparosas in Nogales, I found myself with time to kill in Mexico City. I was there to meet Maria del Coro Arizmendi, an ecology professor at the National Autonomous University of Mexico (UNAM) and Mexico's leading hummingbird researcher. I hoped to discuss the potential impact the trade in chuparosas was having on Mexico's hummingbird populations and, more positively, Arizmendi's hummingbird garden project. In recent years she has spearheaded the creation of small green spaces dedicated to attracting and feeding hummingbirds in the sprawling urban vastness of Mexico City, hoping both to provide those species that are adapting to live in close proximity to humanity with vital feeding stations and, critically, to allow their human neighbours opportunities to see the hummingbirds for themselves.

The first garden was created in 2014 on university grounds in the heart of the heavily built-up urban area of Tlalnepantla, to the north of Mexico City. Within days of the garden being planted with nectar-rich flowers beloved of hummingbirds, the birds had found it. In 2016, buoyed by this early success and working with teachers and students at the Instituto de Educación Media Superior (IEMS) Iztapalapa IV high school in the city, Arizmendi and her team designed and created another hummingbird garden, incorporating recycled waste materials alongside dedicated planting of suitable flowering plants. Arizmendi recalled that, within a few hours of being planted, this garden was visited by its first hummingbirds.

There are now five similar dedicated hummingbird gardens in Mexico City, with private individuals inspired to create dozens more in their backyards. Arizmendi said the germ of her idea for the hummingbird gardens came from none other than Michelle Obama, wife of former US president Barack Obama. In 2009, the then First

Lady created a vegetable garden in the grounds of the White House and, in it, made a point of planting nectar-rich flowers in order to attract bees. Speaking when the Obamas left the White House, she said, "I take great pride in knowing that this little garden will live on as a symbol of the hopes and dreams we all hold of growing a healthier nation for our children."

Arizmendi's hummingbird gardens continue to be an unqualified success at connecting people with hummingbirds. She concluded that one did not need to live in the White House, and it mattered not if one had a big garden or just a flowerpot—as long as people attracted and fed the birds in the city, it would contribute enormously to conserving their kind.

I had visited the gardens at UNAM, more in hope of seeing a hummingbird than any great expectation. The day on which I had arrived in Mexico City was overcast and cold, and students hurried past me huddled in thick jackets. This did not feel like a particularly auspicious day to be looking for hummingbirds. I should have known better, for by necessity they are tough creatures and, come rain or shine, they have to feed if they are to survive and not sink into a terminal torpor. I had not been walking the paths of the gardens for long before I heard a familiar battle cry—the angry squeak of a territorial hummingbird seeing off a rival.

At first I could not find him—looking for movement amongst the trees and shrubs, but seeing nothing that betrayed where he was to be found. Suddenly a blur of bare branches and twigs above my head resolved themselves and, amongst the background chatter, I could see the unmistakeable silhouette of a perched hummingbird. I slowly moved around the tall shrub, bringing a larger tree in the background behind the hummingbird and allowing me to see him more clearly—a male Berylline Hummingbird. The encounter was a typically brief one. He had things to do, and flowers to see—moments after I had registered his identity, he was off, flying purposefully through a break in the trees, heading deeper into the gardens. For the next half hour I tried to relocate him, but the chase was completely one-sided—I could hear him, or his companions, more often than I could see them, and those sightings, when they came, were fleeting. Hummingbirds flew past me like small dark motes on the edge of vision, determined and not stopping.

Eventually, cold and with an hour remaining before I was due to leave Mexico City, I decided it was my turn to not linger. The chuparosas continued to bother me. I had heard dark stories of their open, brazen sale at the Sonora witchcraft market in the city and, whilst friends familiar with Mexico City had warned me it was no place for an unaccompanied tourist to visit, I felt I owed it to the hummingbirds to see for myself if the stories were true. Researchers, scouring the Sonora market for chuparosas in 2009, found more than 650 dead birds for sale. I wondered if times had changed, whether the growing global environmental conscience had suppressed the demand for these tragic love tokens, or perhaps the positive hummingbird public relations work done in recent years by Maria del Coro Arizmendi in the city was now bearing fruit.

The outside of the Mercado Sonora seemed relatively cheerful, the arched gables painted gorse yellow, the market's name emblazoned the length of them in large black letters. Beneath, yellow tarpaulins provided a canopy for stallholders clustered around the entrances to the large building beyond. I picked my way through puddles on the tarmac to one of the entrances, overshadowed by a looming blue billboard depicting a swimming sea turtle and the positive message, "Menos plastico, mas vida"—Less plastic, more life.

Inside the Sonora market I found closely packed aisles of stalls stretching away from me, the walkways packed with jostling shoppers and the occasional wide-eyed young American tourist and a camera. Bearing in mind the warnings my friends had solemnly shared, I was trying not to look like a gringo tourist, so instead of dawdling at the Instagram-friendly displays of lurid plastic Dia de Muertos merchandise that made a mockery of the billboard outside,

I allowed myself to follow the flow of *chilangos* or Mexico City residents who shuffled deeper into the market. All the meantime, I was looking for hummingbirds.

As the tide of people carried me away from the entrance and into the heart of the market, I noticed the tenor of the stalls changed the further in we travelled. Items for sale became less plastic and more organic—some stalls reminded me of the Nogales botanica, offering tubs and bins of myriad dried herbs and spices. Other stalls were less ambiguous, selling candles of black, red, or ivory wax, each with an oracion printed on the side, some with a picture of a hummingbird on the packaging. Were these an alternative to chuparosas involving real birds? The candles promised love, good luck, health, wealth, revenge. Every human base was covered here.

The smell hit me before I caught sight of the cages. At the back of the market, I found myself swept along an aisle flanked by walls of cages containing birds—parakeets of some kind, chickens and bantams, colourful honeycreepers and tanagers—and mammals too. Squirming knots of kittens too small, surely, to be parted from their mothers; sprawling puppies on bare concrete in puddles of urine that ran out onto the path at my feet; listless chinchillas; and crouching rabbits with wide, frightened dark eyes.

It was in this dark place that I found the first stall offering the husks of hummingbirds, threaded onto red string one above another like some kind of macabre fruit hung out to dry. They stopped me dead in my tracks. The stall's owner, a middle-aged woman, began to expound their virtues while her plump, twenty-something son eyed me suspiciously over his mobile phone from his perch on a stool to one side.

"They are good for love, but also for your health if you are ill. You can eat their hearts in a soup. Very strong. They are good for travellers; they open the way ahead. You will have good fortune if you carry one with you . . ."

The potency of hummingbirds for facilitating more than mere love was a further revelation to me, but later I learned that dead hummingbirds had been found on *narcoaltares*, the altars of shrines used by Mexican drugs cartels when praying to Santa Muerte, their favoured patron saint, for good luck, smooth passage, and protection from the police. The *narcocultura* of Mexico collides again with hummingbirds in the songwriting of virtuoso accordion player Juan Villarreal, known to his legions of fans as Don Juan. While Don Juan does not publicly consider himself a writer or singer of *narcocorridos*, or drug ballads, some of his songs certainly have antiestablishment themes that broadly appeal to the lawless. Both Don Juan and his group Los Cachorros are popular in Sinaloa, home to the Sinaloa Cartel, considered by the US intelligence community to be the most powerful drug-trafficking organisation in the world. His song "La Chuparosa" is a particularly popular piece and has been widely recorded by other artists.

One such cover version was made by Fabian Ortega, otherwise known as *El Halcon de la Sierra*, the Falcon of the Sierra. Ortega's bullet-riddled body was found on a roadside in Chihuahua less than a year after his arrest in 2009 on board a yacht off the coast of Baja California, in possession at the time of a quantity of crystal meth, $20,000 in cash, illegal weapons, and more than eight hundred assault rifle rounds. To make matters worse still, he was in the company of a *sicario* or hitman for notorious Mexican drug lord Teodoro "The Stewmaker" Simental—so named for his penchant for disposing of the bodies of his tortured rivals in barrels of acid.

Ortega's rendition of "La Chuparosa," to my untrained ear, was more strident than Don Juan's original, but one had to assume from Ortega's recent criminal record that his death owed more to his lifestyle choices than the actions of a music critic unhappy with a song about a metaphorical hummingbird. The state of Chihuahua is Sinaloa Cartel territory . . . Nevertheless, the inclusion of "La Chuparosa," in a set list that typically glorified narcocultura spoke volumes about the place chuparosas held in the Mexican psyche.

More positively, the quality of bravery so often associated with hummingbirds once found a place in the Mexican *lucha libre*, or wrestling culture. One of the most renowned *luchadores*, or wrestlers, of all time is Oscar Gutierrez, currently plying his trade for World Wrestling Entertainment under the ring name Rey Mysterio. This was not always his ring name. When he started out in Mexico, under the tutelage of his uncle, also known as Rey Mysterio, Gutierrez was considerably smaller than many of the wrestlers he fought. His uncle gave him the ring name Colibrí, or Hummingbird. This was a canny piece of marketing, as children loved watching the plucky Colibrí fighting, and beating, much larger opponents. Soon he had graduated from fighting in small shows at carnivals to weekend shows in auditoriums in Tecate and Mexicali in Baja California. He would go on, as Rey Mysterio, to be regarded as the greatest cruiserweight pro-wrestler of all time—but his fledgling fights were as the Colibrí.

Back in the Mercado Sonora, confronted by all too real chuparosas, I casually made my excuses, feigning disinterest, and moved on. I could not get out of the building quickly enough, but did not want to draw attention to myself. The sounds, colours, and odours of the market were, suddenly, pressing in upon me from all sides. I felt nauseous as I made my way towards the exit, the air swimming greasily around me.

I walked back out into the street outside, gratefully sucking cold exhaust fume–flavoured air into my lungs. Anything was better than the stench of despair and fear I had found within. The strings of dead hummingbirds were bad enough, but the cages of frantic birds, the flat-eyed animals with fur drenched in urine and matted with faeces . . . I knew I should feel angry at their treatment, at the way their lives were reduced to mere commodities, but instead I was overwhelmed with a desperate helplessness. I knew there was nothing I could practically do, there and then, to help any of those animals I had left behind me, let alone bring back to life the dozens of hummingbirds I had found suspended like strings of chillies above displays of candles, bundles of herbs, and luridly coloured *calaveras* and *calacas*. I hated the Sonora market. I hated the stallkeepers. I hated their customers. And I hated myself for my helplessness in the face of it all.

The balance of my time in Mexico was short. I took myself to the Pacific coast, looking for an endemic hummingbird so profoundly associated with the nation that it bears its name—Mexican Hermit. Once considered merely a subspecies of the Long-billed Hermit, in 2013 taxonomists determined that it was, in fact, a species in its own right and one found only in Mexico, and there only on the Pacific coast. They are a relatively large hummingbird, but like all of their kind, an extremely shy one. Hermits are well-named—typically they shun artificial feeders and, when they do deign to appear in front of an observer, their visits are brief and they flee into dense cover at the slightest cause for alarm. Unlike most hummingbirds, their plumage is atypically dull, a muted spectrum of olive greens and buff browns ideally suited to a life lurking unseen in dense forest understory.

While I was becoming addicted to the confectionary bright colours of other hummingbirds, the European birder in me felt strangely reassured by the drabness of the hermits. They reminded me of our warblers, dingy of plumage and skulking of behaviour. I also relished the challenge inherent in trying to see a notoriously shy bird like a Mexican Hermit. Finding a hermit is like solving a particularly knotty cryptic crossword clue.

First, though, before I could look for one of the smallest birds in the world, I had a date with one of the largest living animals on the planet. Boarding a small boat with a handful of other pilgrims as the sun began to rise, I hoped we might encounter some of the Humpback Whales that gather during the late winter in the Bahía de Banderas, a large bay on Mexico's Pacific coast. The sea was glassy, a smooth opalescent sheet of dawn mother-of-pearl. Our boat cut quietly across it, heading away from the shore into the open ocean. The first animals we found were enormous manta rays, barely breaking the surface and, had the sea been anything but as calm as it was that morning, surely invisible to the naked eye. We soon saw the fins of Bottlenose Dolphins from some distance away, apparently feeding actively but, when we drew closer, we realised they were, instead, teasing a young Humpback Whale. Not a fully grown animal, it was nonetheless still a substantial cetacean, and an angry one at that.

The dolphins thronged around it at the surface, their clicking, squeaking voices betraying their excitement. The whale clearly did not want their exuberant company, beating the surface of the water with enormous gnarled pectoral fins and thrashing his head at the dolphins. From a distance, I could look him in the eye and, for the first time, I heard a whale's voice—a deep, foghorn bellow that seemed to come from some other, more ancient and innocent time. I did not need to speak whale to understand the frustration he was vocalising. The dolphins seemed spurred to fresh heights of delirium. It was like watching children turn on one of their number in the playground.

We moved further along the coast, following a report of further whale activity. Our boatman's sensitivity to the whales' welfare was exemplary, taking us slowly towards the area in question and then, when we found activity at the surface, standing well off with the engine cut. What followed was humbling—Humpback Whales displaying to one another in front of our awed boat, breaching fully out of the water before crashing thunderously back into the sea. Our boatman, in between taking photographs of the underside of the whales' tails to enable later identification of individual animals, told us that this appeared to be a number of males courting one female. The obvious affection and admiration he felt for these whales was a welcome antidote to the casual animal cruelty I had witnessed the previous day.

Later that afternoon I made my way along the coast, taking a bus to the Vallarta Botanical Gardens where I hoped I would find my Mexican Hermit. I had the gardens more or less to myself—an isolation that allowed me to pretend I was somewhere a little wilder still, a pleasant fantasy that the abundance of birdlife I found there helped to reinforce. Glossy jet-black and lemon-yellow caciques provided a raucous soundtrack of whistles and rattling chatter, while

Orange-fronted Parakeets and Mexican Parrotlets flew from tree to tree ahead of me. Many of the trees had vanilla orchids scrambling up their trunks, their shiny leaves like lush green ladders leading to the canopy.

The hummingbird feeders that hung from the veranda of the nearby restaurant were bustling with Cinnamon Hummingbirds and one shy Plain-capped Starthroat, but these were not the hummingbird I hoped for above all others. Some hermits come to artificial hummingbird feeders, but others prefer not to. I had no idea what the preference of Mexican Hermits was, and so, after a while watching the feeders, I decided to cast my net further and return to the gardens.

An avenue of flowering prickly pear cacti was also proving attractive to the Cinnamon Hummingbirds. I cautiously made my way around the tall, woody-stemmed cacti, keeping my distance from them—partly not wishing to disturb any feeding hummingbirds, but also from a healthy respect for the armoury of long, sharp spines on each plant. The Cinnamon Hummingbirds had no such reservations, boldly careering around the tops of the plants and dipping their heads assertively into the large tangerine flowers they found there, heedless of the long spines that flanked them on all sides.

I became aware of a very different tone to the regular buzzing hum of the Cinnamon Hummingbirds' flight—a deeper, more urgent sound, coming from lower down in the surrounding undergrowth. Turning, I found myself confronted by a Mexican Hermit, hovering at waist height and, unmistakeably, looking sideways up at me. I recognised him for what he was—his head, in profile was distinctive, with a dark bandit mask that extended from the base of his bill back beyond his glossy black eye, flanked with dark buff counterpoints above and below. His bill itself was long and elegantly down-curved.

The hermit turned, affording the briefest of views of his dark, olive-green upperparts before he sinuously threaded his way back into the dense bushes, his long white tail a tracer of light as he vanished into the greenery and was gone. The entire encounter had lasted mere seconds, but it was enough. I felt utterly connected in the moment with that bird—it was almost as if he had sought me out, for there was no skill on my part in finding him. Curiosity seemed to have brought him to me and, once satisfied, he had departed. That thought was to prove consoling for me as, despite searching the area for a further hour, and lurking hopefully around the prickly pears, I could not find him or another Mexican Hermit in the Vallarta gardens. I had seen my Mexican Hermit and was more than happy with that. A day that combined Humpback Whales and hummingbirds was, by any standards, one of the very best.

This had been a timely reminder that, for all the darkness I had found in Nogales and Mexico City, the country as a whole still had wonderful areas of habitat where incredible hummingbirds remained to be found. Reassuringly, I found I was not the only one to have harboured reservations about the uncertain future faced by hummingbirds and, for that matter, the natural world as a whole in Mexico. Kenn Kaufman, once the maverick young teenager who hitchhiked his way around the United States looking for birds, and now one of the most highly respected birders in the world, told me:

In the late 1970s and 1980s, starting when I was just a teenager, Mexico was my magical birding retreat. Living in Arizona, I could easily get to the border and then travel all over that country, for very low cost, by public transportation. Not many people were birding Mexico then, mostly visitors from North America and Europe, and hardly any locals; so wherever I went, it always seemed there was a chance for discovery, or for learning new things about little-known species. First on my own or with friends, later as a leader of birding tours, I explored every corner of Mexico.

One of my favorite areas was a forested stretch on the Atlantic slope of Oaxaca. For many people, the name of that state conjures up images of elegant old Oaxaca City, which lies in a dry interior valley. But a long, narrow, paved road—Highway 175—runs northeast from the city over a high ridge, then through montane valleys, then over an even higher ridge before it starts to wind and twist down, down, down for a hundred kilometers, finally flattening out practically at sea level at the town of Valle Nacional.

When I was visiting in the 1980s, beautiful forest lined both sides of the highway almost all the way from Valle Nacional up to the crest. The habitat changed with the changes in elevation, from steamy tropical forest up to misty, mossy cloud forest, and birdlife changed with the scenery, so it was worth stopping and birding at every possible pulloff. For me, the two emblem birds of this highway were two hummingbirds: the tiny Emerald-chinned and the big, flashy Garnet-throated.

Emerald-chinned Hummingbird was a species I hardly knew before I started finding them regularly above Valle Nacional. They were never conspicuous, but they were always there—in middle elevations along the highway, in places where roadside banks were in deep shade of over-hanging trees, the little Emerald-chins would come out to hover at tiny flowers near the ground before zipping back into the forest. The brilliant green on the male's chin was an elusive color, just as the birds themselves were elusive, but with enough patience we could always find these sprites of the understory.

Garnet-throated Hummingbirds always appeared singly, in cloud forest near the top of the road, and they seemed to favor the tops of trees. There was a gnarly dead snag near a wide pulloff where we found a male perched in three different years, a welcome stakeout. If the light caught it right the bird looked incredibly gaudy, its green back setting off three different shades of purple on its underparts. When it flew out to catch insects in midair, its wings flashed bright cinnamon-red.

Hundreds of other bird species lived along that road, and we would see scores of them on every transit. It should have been a pure joy to bird there. But on one of my last visits in the early 1990s, I was overcome with a sense of melancholy. Looking across a valley from a gap in the trees, gazing at the intoxicating sight of slopes covered with unbroken forest, I thought to myself: *This won't last.* I had seen habitat gradually diminishing all over Mexico, and it seemed no one could do anything about it. With so little public interest in birds, it was hard for the few conservation groups to gain any traction. I made a grim prediction: *All this habitat and all these birds will be gone in 25 years.*

This despondency felt all too familiar to me. I had tasted it for myself in Alaska, where climate change had been complicit in allowing vast expanses of the boreal forest to burn that summer, the very sea itself was heating up, and the distribution patterns of hummingbirds were visibly changing within a matter of decades rather than millennia. I had, forcibly, been reminded of the wilful harm mankind could wreak upon innocent wildlife in the botanicas and mercados of Mexico.

Kenn continued, and there was hope to be found in his words:

Set aside that glum outlook. Fast-forward more than 25 years, to 2020, and the forest is still there. The birds are still there. And now if I want to know the status of a spot in Mexico, I don't have to wait for a friend from the US or the UK to go there, because now there are legions of Mexican birders, with local clubs and experts all over the country. They know the birds of their nation better than we visitors from outside ever did, and they're paying close attention to the conservation of their special fauna.

I contacted Eric Antonio Martinez, a birder in Oaxaca City, to ask about the road above Valle Nacional. He told me, "Yes, there is still a good amount of nice cloud and tropical forest. It has diminished a bit but very little. The steep terrain has been important to keep that forest still around, hence no new towns have been established."

I have never been happier to be wrong. My sad forecast turned out to be way off. That magical birding road is still there, wonderful hummingbirds still live there, and a new generation of active Mexican birders will keep tabs on the scene. Action to protect this forest may be needed in the future, of course. But for now, the tiny Emerald-chins still flit and hover in the shadows, the big Garnet-throats still zoom through the fog of the cloud forest, and for the moment at least, all is right with their world.

After I left Mexico, my spirits lifted by my Mexican Hermit, and greatly heartened by Kenn's uplifting hummingbird story, I spoke briefly with Pepper Trail. I wanted to know if there was any glimmer of light and hope in the case of the chuparosas. His response was guarded, but provided a little more cause for optimism.

The sale of chuparosas is, I believe, the most significant wildlife trade issue affecting hummingbirds. Investigations of this trade by the Office of Law Enforcement of the US Fish and Wildlife Service are ongoing. This limits the amount of specific information that I can share.

The use of hummingbird love charms likely dates back centuries. Such deeply rooted traditions are difficult to overcome with conservation-based arguments, but there is some anecdotal evidence that this tradition (like many others) is fading among younger Mexicans. Given the low priority given to the trade by Mexican authorities, this may be the best hope that the killing of hummingbirds for chuparosas will decrease over time.

I badly wanted to believe Trail was right about this. Some traditions are best left to wither, after all, as tradition and morality do not necessarily go hand in hand. This was far from uniquely a Mexican issue—I did not have to look far from home to find birds of prey routinely and illegally shot, poisoned, and trapped on the grouse moors of the British uplands, a hangover of a Victorian culture of persecution. At least, in love, the chuparosas offered the promise of something good—our domestic British wildlife crime did not even have that thin veneer of superstitious promise to absolve it.

Anecdotal evidence such as that recounted by Trail does not, however, provide an enormous basis for confidence in the process of change for the better. I had seen and heard for myself evidence of the ongoing resonance that hummingbirds held in Mexican culture—and with a resurgent national pride in indigenous pre-Hispanic religion, philosophy, and traditions epitomised by the Mexicayotl movement, there seemed to be as much subjective cause for concern as for optimism. Chuparosas, purporting to help with the most fundamental, emotional aspect of the human condition, love, would surely resonate with contemporary Mexicans who embraced Mexicayotl.

The Mexicayotl movement coalesced in the 1950s amongst Mexico City intellectuals, and has gained traction in the decades that followed, but its origins lie earlier in the twentieth century in the Mexican Revolution and, latterly, the concept of Mexicanidad, the cultural precursor of Mexicayotl, championed by artists Diego Rivera and his wife, Frida Kahlo. It was in 1940, in the aftermath of her divorce from Rivera and the end of her affair with photographer Nickolas Muray, that Kahlo created one of her most emotionally charged works of art.

Her painting *Self Portrait with Thorn Necklace and Hummingbird* features her looking squarely from the canvas, her gaze direct and challenging, a black monkey behind one shoulder and a black cat behind the other, and a black hummingbird hanging, at her throat, from a necklace of thorns, a marriage of traditional Mexican and Christian iconography. Blood runs from the scratches the thorns have made in her skin. Her suffering is all too evident, but she has an air of proud determination about her too.

Kahlo had been powerfully influenced by the concept of Mexicanidad, and the symbolism of the animals incorporated in the painting is, therefore, significant—the black monkey representing evil, the black cat bad luck and death, and the hummingbird perhaps combining two associations in one fell swoop—it is plainly a chuparosa, but perhaps it also represents Huitzilopochtli, the Aztec god of war. A little later, Kahlo and Rivera remarried, her invocation of the power of the chuparosa appearing to have borne fruit.

This, I concluded, was the only place I was comfortable with chuparosas appearing—in art, be it paintings, songs, or literature. In a time of increasing pressure on the natural world, they had no place hanging from the necks of the lovelorn or travellers hoping for safe passage. I would make my way further into the Caribbean and Costa Rica without the need for any such superstitious token.

Chapter Four

THE SMALLEST BIRD
IN THE WORLD

~

Cuba, Matanzas. 22° N
Costa Rica, various. 9° N

*I*N 1936, AN AMERICAN ORNITHOLOGIST CALLED JAMES BOND published the definitive field guide to the birdlife of the West Indies entitled, appropriately, *The Birds of the West Indies*. One of those who would come to own a copy of his book was former military intelligence officer and writer Ian Fleming.

Casino Royale, Fleming's first novel starring his ruthless, womanising British secret agent James Bond, codename 007, was published in 1953. Bond was based upon a number of individuals Fleming had met during the Second World War whilst working in the Naval Intelligence Division—Fleming described his character as a mixture of all the secret agents and commando types he had met during the war.

Amongst the books that followed was *For Your Eyes Only*, published in 1960. The opening paragraph is anything but what one might, by now, expect of Fleming—there is no sign of the suave, sardonic, hard-drinking British secret agent. Instead there is a description of what Fleming considers the most beautiful bird in Jamaica, if not the entire world—the Red-billed Streamertail or doctor bird. The description is almost worthy of a field guide, accurately detailing the hummingbird's plumage and dimensions, and examining the etymology of the local name for them, doctor bird—we are told this is on account of their long black tails recalling the tailcoats worn by physicians in a bygone time.

We are then introduced to the aging Colonel Havelock and his wife, taking afternoon tea in the garden of their Jamaica home. While Colonel Havelock ruminates about the protracted revolution mounted by Fidel Castro and his supporters against the Batista dictatorship in neighbouring Cuba, Mrs. Havelock is watching two of the Red-billed Streamertails feeding and fighting around the flowering Japanese Hat and Monkeyfiddle bushes beside the veranda. She has named them Daphnis and Pyramus, after romantic mythological figures.

This bucolic scene is shattered by the arrival of three armed henchmen, sent to the Havelocks by a ruthless Cuban to insist they sell him their plantation home. When they refuse to accede to his demands, they are gunned down in cold blood. It transpires that they are personal friends of James Bond's superior officer, M, and in due course Bond decides to seek vengeance. The scene for the remainder of the short story is set.

The inclusion of hummingbirds at the start of the story is far from accidental. Fleming was an avid birdwatcher, and spent a portion of each year living at his Jamaican home, Goldeneye—itself a bird name, one shared with the codename of a major intelligence operation Fleming had been involved with during the war. On his bookshelf at Goldeneye was a copy of the second edition of *The Birds of the West Indies* and, when Fleming sat down to write the opening lines of *Casino Royale* on his elderly Royal portable typewriter, it caught his eye. He needed a "flat and colourless" name for his main character, and in James Bond he had found exactly what he needed. He later explained, "I wanted the simplest, dullest, plainest sounding name I could find. James Bond was much better than something more interesting, like Peregrine Carruthers. He would be a neutral, anonymous blunt instrument wielded by government."

It was only years after the first of the 007 novels had been published that the ornithologist Bond, hitherto quite oblivious to his fictional counterpart's escapades, became aware of the appropriation of his name. His wife Mary wrote to Fleming, complaining lightheartedly that he had "brazenly taken the name of a real human being for your rascal!"

Fleming replied to Mary, reassuring her that he could offer her husband, by way of recompense, the unlimited use of the name Ian Fleming for any purpose he might think fit, suggesting that perhaps one day Bond would discover some particularly horrible species of bird that he would like to christen in a suitably insulting fashion.

While the real James Bond never took Fleming up on this generous offer, he did receive from the novelist a first edition of *You Only Live Twice*—the very title itself surely a wry allusion to the duality of Bond's fictional and real-life existence at the time. Fleming wrote an inscription on the frontispiece for Bond: "To the real James Bond, from the thief of his identity."

While Fleming considered the name of an ornithologist to be suitably bland to appropriate for the purposes of a fictional character in a series of thrillers, the naturalist and philosopher Alexander Skutch helped to redress the real-world balance. He said of birders, "Our quest [to see birds] takes us to the fairest places; to find them and uncover some of their well-guarded secrets we exert ourselves greatly and live intensely."

This was a sentiment I could wholeheartedly relate to in my quest to spend time with the most remarkable representatives of the hummingbird tribe. Until 1844, if I had wanted to see the smallest bird in the entire world, I would have needed to visit the island on which, one hundred years later, the spy James Bond would have come into existence. From at least the early 1700s Jamaica's diminutive and rather plain Vervain Hummingbird held the unofficial title of the world's smallest bird—measuring a mere six centimetres long, and weighing some two grams, it appeared inconceivable that a smaller bird could possibly exist. The Vervain Hummingbird had the additional distinction of being one of the very first hummingbirds to be accorded a binomial Latin name by taxonomist Carl Linnaeus. *Mellisuga minima* commemorated not only the smallness of the bird, *minima*, but also the feeding habits of its kind—*melli* being the Latin for honey, and *suga* meaning to suck.

German-born ornithologist Johannes Gundlach moved to Cuba in 1839, and wasted little time before exploring the birdlife of the island. A keen collector and taxidermist, he was aided in the grislier aspects of his work by a fortuitous side effect of an accident whilst working in the field—a small gun discharged so close to his nose, he was left with no sense of smell thereafter. From the first day he set foot on Cuba, he would have been unable to miss the ubiquitous Cuban Emerald hummingbirds—a bright metallic-green species that is found across the island. It was not, however, until 1844 that he stumbled across their much smaller counterparts—tiny blue and white hummingbirds that, in the case of the adult male birds, sported a shiny wine-red gorget that extended into drooping moustaches. Gundlach, when newly arrived on the island, was befriended by Charles Booth, the owner of a sugar plantation, and it is Booth's wife Helen after whom Gundlach named the new hummingbird, *Mellisuga helenae*, the Bee Hummingbird.

Whether the Bee Hummingbird is actually smaller than the Vervain Hummingbird remains, to this day, a matter of some conjecture—the two may be approximately equivalent in dimensions and mass, with the male of each species being the smaller of the two genders. However, the Cuban Bee Hummingbird had both the advantage of novelty and aesthetics over its plainer Jamaican counterpart, and has been considered the world's smallest species ever since its discovery. The Vervain Hummingbird, unhelpfully,

lives exclusively in the inaccessible Jamaican tree canopy and so remains something of a poorly known enigma to this day. If I was to
see the smallest bird in the world, it was in Cuba I would need to
search for it.

A visit to Cuba sounded, on the face of it, like the very definition
of Alexander Skutch's description of birding—the island, nestling in
the heart of the Caribbean, has a reputation amongst holidaymakers
as one of the "fairest places." My previous experience of Cuba, on the
other hand, had not led me to share that particular opinion. In the
duration of a weeklong stay at the turn of the century I had suffered
a bed infested with bed bugs; an attempted robbery at knifepoint
in broad daylight; an attack of amoebic dysentery that took weeks
to overcome and prompted my doctor to marvel at the "particularly
persistent amoeba" in question; and, finally, on the flight home to
the UK, a technical failure in one of the plane's engines that necessi-
tated an emergency landing at the nearest airport, Shannon, on the
west coast of Ireland.

This had been my honeymoon and, as omens went for a marriage,
it proved to be both appalling and accurate in equal measures.

I could, I felt, have been forgiven for not feeling particularly
thrilled about the prospect of returning to Cuba but, on the contrary,
I found myself looking forward to laying some ghosts to rest. That
and the prospect of seeing not only the smallest bird in the world,
but also some of Cuba's other endemic and colourful birdlife. My
previous visit had involved no looking at wildlife whatsoever—I was
still trying, back then, to downplay my interest in natural history,
that being a time when, unlike the present day, professing any interest in the natural world remained likely to make one the object of
ridicule.

I would return, on this occasion, with some confidence about how
my visit to the island might unfold. Many years ago I spent some
weeks birdwatching on the Orkney island of North Ronaldsay, staying at the bird observatory on the island and, while there, met Andy
Mitchell, then the observatory's assistant warden. Years later, our

paths crossed again and, when I mentioned my plans to return to Cuba, Andy kindly offered to organise everything from the moment I landed to the point of my departure. It transpired that Andy had been making annual visits to the island for decades and had a network of close friends in Cuba who could help me.

Foremost amongst these were two brothers, Orestes and Angel Martinez, who had grown up with their nine brothers and sisters in a small village in the heart of the mosquito- and crocodile-infested Zapata swamp. The two brothers had taken their childhood interest in birds and used it to form the basis of a career as local wildlife tour leaders. The Zapata Peninsula, jutting from the south coast of the island, is a particularly biodiverse area of Cuba, and amongst its many avian delights was a good population of Bee Hummingbirds, known locally as *zunzuncitos*. An approximate translation of zunzuncito is, charmingly, little buzz—as I was to learn in due course, this onomatopoeic name was well deserved for a bird dwarfed by many flying insects.

Local folklore had it that the zunzuncitos were living incarnations of *guanín*, an alloy of copper, gold, and silver prized in pre-Columbian Central America for its lustrous shiny red colour and smell. While I would not be likely to smell a Bee Hummingbird, I hoped I would get to see for myself the metallic-red plumage of a male bird, and my anticipation was building by the time I arrived, late one night, in Havana.

The following morning I sipped coffee on the veranda of Dona Amalia, a small guesthouse on the outskirts of the city, and watched a Cuban Emerald feeding from the flowers of one of the bushes planted around the garden. My first Cuban hummingbird, and it was barely daylight on the first day of my stay on the island. Feeling tired after my late arrival, I took a leaf from the emerald's book and added extra sugar to my coffee. If a sweet diet was good enough to power a bird capable of hovering and flying backwards, it was good enough to see me through the morning to come. I flicked through the pages of *Birds of the West Indies*, familiarising myself with some of the Cuban endemics besides the Bee Hummingbird, and dared to imagine I was the fictional James Bond—in *Die Another Day*, Pierce Brosnan's Bond browses that seminal work during a scene in Havana, and introduces himself to American secret agent Giacinta "Jinx" Johnson, played by Halle Berry, as an ornithologist.

The only other guest present at this early hour was, however, no Halle Berry. Rick, an older American man, was grief-stricken at the death of his dog, a boxer called Chloe.

"She died a few days ago. She's buried right over there . . ."

He gestured towards the furthest reaches of the garden.

"She was my service dog. I'd had her since she was a puppy, fourteen years. We'd lived all over . . . we tried Mexico, but we didn't like it there. Then Canada for a while. Chloe loved it here in Cuba, and I do too, but we couldn't stay here, only visit it from time to time. I don't know where to live now. The world isn't a safe place anymore."

I sympathised with that latter sentiment. Without any mobile data on my phone, I was looking forward to a spell in the coming days disconnected from the febrile and increasingly depressing news of global politics and environmental disasters.

Orestes "Chino" Martinez arrived shortly after this sobering encounter and, initial introductions exchanged, we began the long drive to his home on the shore of La Bahía de Cochinos, the Bay of Pigs, infamous for the CIA-backed invasion of 1961 that failed to overthrow the fledgling Cuban state headed by Fidel Castro after the conclusion of the protracted Cuban Revolution that Ian Fleming's fictional Colonel Havelock had discussed in the opening moments of *For Your Eyes Only*. As we drove southeast out of Havana, Chino told me about the changing fortunes of the Bee Hummingbird.

"Their numbers declined between 1960 and 1980. There were some bad hurricanes, but the birds have recovered a little since 1990."

I asked about the effects of agriculture—I had heard that the growth of the sugar, coffee, tobacco, and cacao industries had all led to deforestation and habitat loss across Cuba, impacting many species, Bee Hummingbirds amongst them. On the other hand, I had also heard positive things about the late Cuban leader Fidel Castro's "green revolution." Addressing the landmark United Nations Conference on Environment and Development in Rio de Janeiro in 1992, Castro berated the leaders of developed countries for the ravages to the environment caused by their consumerist societies, and urged them to change their ways. He concluded his unusually short, five-minute-long address to the world's delegates by saying, "Tomorrow will be too late to do what we should have done a long time ago."

On his return to Cuba, Castro set about matching actions to his words, amending the Cuban constitution to place emphasis on the protection of the atmospheric, marine, and terrestrial environments. The changes wrought by the new Law of the Environment, formally enacted in 1997, appear significant—the area of land in Cuba under forestation has grown dramatically, increasing from 14 percent in 1959 to 19.2 percent in 1990, but accelerating to over 30 percent by 2015; over one hundred protected marine areas have been established; and, as a whole, Cuba now has an estimated 20 percent of the country under legal protection, compared with 13 percent in the United States—the latter's environmental protection being systematically eroded under the presidency of Donald Trump. Organic agriculture in Cuba is on the rise and, according to the Cuban government, over fifty thousand hectares of brownfield sites have been transformed into urban agricultural areas, producing an estimated 60 percent of the fruit and vegetables consumed in Havana alone.

It sounded to me that Cuba, perhaps thanks to a Damascene moment of environmental clarity on the part of Fidel Castro, or perhaps due to sheer economic necessity, had become something of a model for a more sustainable food production system, one where the broader environment was recognised as being of paramount importance. As Miguel Altieri, professor of agroecology at the University of California, Berkeley, concluded, no other country in the world has created a comparable agricultural system that produces food for local consumption with minimal food miles, limited energy use, and placing such value in the biodiversity of the surrounding countryside.

I wondered whether the Bee Hummingbirds' recovery in recent years was due to these more enlightened development policies. Chino shrugged. "The government is all talk about the environment. In reality, they are neither good nor bad for it. Just average."

I was not sure where the truth lay about the changing fortunes of the environment the Bee Hummingbirds depended upon—perhaps somewhere between my idealistic enthusiasm for enlightened, environmentally sensitive approaches to development and Chino's more guarded and natural cynicism about the policies of the Cuban government. I understood that it would naturally be difficult to be unreservedly positive about a government in a country where fuel shortages impacted everyday life for all citizens, to name but one inescapable routine detail. Furthermore, while Chino thought that Bee Hummingbird numbers were recovering, the birds remained listed on the International Union for the Conservation of Nature (IUCN) Red List as Near Threatened, with their population still officially considered to be in overall decline. The truth appeared as oblique as a hummingbird's wings in flight, a blurred impression of what lay beneath.

Another history, a more human one, unfolded as we approached Playa Larga. The road was lined with memorials to those who had fallen in the Bay of Pigs conflict, interspersed with small billboards bearing rousing slogans. "Aquí se libró un combate por la Victoria"— Here a battle was fought for victory. As we came into the town itself, a Soviet SU-100 tank stood proudly by the roadside, with a group of American visitors posing for photos beside it. Crossing the town to Chino's home took some time, for he drove slowly with the window down, exchanging pleasantries with many of the pedestrians and cyclists we passed.

"Ay, Chino!" they chorused in greeting, as garrulous as the colourful Cuban Parakeets we had passed in the countryside. I had the feeling I was about to go birding with a local celebrity, an impression borne out by the appearance of his home on the shores of the bay—painted bright red, its street-facing wall featured a large mural of him standing alongside a Zapata Wren, one of the endemic birds of the area.

I hoped we might see a Bee Hummingbird in the forested areas about the Zapata swamp, but Chino was quick to manage my expectations. "They are very, very difficult to see in the forest. Almost impossible at this time. We would have to be very lucky indeed."

Failing an outbreak of extraordinary good fortune, Chino reassured me, the best place to encounter them was in the garden of Bernabé Hernández, in the nearby village of Palpite. Bernabé and his wife, Juana, have a large flowering tree in their back garden that, in addition to a number of hummingbird feeders they have hung from their washing line, has in recent years proved potently attractive to Bee Hummingbirds. So much so that their home is now known as La Casa de Zunzuncito—the Bee Hummingbird House. "You will see them there, no problem. And I have a friend here in Playa Larga too with feeders, and Bee Hummingbirds in his garden. It is a little quieter there, maybe better for photography. There will be less visitors."

Before we fell back on the dead certainty of these gardens and their welcoming owners, I was determined that we should try to find my first Bee Hummingbird in the forest. A short drive out of Playa Larga brought us onto gravelled roads and then, as we entered the forest itself, damp muddy tracks that wound through the trees. Abandoning Chino's car, we continued on foot, following nothing more than his instinct as we made our way through the enveloping trees. Chino, his head cocked to one side, was birding with his ears as much as with his eyes.

"Cuban Tody!" he said quietly, stopping dead in his tracks. "He is nearby . . ."

Somewhere in the tangled undergrowth ahead of us a bird was calling, a rapid staccato succession of hard, flinty notes like pebbles being struck together. His lips pursed, Chino imitated the call and then, with the air of a conjuror, pointed at a nearby tree.

"There!" he hissed. "Cuban Tody, the male . . ."

I followed his directions, finding myself confronted with the most incongruous, outrageous bird I had ever seen. Smaller than a tennis ball, but just as circular, perched in front of me was a fluorescent green creature that seemed to be all head, with a minimal body and a frankly laughable stub of a tail. His throat was blood red, his cheeks sky blue, and his belly snow white, with flanks of bubblegum pink. He seemed completely unafraid of us, and continued to call incessantly. As introductions went, this was an excellent start to my time in the forest.

Also making their introductions were hordes of mosquitoes— hungry enough to settle on clothes and bite through them. Insect repellent seemed ineffective and, judging by the clouds that surrounded me but not my companion, they were keen to sample fresh, exotic blood. Eventually I resigned myself to their attentions—the avian distractions of the damp forest made this submission almost tolerable. Cuban Green Woodpeckers scrambled through the canopy above our heads, while at the edge of open clearings we found sombre ashen Cuban Pewees fly-catching for insects. What we could not find, however, was a Bee Hummingbird. Given the immensity and density of the habitat, I appreciated now why Chino judged it almost impossible to encounter one here—with a bird so small, this really was like looking for a needle in a haystack.

My lodgings for the night were in a *casa particular*, or bed and breakfast, run by another of Chino's brothers, Ramon, known to all as Mongui. A mural on my bedroom wall suggested that mine was the honeymoon suite. A kneeling, naked woman, surrounded by love hearts, her modesty only preserved by a strategically positioned bouquet of roses, bore the legend, "Mi cuerpo esta presente y tu mente asiente"—My body is present, and your mind assents.

The following morning both body and mind were in agreement—I was determined that today should be the day I would see my first Bee Hummingbird. Chino was much calmer about this than I was, safe in the knowledge that they would, in time, be a mere formality. He added to the sense of mounting anticipation by taking me into the heart of the swamp in which he had grown up, spending the first hours of daylight searching for some of the Zapata Peninsula's other famous bird inhabitants. We readily found a singing Zapata Wren—a large barred brown bird that dwarfed the small wrens I was familiar with around my Shetland home, but with a song every bit as sweet and tuneful as theirs. Zapata Sparrows were another Cuban endemic species, harder to find as they fed at ground level beneath dense bushes that edged the deep water-filled channels of the swamp, but they too succumbed to Chino's keen eye and ear.

We paused for an early lunch outside Palpite, enjoying plates of rice and black beans. I asked a question that had been in the back of my mind since the moment I met Chino and glanced to see his hand resting on the steering wheel of his car.

"If you don't mind my asking, Chino, how did you lose your finger?"

Chino paused, swilled some beer reflectively about his mouth and replied succinctly, "Crocodile."

We had spent the morning at the very edge of the water in the swamp, and I had not given crocodiles a second thought at any juncture. My copy of a more recent field guide to Cuba's birds, *Endemic Birds of Cuba* by Nils Navarro, had given no warning that they might be present, let alone bothersome. Navarro stated, blandly, "Cuba has no dangerous or highly poisonous animals, which makes the archipelago a paradise."

Perhaps Chino's accident was an aberration. I asked if crocodile attacks were unusual.

"Oh no, they're common around here," he replied airily, proceeding to tell me a succession of stories of friends who had been attacked with varying degrees of severity.

"One man, he was bitten in the testicles. Before this, he made two children. Afterwards, no more.

"Another, he was bitten in the leg while he was camping in the swamp with a friend. It was a very bad wound, so the friend walked out of the swamp to get help to carry him. We returned the following day, with a stretcher, but we found him halfway back to the road already—he'd put thirteen stitches in his own leg. The doctor looked at it and said he couldn't have done a better job himself."

With two close encounters with predatory animals already behind me whilst looking for hummingbirds, I was not keen to add another to my résumé, and was pleased that after lunch we would not be returning to those watery places where very hungry crocodiles lurked, unseen. Our surroundings would be the considerably safer and more comfortable garden of La Casa del Zunzuncito and, here, Chino assured me, I would easily see Bee Hummingbirds.

I had heard enough similarly blithe statements from birders over the years to not entirely trust such reassurances in practice—indeed, I had uttered the same sorts of platitudes myself to guests on wildlife tours I was leading, only to discover that the bird or butterfly or plant I guaranteed would be in a certain location was nowhere to be seen. Until we walked into the garden of Bernabé and Juana's small house, I remained innately cautious.

We had no sooner rounded the corner of the house, following on our hosts' heels into their small, enclosed back garden, when Juana exclaimed, "Ooh, mira, mira! El zunzuncito, el macho!"

Sure enough, just inches away from us, hovering at a hummingbird feeder at eye level, was an impossibly small, cobalt-blue and white hummingbird. He circled the feeder, quite unconcerned by our presence, his throat appearing black in the shadow of the eaves of the house. I found I was holding my breath, releasing it only when he flew up into the sheltering branches of the famous flowering tree I had heard so much about. This was a *ponasi* or firebush, a tree some four metres tall that dripped with long, tubular coral-coloured flowers, the original lure that attracted hummingbirds into the garden before Bernabé and Juana supplemented its flowers with feeders filled with an inexhaustible supply of sugar water.

Now, as it moved momentarily out of sight, it was the size of the bird that had made the most impression upon me. I was prepared for a Bee Hummingbird to be small, but I had assumed that the hyperbole would have created a sense of anticlimax when the moment of seeing one first came to pass. I was very wrong, for the bird truly did seem to be the same size as one of the larger bumblebees or carpenter bees I was familiar with in Europe. Thrilled at the immediacy of my first encounter with a Bee Hummingbird, I nonetheless found it hard to comprehend that a bird could, in practice, really be this tiny.

Cuban ornithologist Juan Lembeye, writing about the Bee Hummingbird for the first time in 1850, was similarly ill-prepared for the powerful impression the bird had made upon him.

Until now, the beauty of the Cuban Emerald hummingbird knew no rival in ornithology. To contemplate these diminutive beings as brilliant as the most refulgent star in our constellations, rapid in their movements like a fleeting breath crossing the firmament, to see them, I repeat, so nice and gracious, it would barely be possible to conceive an ensemble of greater beauty.

In the varnish of their iridescent throats, all the appeal of nature seemed to have been exhausted; but just when we believed we found in them the most beautiful type of Cuban being, there appears in the middle of our perpetual garden this new species, manifesting to us with its diminutive proportions and peerless livery, that there always exists one more beyond in the marvellous works of creation.

I peered into the branches of the firebush, trying to see where the Bee Hummingbird had perched to rest between feeds. Bernabé, familiar with the habits of his hummingbirds, drew me to one side and indicated that I should look through a window in the leaves. There, above me, sat the male bird, his throat now glowing like a hot coal, a rich fiery crimson in the sunlight. These flaming feathers extended on either side of his throat, creating a drooping moustache of lava tones. He was small, but utterly magnificent. His head cocked to one side, constantly scanning for interlopers in his territory, he reminded me of Chino looking for birds in the forest the day before, his entire being exuding concentration. I wondered what superlatives could do such a compact, perfect bird justice.

Juan Lembeye reserved his purple prose for the Cuban Emeralds he had hitherto considered "the most refulgent star" in the birding firmament, and seemed uncharacteristically lost for words when describing the Bee Hummingbird. It had "diminutive proportions and peerless livery," but there words seemed to fail him. In 1966 Spanish poet Blas de Otero devoted an eponymous poem to the zunzuncito, in which he exercised similar restraint. De Otero first came to Cuba in 1964, remaining there until early 1968, when he returned to Spain. In Cuba he encountered a form of poetry long since lost to Spain—poetry formed of tenths, or stanzas consisting of ten octosyllable verses that rhyme in consonant, in the form *abba accddc*, created by the Spanish priest, musician, and poet Vicente Espinel in the late sixteenth century. This form remained popular in Cuba, and songs celebrating the struggle for independence from Spain and the socialist revolution of 1959 were set to it. De Otero would have encountered these songs in bars and at public gatherings during his time in Cuba, and adopted the form for his poem "El Zunzuncito." It was published in the magazine *Bohemia de la Habana*, alongside a poem by Cuban poet Nicolás Guillén, entitled "El Zunzun"—the latter being the local name for the other hummingbird resident in the island, the Cuban Emerald.

For de Otero the zunzuncito was more than merely the world's smallest bird. He suggests its flight airs the misfortunes of the past, referring to the memory of less happy times in Cuba, and infers that the zunzuncito is a symbol of freedom. The first stanza of the poem establishes the brotherhood felt between the Cuban and Spanish people; and the stanza that follows yearns for a better future for Spain, at the time a right-wing dictatorship under the boot heel of General Francisco Franco. The Bee Hummingbird represented far more than the traditional Cuban folkloric association with the precious metal guanín—for de Otero, resident in Cuba but looking across the ocean to his homeland of Spain, it was the very embodiment of freedom.

The foreigner in exile was a recurring motif in the writing of Cuba's most famous foreign writer in residence, Ernest Hemingway. While Robert Jordan in *For Whom the Bell Tolls* and Frederic Henry in *A Farewell to Arms* were, like their creator, American exiles in their adopted countries, Santiago, in *The Old Man and the Sea*, was like de Otero, a Spaniard adrift in Cuba. At first glance, Hemingway appeared to have a more pragmatic view of the wildlife that abounded in the vicinity of his rural Finca Vigía home than de Otero. He was renowned for an appetite for sport-fishing for marlin and barracuda in the waters off Havana that matched his hunger for women and a thirst for double frozen daiquiris, the great potency of which he likened to rushing through powder snow when skiing down a glacier.

His son Patrick, meanwhile, recalled the simple pleasures of walking out of the gates of Finca Vigía to shoot guinea fowl in the immediate countryside. However, there are clues that the hard-living Hemingway, while happy to fish and shoot the wildlife around his adopted home, was more sensitive than his public persona may have suggested. Hemingway refused to allow the trees that dotted the baseball field created in the fifteen-acre grounds of the finca to be cut back, preferring that they continue to provide cover for the birds on his estate. Hibiscus bushes lined the veranda of his home, and were a source of nectar for the Cuban Emerald hummingbirds that preferred their daily drinks to be strictly nonalcoholic.

How much of this was Hemingway's doing is a moot point. Finca Vigía, a dilapidated limestone Spanish colonial house on a hillside overlooking Havana, was chosen by his soon-to-be third wife, war correspondent Martha Gellhorn. She described the finca's grounds—choked with flowering bougainvillea, orchids, and vines, thronged with nesting hummingbirds, and littered with rusty tins and empty gin bottles—as being like a beautiful desert island. The house had not been lived in for years, and Hemingway's initial reaction to it was a profound rejection that manifested itself in his taking himself to sea to fish—he was said to prefer the distractions of life in Havana to the wild solitude the finca offered. However, Gellhorn, in this instance at least in their turbulent relationship, prevailed—a decision that found favour with Hemingway's youngest son, Gregory, who recalled finding tiny hummingbird nests in the foliage that draped the house and spending hours watching the female birds incubating their eggs, a sight he recalled as being one of the most beautiful things he had ever seen.

For Hemingway as a writer, nature was alternately challenging and inspiring—no stranger to semiautobiographical writing, one suspects that this mirrored his own feelings towards the natural world. Gellhorn's insistence that they move into the hummingbird-infested Finca Vigía was, for all Hemingway's initial outward reluctance, in reality a gift to him as a writer. This could be a quiet place where, surrounded by nature, he could write from first light until the early afternoon, a time when he allowed those other compulsions that drove him to dictate the shape of the remains of the day. We do not know if the hummingbirds that haunted the veranda of his finca moved him as they did Martha Gellhorn or his son Gregory. Certainly, hummingbirds did not feature prominently in his written work—but perhaps Hemingway's Finca Vigía hummingbird legacy lives on in his granddaughter, Mariel. She speaks movingly of the hummingbirds that come to the feeders she fills early every morning in the garden of her Californian home, set deep in a canyon on the outskirts of Malibu. She describes the sense of peace she finds when sitting, with a cup of tea, on her porch watching those hummingbirds, and concludes that where there is peace, there is joy; and where joy is to be found, there is happiness.

Back in Palpite, in Bernabé's back garden, I spent the afternoon happily lost in the comings and goings of a succession of Bee Hummingbirds, and could relate to Mariel's sentiment. I found their size impossible to take for granted—knowing in advance that these were the smallest species of bird in the entire world simply didn't prepare one for the Lilliputian reality. The periodic appearance of a dragonfly in the garden airspace brought sharp perspective—considerably larger than the Bee Hummingbirds, its appearance caused alarm amongst them and, in a chorus of shrill squeaks, the tiny birds fled for cover in the ponasi tree, like a maelstrom of sparks whirling out of sight up a chimney.

One might assume that hummingbirds, even ones as small as Bee Hummingbirds, have little to fear from insects. They are, after all, remarkably fast and agile, and would surely be difficult to catch, their bulk notwithstanding. Dragonflies, on the other hand, are famously fast and agile aerial predators, and the Bee Hummingbirds' reaction I witnessed certainly spoke of a healthy respect for the insect. Tales of dragonflies taking hummingbirds have been spoken of for years, though documentary evidence of the act itself has yet to be seen. Naturalist Joseph Kennedy came close in 2015, with a photo he took in Texas of a Green Darner dragonfly consuming a Ruby-throated Hummingbird. The dragonfly is approximately the same size as the hummingbird, so it is conceivable—though still unproven—that it may have delivered the coup de grâce.

None of which is to say that invertebrates do not routinely consume hummingbirds. Many hummingbirds use spider silk, taken from webs, to bind their nests together. The silk, combined with tendrils of soft moss, forms an expansive and strong nest that allows an adult bird to comfortably incubate her two eggs, and room for the nestlings to grow until they have fledged. Unfortunately, some hummingbirds become entangled in the webs they are harvesting silk from and, if the spider in question is large enough, it may treat the hummingbird as a welcome meal.

There are some insects, however, that are more proactive. A study of birds taken by praying mantises revealed that, of 147 cases examined, 114 involved hummingbirds. Mantises were observed hunting hummingbirds both on nectar-rich flowering plants and artificial hummingbird feeders—adapting their feeding behaviour as adeptly as the hummingbirds have learned to do.

The zunzuncitos, scattering at the dragonfly's approach, seemed at once incredibly vulnerable and, at the same time, immensely capable and enduring. I wondered at the evolutionary path that had led them to this tiny pass. I was aware that on islands many species of animal were known to become smaller, in the passage of millennia—island or insular dwarfism was thought to be a gradual response to limited food sources. Then again, most hummingbirds were hardly giants in the avian world—their chosen food source and the mechanics of their flight limited the size a hummingbird could, realistically, possibly be. The Giant Hummingbirds of South America are the largest of their kind—I would see them in due course on my travels, and could expect to find a hummingbird approximately the same size as a European Starling, though considerably slimmer and lighter in weight, weighing a mere twenty-four grams. For a hummingbird, twenty-four grams makes the Giant Hummingbird a lumbering behemoth, with wings that flap at just fifteen beats per second. Charles Darwin, observing them in Chile, noted, "Whilst hovering over a flower, it flaps its wings with a very slow and powerful movement, totally different from that vibratory one common to most of the species, which produces the humming noise. I never saw any other bird, where the force of its wings appeared (as in a butterfly) so powerful in proportion to the weight of its body."

It is believed that Giant Hummingbirds are probably at the cusp of the upper limit of viability of size for a hummingbird—hovering, for them, requires an exponentially larger input of energy than for smaller hummingbirds, as energy requirements for hummingbird flight do not scale evenly with increases in size. Scientists have estimated that the Giant Hummingbird needs 4.3 calories per hour to sustain flight. If humans had similar energy requirements, we would need to consume over 150,000 calories every day. Being a smaller hummingbird, like the Bee Hummingbird, particularly in an island environment where nectar sources may be restricted at certain times of year, begins to make sense.

A tiny Mesozoic dinosaur fossil, found encased in amber in Myanmar, and described by scientists in 2020, suggests that miniaturisation was always a likely and potentially advantageous outcome for latter-day birds on isolated islands. The animal's bird-like skull, complete with a beak lined with dozens of tiny, sharp teeth, is under two centimetres long—comparable to the Bee Hummingbirds of today.

Watching the Bee Hummingbirds, it was easy to feel a little like Alice in Wonderland after she had foolishly imbibed a concoction that made her a giant in the world in which she found herself. Being in the presence of the smallest bird in the world had that effect on me and, judging by the delighted and slightly disbelieving expressions on the faces of visitors to the garden, on others too.

In time, I came to recognise individual hummingbirds, particularly young males with patterns of marbled juvenile and adult feathers on their gorgets as distinctive as fingerprints. At one point Juana brought me a coffee, though it grew cold while I concentrated on the birds themselves and the constant stream of admirers who came to see them. It was intriguing to see what a powerful draw these tiny birds were for visitors to Cuba from all over the world. Tourists from France, Italy, Colombia, the United States, and Russia visited as the afternoon wore on. If no Bee Hummingbirds were immediately apparent in the garden, Bernebé would take one of the hummingbird feeders in his hand and entreat the birds with a soft, susurrating call—*pssh-pssh-pssh*—that would, in seconds, lure at least one Bee Hummingbird to come and hover beside him, wings buzzing.

As the light began to fade, the activity at the feeders intensified as the birds topped up their energy levels for the night ahead. The last visitors to the garden, a Russian family with two young daughters, stood beside me as the birds flurried around us. They had taken a taxi from Varadero, on the north coast of the island, just to see the Bee Hummingbirds, a four-hour roundtrip journey. They were pleased they had made the effort. I remarked on how many Russians I had met in the course of the past few hours. The father, a tall man with short *Spetsnaz* silver hair and piercing blue eyes, replied dryly, "Well, lots of Americans vacation in Vietnam. Plenty of Russians come to Cuba . . ."

The most visible American influence in Cuba was, undoubtedly, the serried ranks of early twentieth century cars to be seen making their stately way along the crumbling roads of the island. Imports of these colourful, grand vehicles stopped abruptly at the time of the revolution in 1959—a political moment that, in a strange way, created the circumstances for an evolutionary and taxonomic event that bore comparison with the creation of Cuba's many endemic bird species, the Bee Hummingbird amongst them. Isolated on the island, with relatively little external influence, time and adaptation to local conditions allowed a range of colourful and unique birds to evolve in Cuba, from the outlandish Cuban Tody to the nation's official national bird, the Cuban Trogon—a wonderfully tame and approachable creature that, by happy coincidence, is clad in plumage that matches exactly the red, white, and blue colours of the Cuban flag.

As it was with the birds, so it was with the Buicks, Cadillacs, Mercuries, Oldsmobiles, and Plymouths. Isolated after the revolution by the Cold War and the American trade embargo of Cuba, these venerable vehicles began to evolve by necessity—their mechanics maintained or replaced when worn out entirely, their paintwork refreshed, their bodywork enhanced with new lights, fins, and hood ornaments, and sometimes even their very substance cut or stretched to reflect the day-to-day practical requirements of their owners. I encountered some that had been turned into pickup trucks, and others into homemade minibuses. It was like stepping into a beautiful automobile equivalent of H. G. Wells' *Island of Doctor Moreau*, a place where cars had evolved at the hands of man into something uniquely Cuban.

I would be sorry to leave Cuba, but before I did Chino took me to the house of a close friend, Adrian Cobas Arencibia. The garden of Casa Ana was much quieter, both in terms of hummingbird activity and human traffic, but the setting was altogether more peaceful, set on a rocky promontory above a slow-flowing black river on the outskirts of Playa Larga. Adrian had created a small clearing enclosed by low, flowering bushes from which hung a handful of hummingbird feeders donated by Chino and, curiously, several large hypodermic syringes. Around the edge of the clearing were half a dozen short logs, stood on their ends, each with a half coconut shell full of water sitting in a hollowed concavity.

These drinking stations were proving irresistible to a seething mass of warblers, as varied and colourful as the sweets in an old-fashioned newsagent's window. They had none of the hummingbirds' iridescence, but made up for this with their bright, clear colours—confections of lemon sherbet yellow, fruit salad orange, humbug black and white, and the improbable blue of raspberry bonbons. I stood surrounded by a nebula of drinking, bathing, and squabbling Northern Parulas, American Redstarts, Cape May, Black-throated Blue and Yellow-throated Warblers.

It was hard to look beyond them, but it was the hummingbirds I was there to see. Cuban Emeralds made regular neon forays to the feeders, while two female Bee Hummingbirds plied their trade at the hypodermic syringes. I realised now that Adrian, displaying the same resourcefulness Cubans applied to keeping their aging American cars roadworthy, had made his own hummingbird feeders from redundant medical equipment. The Bee Hummingbirds seemed to prefer the syringes to the conventional feeders, blissfully unaware of the irony of their extracting vital liquids from instruments themselves usually associated with the injection and withdrawal of fluid.

Occasionally a male Bee Hummingbird would deign to enter the clearing, and I came to realise I could recognise his arrival by sound alone—the buzzing of his wings had a slightly deeper tone to it than that of the females. His visits were more fleeting than those of the birds I had seen the previous day in Bernabé's garden, frustrating my efforts to better the images I had taken there. At one point he flew straight at me where I stood, camera raised and poised, fruitlessly trying to track him in flight. The thrum of his wingbeats intensified tenfold, and I realised he was inside the large hood on the end of my telephoto lens, the enclosed space acting as an amplifier. The close encounter was over as quickly as it had begun when, with a shrill chatter he flew away from me and over the encircling bushes, an enraged tiny comet who had met, in his reflection in the glass of my lens, a rival who would not back down from his challenge.

I gave up with the camera, not wishing to disturb the ebb and flow of the Bee Hummingbirds' routine. I contented myself with sitting in the warm sun, alone with them for the last of my time on this wonderful island. I had met the smallest birds in the world, and I had laid the ghosts of my previous Cuban experience to rest.

If Cuba had provided just two hummingbird species, I anticipated that two days in Costa Rica would prove to be the polar opposite where volume and variety of hummingbirds was concerned. I had read a blog written by an expatriate American birder living there, Pat O'Donnell, that had piqued my interest. Pat had asked, rhetorically, "How many hummingbird species can you see in Costa Rica in just one day?"

He considered the virtues of Costa Rica in this regard—with a range of habitats accessible in a relatively small area, it should be possible to see something in the region of fifteen to twenty species of hummingbird in the space of one day.

Pat went on to suggest a potential route that might work. That baited hook proved utterly irresistible to me as I passed through Central America—if Pat was still interested in finding out, I wanted him to accompany me on a breakneck hummingbird race in his adopted homeland. I wrote to him to see if he was interested in turning that hypothetical question into a practical reality—better still, we would have not one but two days to play with. Pat's initial reply was a little tentative—was I really serious about realising this intensive hummingbird quest? I managed to convince him that this was a genuine enquiry and, moreover, I would be with him soon.

Nonetheless, having arrived in San José at midnight and had only four hours sleep, I was still enormously relieved to see Pat's car pull up outside my guesthouse. I felt exhausted and badly in need of a coffee, but the surge of adrenaline as we set off into the darkness heading towards the coast was invigorating. As we drove, Pat explained that, with two days ahead of us, we could afford to spend a little more time looking for some of the trickier species.

"The original idea involved a roundabout trip that went from the San José area to the wet foothills and lowlands of the Caribbean slope, then back up to cloud forest, high-elevation forest, way back down to the hot habitats of the Pacific coast, and then up to San José.

"I've realized that this wacky jaunt from one side of the mountains to the other and back up again would involve more driving than birding, so splitting that route into a pair of days is definitely going to take the edge off the craziness."

Our first target was a Costa Rican endemic, the Mangrove Hummingbird.

"It's one every birder who visits wants to see," explained Pat, "and while most birders go away having ticked one, that's not to say they've actually seen a Mangrove Hummingbird. They see a Scaly-breasted Hummingbird at the edge of the mangroves, they've come here to see a Mangrove Hummingbird . . . well, you get the idea.

"They're an endangered endemic, and they're always tough to find even right in the middle of the mangroves. Unlike other hummingbirds, they refuse to come to feeders, and it's rare to find one feeding from a flowering bush. They're far from common or easy to see."

This appealed enormously to me. I like a birding challenge and, while some hummingbirds might give themselves up readily at feeders, the unpredictability, rarity, and cachet attached to a genuine Mangrove Hummingbird ticked all of my boxes.

We arrived at the edge of a mangrove forest on the outskirts of Mata de Limon, on the shores of the Gulf of Nicoya to the west of San José, just as the sun was rising over the horizon. Day breaks quickly in Costa Rica, and the resident hummingbirds were wasting no time in sallying forth. Several Scaly-breasted Hummingbirds were feeding at the outskirts of the mangroves, and a Plain-capped

Starthroat flew overhead. From a distance, I could see how the Scaly-breasted might be a trap for the unwary but, forearmed by Pat, I knew what we were looking for would have cleaner, whiter underparts. The question was, if Mangrove Hummingbirds rarely deigned to feed at flowering bushes, how would we find one apart from through sheer, blind luck?

The whine of wakening mosquitoes was punctuated by the sound of Pat attempting to lure a Mangrove Hummingbird from the dense thickets of mangrove trunks that rose from the dark water below us. He had two weapons in his armoury—pishing and pygmy-owls. Pishing is hard to explain to the nonbirder, and harder still for birders, like me, who are resident in Scotland. There the word has a very different meaning indeed, and as such elicits strange looks when one says that one is pishing to attract hidden birds. For a birder, it means the act of pursing one's lips and blowing out, making a repetitive *pssh-pssh-pssh* noise. For some otherwise skulking birds this can prove irresistible—they come out of hiding to investigate the noise. Nobody is quite sure why they should do this—maybe it sounds like other birds mobbing an owl, or a bird of prey. It does not work with all birds, and seems more effective in the Americas than it does in Europe—though, at home, wrens are particularly keen on a good pish.

Mobbing predators is something that many small birds do. There is a collaborative benefit to gathering and making a fuss about a predator, whatever form that threat might take—the more attention that is drawn to, say, an owl, the less likely it is to catch prey by surprise and, if the local birds are particularly tenacious, they may be able to annoy it enough that it moves on entirely, leaving their immediate territories a little bit safer. The sound of a Ferruginous Pygmy-owl in Costa Rica has the potential to draw even a shy hummingbird into the open. Pat deployed both sounds, pishing and issuing the monotonous *hoo-hoo-hoo-hoo-hoo* pygmy-owl call, in a sustained, determined, and for some forty-five minutes, completely fruitless attempt to draw a Mangrove Hummingbird out of the swamp.

It was only when we were both passing from a state of initial optimism, through a period of grim determination, to the point of giving up on Mangrove Hummingbird that, with a whirr of wings through the vegetation, a female appeared and alighted on a branch nearby. A subtly beautiful bird with the promised clean white underparts contrasting with delicate, metallic-green upperparts and a faint suggestion of white moustachial stripe running from the base of her bill down her cheeks, she was almost too close to focus our binoculars upon. Not my first Costa Rican hummingbird, but my first endemic species of the weekend, and we could now move on to look for other targets. The hummingbird race was no longer stalled in the mangroves, and my spirits began to lift.

We swapped the watery environs of the mangroves for a very different habitat indeed, searching dry forest for Canivet's Emerald, another understated and largely green hummingbird. According to some taxonomists, we were searching for a different species entirely, named after an entirely different naturalist: Salvin's Emerald, a bird that is sometimes treated as a subspecies of Canivet's Emerald. Emmanuel Canivet was a French ornithologist for whom the Emerald represents the only bird to carry his name into posterity—Osbert Salvin, on the other hand, was a determined English naturalist with a prodigious output of new species to his credit during the nineteenth century, many of which, as was the custom, he shot for posterity. He recounted that he was, "Determined, rain or no rain, to be off to the mountain forests in search of quetzals, to see and shoot which has been a daydream for me ever since I set foot in Central America."

Happily for Salvin, he was one of the first Europeans to record setting eyes upon a Resplendent Quetzal—the bird whose long green feathers the Aztecs placed in such high esteem—describing it as "unequalled for splendour among all the birds of the New World." Salvin proved to be as good as his word and, unhappily for the quetzal in question, he promptly shot it.

We had no luck finding the hummingbird that, to this day, depending on which taxonomist one believes, either bears Salvin's name or that of Canivet. Undaunted by this setback, Pat took us a short distance inland to an isolated stand of large trees in fields outside the small town of Tárcoles that he knew were in flower—this level of local knowledge a distinct advantage of using a local guide. Here our hummingbird fortunes significantly turned, for the air above the trees was boiling with hummingbirds. Green-breasted Mangos jostled for airspace with Steely-vented and Rufous-tailed Hummingbirds. Ruby-throated Hummingbirds, famous for their annual migration north from their Central American wintering grounds across the Gulf of Mexico to their breeding grounds in the eastern United States, were also present in low numbers over-head, and amongst this seething mass of birds was one more new hummingbird—Blue-throated Goldentail, a hummingbird as entic-ing as its name suggested, its body a suffusion of rainbow shades from golden tail to sapphire-blue throat.

The importance of Costa Rica to the Ruby-throated Humming-birds has been emphasised by a ringing program at the Nicoya Pen-insula Research Station on the Pacific coast of the country. There, researchers have shown that individual birds return, every year, to overwinter in the same small areas of forest. If that habitat has been lost in the meantime, the birds are in trouble.

Within those Costa Rican forests the hummingbirds, unbeknown to themselves, have hitchhikers riding on board as they travel from flower to flower, and plant to plant. There are in the region of one million known species of mite found worldwide, each of which oc-cupies a tiny ecological niche. Amongst this horde of mites are hum-mingbird flower mites, each vanishingly small, smaller even than the full stop at the end of this sentence. Each feeds on the nectar of a flower species particular to the tastes and evolution of its re-spective species. Mites can, collectively, consume up to half an in-dividual flower's nectar—as such, they're competition for hungry hummingbirds.

What to do, then, when the nectar in a flower is running dry? The mites wait for a visiting hummingbird to thrust its bill inside the flower they're currently occupying. In the space of the few seconds the bill is present, the mites leap upon it, race up the bill, and clasp tightly to the hummingbird's nostrils, hanging on grimly there while the bird flies to another flower of the correct species. There, they have mere seconds to disembark from the beak and tuck into the new nectar source. Jump off at a flower of the wrong species, and there's a good chance the resident mites of a different species will attack and kill the mistaken hummingbird flower mite. Life can be tough for the hummingbird flower mite that doesn't catch a lucky break or, indeed, beak.

Our fortunes also rose and fell as the day progressed—this was emphatically not straightforward birding. Pat's plan to check flowering heliconias for hermits drew a blank—we couldn't find any flowering plants in the places he expected them to be, let alone shy hermits attending to them. The afternoon continued in similar vein, with the roads around and through Carara National Park proving largely devoid of flowering trees, and still not a flowering heliconia in sight. We picked up new hummingbirds, a Long-billed Starthroat and White-necked Jacobins, but the hermits would have to wait until the following day—a day that, with hindsight, I was glad we had built into the itinerary.

In the last hour of daylight Pat found us a large flowering tree on a sharp hairpin bend, and we decided to stake it out for what was left of the day. The air was dry and dusty. While we stood, watching another Ruby-throated Hummingbird working its way around the flowers above us, a pair of Scarlet Macaws passed overhead, a reminder that, whilst we were focusing on hummingbirds, we were still seeing significant numbers of magnificent birds besides. That came as no surprise—despite representing only 0.03 percent of the world's landmass, an enormous 5 percent of the world's biodiversity is found in Costa Rica.

The country prides itself on its biodiversity and the way in which it has embraced environmentalism—it is the only nation in the world to meet the United Nations Development Programme's five criteria for environmental sustainability. It currently generates 98.1 percent of its electricity from renewable sources, and aims to be entirely carbon-neutral by 2021. Having had no standing army since 1949, the country offers an enticingly utopian alternative approach to life that held considerable appeal to me.

"It's not perfect here," Pat conceded as we discussed the country whilst we waited, heads craned up towards the flowering canopy above us, "but it's pretty good."

His confidence in the tree and pride in the country's abundant birdlife soon paid off. A small hummingbird flew into the treetop, circled around the back of the crown where we could not see it, and then landed on an exposed twig protruding from the treetop.

"That's exactly what coquettes love to do . . ." muttered Pat. "Yes! White-crested Coquette!"

This was my first coquette and, while distant and seen from below, it was still a fabulously attractive tiny, long-tailed bird, with underparts of soft apricot, a gleaming white throat, a short white quiff on his forecrown, and long, spiky green cheek tufts that protruded far beyond the nape of his neck. Even from that distance, his blood-red bill gleamed against the darkening blue sky. From where we watched, he was a small hummingbird comprising acute, sharp angles. For some birders, this would have been just another tick in a column on a life list. I took more from the experience than that—this was no mere number, this first example of an entirely new hummingbird genus to me. He was spectacular.

The same, with the best will in the world, could not be said of Charming Hummingbird. Was ever a plainly marked hummingbird given a more optimistic yet, simultaneously, slightly desperate name? Previously considered to be a subspecies of the similar Blue-chested Hummingbird, and at one time known as Beryl-crowned Hummingbird, this was another bird that owed its first description to the trigger-happy quetzal-bagger, Osbert Salvin. First one, and then two more of these grey-bellied, sombre-hued birds came to feed in the treetop above us, occasionally perching and, as they looked around them, allowing glimpses of their shining turquoise crowns.

We finished the day with thirteen hummingbird species in the bag, a total that Pat assured me could have been much higher had we picked up the pace and incorporated any feeding stations into our route. The following day would, he said, dramatically increase our tally, and we would start at a site that was legendary amongst birders, El Tapir.

If there was one hummingbird I wanted to see in Costa Rica above all others, it was the Snowcap. Other hummingbirds have longer, more elaborate names, but the Snowcap has, in its name, a simplicity that fits the bird perfectly. Snowcaps have a plumage that is unique amongst hummingbirds—at first glance, the male's body is entirely a deep, rich burgundy, topped by a searing white crown, the eponymous snowcap. Look more closely, and the burgundy plumage shows gold and bronze tones. Like most of the hummingbird tribe, Snowcap plumage is iridescent.

This iridescence has been the focus of study in recent years to understand how hummingbirds, unlike all other birds, have feathers that display such complexity and intensity of colour. Sampling feathers from a representative range of thirty-four hummingbird species, scientists examined the feathers under transmission electron microscopes, paying particular attention to the melanosomes present in the feathers' tiny filaments, or barbules. Melanosomes are the cells that contain melanin, the pigment that gives feathers, fur, and skin its colour. How those melanosomes are shaped, structured, and arranged makes a world of difference to the colour the eye perceives. The study's authors were consumed with curiosity about why some groups of birds were more colourful than others and, in particular, why hummingbirds glittered and flashed so brightly. They wondered if this colour production was something to do with sexual selection, or the internal mechanisms and physics of their feathers themselves. It transpired that hummingbird melanosomes were uniquely formed—pancake-shaped and containing many tiny air bubbles. In the hair of mammals, the melanin is not particularly organised in any way, but in birds the melanosomes are layered—when light bounces off the different layers, onlookers perceive colours.

In hummingbirds, the pancake-shaped, aerated melanosomes meant that the birds' feathers could exhibit not only a rainbow of different colours, but also display them with an iridescent impact unparalleled in nature. Professor Matthew Shawkey of the University of Ghent, one of the study's authors, used the analogy of soap to illustrate this—a flake of soap is a bland, drab thing, but structured correctly, spread out thinly on the shell of a bubble, it forms shimmering rainbow colours. Melanosomes of the right shape and structure, arranged in just the right way, give hummingbirds their iridescent plumage.

Standing in the grounds of El Tapir, an abandoned former butterfly garden in the depths of the Costa Rican countryside, the mechanics of feather colour, hue, and saturation could not have been further from my mind as I watched a Snowcap systematically working his way up and down the pink-flowered spires of porterweed that grew in impressionist swathes around us. His shimmering burgundy plumage was a colour the likes of which I had never seen before on a bird, and the sight of my first, long-anticipated Snowcap took my breath away. Better still, he was not alone. As Pat had warned as we approached El Tapir, "For hummingbirds, this place is like trick or treating in rich neighbourhoods while Halloween just repeats itself day after day after day. You'll see plenty there besides Snowcaps."

Sure enough, the porterweed bushes were swarming with hummingbirds from the very moment we arrived. Rain was falling torrentially, but this was not stopping the hungry birds first thing in the morning. Green Thorntails, Crowned Woodnymphs, and Violet-headed Hummingbirds mingled interchangeably and, in a moment of panic for me, another new coquette appeared simultaneously with the Snowcap—a male Black-crested Coquette, subtler than his White-crested counterpart of the previous day, but equally ephemeral, making the briefest of feeding pit stops in the porter-weed before towering high above the treeline and away from us. We stood in the dripping shelter of a decaying wooden outbuilding and focused on the Snowcap until he too chose to move on.

With hummingbird numbers mounting steadily, we dropped down to the lowlands and onto an island in the Puerto Viejo River, where Pat hoped to address the shortfall of hermits. After the previous day's dismal attempt to find any flowering heliconias, finding ourselves surrounded by their waxy, flaming blooms was welcome. The intensifying rain was much less pleasant altogether—a tropical downpour that even hungry hummingbirds were not braving. The ground soon became saturated beneath our feet, puddles coalescing into larger sheets of water in which the heliconias forlornly stood alongside us. Now we had heliconias, but still no hermits. This dismal scene was broken only once by a brief hummingbird, a Purple-crowned Fairy that dived through the cascading rain, fed momentarily at the dripping, frosted pink flowers of a ginger, and then was lost to sight as it flickered back into the louring sky. It was difficult not to feel despondent, the euphoria of El Tapir draining from us.

"I thought this would be a good place for hermits," Pat said bleakly. "If it wasn't raining, it would be. We should have had at least a Stripe-throated Hermit by now. Not seeing one of them is simply absurd—it's one of the most common hummingbirds in the country. Perhaps we should move on . . ."

We were walking back towards the bridge that brought us onto the island when Pat stopped abruptly, his head cocked to one side. Over the rush and patter of rain falling on leaves all around us, he had heard something.

"I think that's a barbthroat," he said quietly. "There, singing in the understorey. Can you hear it?"

I strained to make out any birdsong. Following Pat as he slowly walked towards a dense area of bushes, a silvery cascading sound interposed itself over the background noise of rushing water. Something was singing nearby. It took minutes that felt like eternities before, in the near darkness of the understorey, we finally picked out the unmistakeable silhouette of a hummingbird perched just above the ground. Sure enough, Pat's keen hearing had, at last, found us our first hermit of the weekend—and not just any hermit, for Band-tailed Barbthroat is a scarce species that I had not dared to hope we might encounter. Making out any detail in the poor light was challenging—the bird's olive-green mantle appearing black, with just the white-tipped tail and two white facial stripes providing any paler counterpoints in the gloom.

Abandoning our hermit hunt, we headed for a roadside café for a welcome hot lunch of fish and rice, sharing the outside tables with two truck drivers, who sat, like us, mesmerised by the activity at the handful of hummingbird feeders the café owner had hung in the trees beside the covered seating area. The rain showed no signs of letting up, and here, at a much higher elevation, the windchill was noticeable too.

"There should be more hummingbirds here," Pat said, the disappointment weighing heavily in his voice. For the sake of our hummingbird list, the new species were, however, still accruing, with the Violet Sabrewings that fed alongside us a particularly dramatic addition—these were large hummingbirds, as flamboyant as the barbthroat had been subtle, with rich, deep imperial-purple plumage and long, curved dark wings that snapped like castanets as they sheared and sparred around the feeders.

After lunch, our fortunes changed, dramatically. A Coppery-headed Emerald, another Costa Rican endemic, was feeding around a flowery treetop just a few hundred metres from our lunch stop—a shy hummingbird of subtle green and bronze tones that would probably not have held the truck drivers spellbound in the way the confiding and dramatically colourful sabrewings had, but to me was more beautiful still. Less, sometimes, was more where hummingbirds were concerned. The emerald, his feathers looking like the patina developing on a Henry Moore bronze, was a powerful omen for the afternoon ahead. As the rain abated, new hummingbirds came thick and fast, a deluge of species that more than lived up to my expectations.

"I normally avoid La Paz Waterfall Gardens," said Pat as we pulled into a small car park, "because it's sort of like a zoo, and crawling with people. Nevertheless, it's also a necessary part of a hummingbird quest in Costa Rica because the feeders are some of the best in the country. We should do well in here."

This proved to be an understatement on all counts. The gardens were, indeed, full of families grimly making the best of the wet day, dodging showers to show their children caged animals; but, once we reached the small hummingbird feeding area, we found wild birds in abundance and, amongst more sabrewings and thorntails, our two main targets, White-bellied and Purple-throated Mountain-gems. As their names suggested, these were montane species, found in higher regions of Central America. Getting both together, side by side, was pleasingly straightforward, but there was something more unexpected feeding alongside them—a bonus Black-bellied Hummingbird, another hummer that, like the barbtail in the morning, was by no means a bird we would have counted upon seeing. Watching this sooty, dark hummingbird, Pat was visibly elated.

"This is good, Jon! Our luck's changing. We could try for something else while we're here, you never know . . ."

Pat, assessing the possibilities nearby, suggested a speculative diversion to a nearby fast-flowing, boulder-choked river. We scrambled down a muddy, slippery path to the riverside.

"You see that waterfall?" Pat asked, pointing to a small waterfall dropping into a sheltered corner of the river, "That looks like the perfect place for a Green-fronted Lancebill."

The words had no sooner been said than a dainty, dark-green hummingbird flew up from a mossy rock at the side of the water, caught a fly midair, and perched for a few precious seconds on a thin, bare branch overhanging the water. A Green-fronted Lancebill, right on cue, visible for just long enough for us to appreciate its long, needle-thin black bill before it flew into the mist of the waterfall and vanished from sight. My adrenaline was soaring now—the day had transformed, and it now seemed like we needed only to suggest a hummingbird for the Fates to conspire to provide it for us. The hummingbird drug was coursing through my veins once more.

We spent the next hour ascending the slopes of the Poás Volcano, an immense, simmering presence to the north of San José, moving into the very clouds that had disrupted so much of the day with their precipitation. Another roadside café had hummingbird feeders hung along a chain-link fence—not a particularly attractive setting in which to find hummingbirds, but the birds were beyond such human aesthetic judgements—for them, all that mattered was a ready and reliable food source. New species continued to flood in—Stripe-tailed, Talamanca, and Volcano Hummingbirds, Lesser Violetears, and Magenta-throated Woodstars. The promised surfeit of Costa Rican hummingbirds was now a reality. One possibility remained, and this was a species that Pat had never seen on the feeders. It was also a species I dearly wanted to see, for the principles of iridescence in hummingbirds have arguably no finer proponent than the plumage of a male Fiery-throated. An otherwise green hummingbird, when seen facing the observer, the male displays a throat that burns in its centre like a red-hot coal; fades to shades of amber and gold, fringed with turquoise tones; and has a crown of electric blue, like a shard of the sky captured in feathers.

Whilst in normal conditions Fiery-throated Hummingbirds are not uncommon, the weather had deteriorated once more. The higher we went, the wetter and windier it became. Finding just one bird felt, in the end, like a blessing—we had given up, and were walking through the diagonally falling rain back to the shelter of Pat's car when, out of the grey miasma, a hummer buzzed past us, perching in the shelter of a roadside tree. A Fiery-throated and, while this was not quite the photographic opportunity I had hoped it might be, it was a good close view that filled my binoculars.

Pat displayed admirable commitment on the journey back into San José in the last hour of daylight, stopping several times to try to add more species to our final tally. Scintillant Hummingbird and the elusive Canivet's Emerald were both possibilities, as was the mystifyingly absent Stripe-throated Hermit, but our luck had turned once more on the whim of the weather. While forty species would have been a pleasingly round figure, I knew it would be churlish to be anything but delighted with the experience of the past two days—we had seen and heard, in the final reckoning, 223 species of birds, thirty-seven of which had been hummingbirds and, in their number, included some sought-after endemic and iconic species.

It was only later that I learned, from Pat, just how well we had done—he spent a fortnight birding intensively in the country with a friend, tallying thirty-nine species of hummingbird amongst a haul of over five hundred species of bird. We had seen almost as many hummingbirds in just two days. Ours had been an intense birding experience, filled with the emotional peaks and troughs familiar to any birder who has attempted a "big day," as the challenge of seeing as many species as possible in a twenty-four-hour period is known.

We had stretched and modified that format to maximise the hummingbird potential of this wonderfully biodiverse place, a country I already knew I would return to one day, with much more time in hand, to explore more thoroughly. There was so much still to see and, if nothing else, I wanted second helpings of Snowcaps—one of the most beautiful hummingbirds of all.

CHAPTER FIVE

FAKES, FREAKS,
AND PHANTOMS

~

Colombia, Santa Marta. 11° N. Antioquia. 6° N

*A*NY NATURALIST WORTH THEIR SALT WOULD NEED NO EXCUSE to visit Colombia. For a birder, let alone one consumed with a hunger for hummingbirds, Colombia is simply irresistible, with a steadily increasing national list approaching two thousand different species of birds as a whole recorded to date. In living memory, the country was considered too politically unstable and dangerous to safely visit but, as I planned the next stage of my odyssey, these concerns were largely consigned to the past, and I could look forward to a near future studded with some of the rarest hummingbirds South America had to offer, enigmatic species that had been unattainable for birders or even lost entirely to science for many decades. For a birder, their rarity and exclusivity salted them with an additional seasoning that transcended their physical, aesthetic appeal—there is an undeniable frisson in having seen something that very few others have laid eyes upon.

Colombia's reputation for enigmatic hummingbirds stretches back not decades but centuries. Hummingbirds have come and gone, have teased their observers and their acolytes, their identities and stories as elusive and complicated as the very birds themselves. Theirs is a redolent history of fabrication and fraud; human reputations staked, won, and lost; and birds that have defied description, sometimes in a literal as well as a metaphorical sense.

This tale of lost hummingbirds begins in 1788, when the German naturalist Johann Friedrich Gmelin published the thirteenth edition of the great *Systema Naturae* by the renowned Swedish taxonomist Carl Linnaeus. Clearly no academic slouch, Gmelin was simultaneously professor of medicine, chemistry, botany, and mineralogy at the University of Göttingen during the latter decades of the eighteenth century. In the new edition of *Systema Naturae*, he turned his attention to formally describing almost three hundred new bird species, including a number that had previously been described without a Linnean scientific name by an English naturalist, John Latham, in an earlier work, *A General Synopsis of Birds*. This was the moment that the Harlequin Hummingbird, *Trochilus multicolour*, officially existed on the scientific record.

Latham's description of it in 1782 was suitably scientifically dry, for all it lacked Linnean taxonomic clarity:

Length four inches and a half. Bill bent, an inch and a quarter in length, and of a brown colour: crown of the head, chin, breast and middle of the back, green: from the bill, through the eye, is a stripe of fine blue, passing behind almost to the nape; the lower part of this is edged with black: the upper parts of the body and wings are brown: the belly and vent of the colour of cinnabar, but not glossy like the rest of the plumage: the tail even at the end, and of a brown colour: the legs are also pale brown.

Latham based his description upon a specimen of the bird held in the collections of the British Museum, although he issued it with a small caveat, noting that the specimen has "no history annexed to it." Writing again of the Harlequin Hummingbird five years later, in 1787, his accompanying coloured plate of the bird depicts a strikingly particoloured bird—and better still, he had now found a corroborating source for the bird, amongst the drawings of another English naturalist and British army officer, Colonel Thomas Davies. Latham implied that Davies had based his representation upon a different specimen to that in the British Museum, noting some minor differences between it and his own earlier description of the bird, concluding, "The colours of the plumage are much the same as before described . . . The plate herewith is a good representation."

Indeed it was, for Latham's plate is a striking facsimile of the original watercolour painted by Davies, albeit a mirror image as he had depicted the bird facing in the opposite direction to that chosen by Davies. Davies was, in his military career, well-travelled in North America and the West Indies, so Latham may have reasonably assumed Davies had encountered the Harlequin Hummingbird on his travels. Davies' own collection of bird specimens was disposed of shortly after his death, so we will never be sure whether Latham's assumption of a second corroborating specimen was accurate or not.

However, we do know that Davies visited the British Museum at least once during the period 1785–1786, as there is a note in his own hand on one of his drawings to that effect. There is a very good chance that Davies' depiction of the Harlequin Hummingbird was based upon the same British Museum specimen that Latham first described in 1782, and the minor differences that Latham noted in 1787 between their respective descriptions can be attributed to the iridescent nature of hummingbird feathers—viewed from different angles, and in different lighting conditions, they can vary dramatically in colour and tone.

It was Latham's descriptions and 1787 painting of the Harlequin Hummingbird that provided Gmelin with his source material for the bird's inclusion in *Systema Naturae* in 1788. Thereafter, for years, the provenance of the Harlequin Hummingbird went uncontested, and it cropped up repeatedly in subsequent publications.

Writing in 1791 in their *Vivarium Naturae or The Naturalist's Miscellany*, George Shaw and Frederick Nodder described it as "among the rarest species of its genus," and provided very little more detail about the bird—they considered it to hail from South America, an assertion that, given that most of the hummingbirds known to the naturalists of the day came from South America, was not a particularly radical suggestion. Frederick Nodder illustrated the bird, presumably using the specimen held in the British Museum collection—he had been appointed there as Assistant Keeper of Natural History earlier in the year.

In 1801 the Harlequin Hummingbird was included in the sumptuous *Oiseaux dorés ou à reflets métalliques*, a two-volume folio work started by French naturalist and artist Jean-Baptiste Audebert and completed, after his death, by his friend Louis Jean Pierre Viellot. The book containing the hummingbirds was notable for the astonishing quality of the artwork—the plates being etched by Audebert to his own designs and, according to his preface, those of "les plus habiles artistes de Paris"; coloured and painted with oil paints; and then overlaid with fine printed lines of gold and silver to give the hummingbirds' plumage an impression of iridescence. The illustration of the Harlequin, however, was created for Audebert not by one of Paris's "plus habiles artistes," but instead by a natural history illustrator from Monmouthshire named Sydenham Edwards. It is once again strikingly similar to one that had gone before, this time that of Nodder, suggesting that Edwards had more than a passing familiarity with the contents of *Vivarium Naturae*, if not those of the British Museum.

Twenty years later, doubt was beginning to set in amongst the naturalists of the day, including those who had originally promoted the Harlequin Hummingbird as a new species. Perhaps the lack of further specimens forthcoming from the Americas, at a time of prodigious collecting in the region, was unsettling the Harlequin's champions. Writing in 1822, John Latham remarked, "It has been suggested to me that this is no other than a bird made up by the ingenuity of some whimsical person, who has fabricated it from the feathers of others; but which, by every attention paid to it, I cannot detect."

Back in France, meanwhile, in 1829 naturalist René Lesson was much more uncompromising: "The bird that served as the type for Latham's description and for the figure copied by Viellot was the product of a fabrication . . . it had been discovered on deconstructing the specimen preserved in the British Museum."

By the time John Gould, no stranger to hummingbird hyperbole himself, produced his *Monograph of the Trochilidae, or Family of Humming-Birds* in 1849–1861, the Harlequin Hummingbird was an embarrassing side note. Gould scathingly concluded that Gmelin's description of the Harlequin Hummingbird as a new species was taken from a plate, "Which must have been drawn from the imagination and not from any real specimen."

We know, however, that this was not the case. Latham and Davies appear to have both worked from the same actual specimen in the British Museum's collection; and the existence of the specimen at the time is recorded in no other more august record than that of the British Parliamentary Papers. During 1835–1836, a significant parliamentary enquiry was conducted into the unsatisfactory state of the "Condition, Management and Affairs" of the British Museum. In April 1836 John Edward Gray, a zoologist on the British Museum's curatorial staff, was questioned by Conservative Member of Parliament Sir Robert Inglis about technical procedures behind the scenes at the museum.

One such question related to a perfidious technique that Gray's French counterparts were known to practice in order to improve the appearance of exhibition bird specimens—a process known as having them "made up"—in other words replacing, say, a worn tail or wing, with a fresh body part from another bird. Inglis asked, "Looking at the practice [making up] as a man of science, do you consider it advisable or reprehensible?"

Gray replied, "It is very wrong. We had formerly in the collection of the museum a made-up specimen, called the Harlequin Hummingbird, which I believe was destroyed by Dr Leach. It was ejected before my time."

Dr. William Elford Leach was the British Museum curator with responsibility for zoology from 1814 until 1822. Gray had assisted Leach on an ad hoc basis since 1816 until his formal employment at the museum in 1824, and he clearly knew about the Harlequin Hummingbird's chequered recent past. It seems likely that the incident referred to by René Lesson in 1829 in which the specimen was "deconstructed" was one and the same incident. Suspicion about the hummingbird had been aroused at some point during Leach's tenure as curator, and he or his staff had examined the specimen more closely, discovering it was made up of composite parts of several different species of hummingbirds.

Why would anyone perpetrate such a fraud? Given that there was no collector's name associated with the specimen, we can reasonably rule out personal advancement or fame-seeking. Mischief-making seems equally improbable. More likely, the creation of the Harlequin Hummingbird was a calculated attempt to make money—collectors, including museums, paid good money at the time for new specimens for their collections. Somebody, their identity lost to the mists of time, fabricated the Harlequin Hummingbird using the dastardly and supposedly French practice of making-up.

Such skulduggery was by no means confined to France—the inference, perhaps, owing more to recent Napoleonic conflict than any basis in fact. By all accounts, birds were being made up all over the world, from far overseas to much closer to home. One of H. G. Wells' earliest stories, "The Triumphs of a Taxidermist," published late in the nineteenth century, offers us a window into the preceding decades. While it is a work of fiction, so too were the bogus birds that we know were being fabricated. Wells reveals something of the psychology of the fraudsters, the pursuit not just of profit, but also projection of power over those who purchased the specimens—they would have been of a higher social status than the lowly taxidermist. It would have been satisfying to deceive one's social betters, and to be paid for the privilege. In the story, the taxidermist boasts of his fraudulent creations, including extinct, iconic birds like the Dodo and the Great Auk.

"My dear fellow," he confides, "half the Great Auks in the world are about as genuine as the handkerchief of Saint Veronica, as the Holy Coat of Treves. We make 'em of grebes' feathers and the like."

He concedes this pays him handsomely and then, lowering his voice, he reveals: "This is merely imitating Nature. I have done more than that in my time. I have . . . beaten her. I have *created* birds. *New* birds. Like no birds that was ever before. Some of the birds I made were new kinds of hummingbirds, and very beautiful little things, but some of them were simply rum."

The manufacture of fake birds, and hummingbirds in particular during the nineteenth century, was evidently both a notorious trade and a pitfall for the unwary collector or scientific institution. The Harlequin Hummingbird was not the only example of this fraudulent practice to enter the collections of the British Museum. In 1819, when nurseryman and hummingbird collector George Loddiges bid on some of the hummingbirds for sale in the auction of William Bullock's prodigious collection of natural wonders, the British Museum's very own zoology curator Dr. Leach acquired, at significant expense to the museum, an extraordinary seabird, a petrel with abnormally large, duck-like feet.

It was not long before the museum staff realised, to their dismay, that the legs and feet of the petrel were, in fact, those of an actual duck. This must have caused Leach considerable embarrassment. Perhaps the incident spurred an internal review of other unique specimens in the British Museum's bird collection. It may also have contributed to the mental collapse that Leach suffered in September 1820; he was pensioned off early in April 1822 on the grounds of ill health. One suspects that the period after duck-gate was probably a torrid and unpleasant time for Leach in the museum, a quacking figure of fun to his colleagues and a source of professional embarrassment to his superiors.

Yet poor Dr. Leach was not alone in being fooled by hummingbird fraud. Sixty years later, it was still going on. When, in July 1889, Frank Chapman, writing in the *Bulletin of the American Museum of Natural History*, described a new hummingbird species *Amazilia æneobrunnea*, purchased from a Mr. C. S. Galbraith and said to have come from Bogotá, he could scarcely contain his excitement: "This new species is so remarkably distinct as to scarcely require comparison with any other member of the genus."

Months later in October 1889, it was a chastened Chapman who wrote again in the same journal to reveal that he had been the victim of a hummingbird hoax:

Since publishing a description of *Amazilia æneobrunnea* I happened to handle a Bogotá example of *Chrysolampis mosquitus*, and the 'make up' of the skin at once rendered apparent the before unrecognised similarity in the colour of the body of the two birds. A re-examination of the type of *æneobrunnea* showed that the body did belong to this species, while the head and neck were those of *Chlorostilbon haberlini*. [*Chrysolampis mosquitus* and *Chlorostilbon haberlini* were both widely recognised and valid hummingbird species at the time.]

In brief, *Amazilia æneobrunnea* is one of those taxidermal deceptions which not infrequently puzzle and sometimes, as in the present case, completely deceive unsuspecting ornithologists.

Ever the scientist, poor Chapman goes on to attempt to explain his taxonomical reasoning in placing the imposter in the genus *Amazilia*, and then concludes, "Further remark is perhaps unnecessary; but the experience apparently shows that the anatomy and construction of 'Bogotá' skins are as deserving of examination as their external characteristics."

Whatever was going on in Colombia in the nineteenth century? It sounds, from Chapman's conclusion, as if hummingbird specimens emanating from Bogotá had come to acquire something of a reputation for being unreliable. The creation and sale of fake hummingbirds to unwitting overseas collectors seems to have been a thriving cottage industry in Colombia's capital city.

The bustling Mesoamerican trade routes that saw feathers of hummingbirds and other neotropical bird species moved over great distances to feed the Aztec demand for the products of *amanteca* feather craftsmen had their counterparts elsewhere in the pre-Columbian Americas. In the north, a well-established network operated in the Mississippian culture of what is now the eastern and southeastern United States; and in South America, the best-known trade network was that of the Inca peoples of what is now largely Peru.

Bogotá was, during the nineteenth century, a hub for this bird trade that fed the hunger of foreign collectors and institutions for novel bird specimens. Dealers from Britain, France, and Belgium established themselves in the city, exporting countless thousands of bird skins to Europe every year, primarily supplying demand from the fashion industry. Initially, birds would have been collected relatively locally in central Colombia but, with time, from further afield too. Tellingly, there are a number of bird species claimed for Colombia on the basis of so-called Bogotá skins that are normally found in Ecuador and Peru but which have not, to date, been seen again in Colombia. As the global appetite grew for discovering and categorising new species, and with a burgeoning number of potential donor species from which to "make up" a novel hummingbird, the temptation to do so and cash in on the demand evidently proved irresistible for some bird fabricators in Colombia and, indeed, elsewhere.

In time these frauds were uncovered one by one, and species that had formerly been recognised as such were lost. However, another hummingbird specimen, bought at a Bogotá market in 1909, remains lost to this day—a confusing bird created not by the wilful hand of man, but by sheer chance in nature itself.

In 1947 Brother Nicéforo María sent an unusual steely-blue, fork-tailed hummingbird specimen, quite unlike anything he had ever seen before and purchased in Bogotá in 1909, to ornithologist Rodolphe Meyer de Schauensee at the Academy of Natural Sciences of Philadelphia with a request for assistance in identifying the bird.

Brother Nicéforo María was a French-born Colombian missionary and naturalist who, during his lifetime, collected extensive amounts of biological material in Colombia, sending whatever he could not identify for himself to researchers elsewhere in the world for assistance. He described two new species for himself, a coral snake and a fishing snake, but from his steady stream of collected material over 130 new species of plants, spiders, reptiles, fishes, amphibians, and birds were described by other biologists. What would the mysterious blue Bogotá hummingbird prove to be?

Meyer de Schauensee certainly didn't recognise it, and shared the specimen with some equally baffled and intrigued peers, a roll call of the prominent American ornithologists of the day. In the correspondence that ensued, James L. Peters, former president of the American Ornithologists' Union (AOU), suggested it might be of hybrid origin, as hummingbirds are known to regularly hybridise between species, but was perplexed by the blue colouration. From the general structure of the bird he hypothesised that one parent might be a sylph (a long-tailed genus of hummingbird) and the other a sunangel (another genus of hummingbird), but he concluded that the bird was very puzzling indeed, and he felt he had not helped advance the resolution of its identity.

John T. Zimmer, curator of birds at the American Museum of Natural History in New York, also suggested a putative sylph / sunangel hybrid origin for the specimen. However, Alexander Wetmore, renowned ornithologist and secretary of the Smithsonian Institution, was of no doubt that the specimen represented a new species and, perhaps, a new genus of hummingbird too. He summarised that he had never seen a bird like it.

Brother Nicéforo María had first passed the bird to Meyer de Schauensee, and it was he who would have the last word, at least for a while. He concluded that the bird was probably merely a specimen of an extremely poorly known species of hummingbird, Nehrkorn's Sylph, a bird that, at the time, was known from only two museum specimens.

However, the mystery did not rest there. In the years that followed, the enigmatic Nehrkorn's Sylph came to be regarded not as a species but, instead, as a hybrid with Long-tailed Sylph as one of the parents. Maybe the Bogotá hummingbird was, after all, a hybrid as Peters and Zimmer had suggested. We should, perhaps, be simply grateful that the bird made it safely to Meyer de Schauensee in the first place—a shipment of preserved fish specimens sent to him in barrels from Thailand went missing upon arrival in New York harbour when the stevedores handling them apparently drank the alcoholic preserving fluid, after first dumping the fish into the bay.

In 1993, ornithologist Gary Graves wrote a paper entitled "Relic of a Lost World: A New Species of Sunangel from 'Bogotá'" for *The Auk*, the scientific journal of the AOU. In it he made a careful and measured case for the Bogotá hummingbird being not, after all, a hybrid, but instead a valid species in its own right, albeit one that had not been known to be seen alive by any person since its corpse had been purchased in a Bogotá market some eighty years beforehand. He systematically examined the case for it being a hybrid, and concluded that this could not reasonably be so. Graves gave the Bogotá Sunangel a scientific name, *Heliangelus zusii*, named after his friend and colleague Richard L. Zusi, in recognition of his contributions to the systematics of hummingbirds.

Not everybody in the ornithological world agreed with Graves' conclusions, though this is far from unusual in the torrid field of avian taxonomy. Then, in 2009, hard science appeared to vindicate him—a paper was published announcing that, using skin cells scraped from the feet of the centenarian dead hummingbird, researchers had extracted DNA from the Bogotá Sunangel and analysed it in the laboratories of the New York State Museum. The results seemed unequivocal—the DNA indicated the Bogotá Sunangel was indeed a valid species, albeit one that might be inappropriately named. The bird's DNA suggested it was not at all closely related to the other sunangels and, in fact, had far more in common with the sylphs.

While the Bogotá Sunangel now appeared to be a valid species, it was represented only by a single specimen residing in a museum drawer, and one that told us nothing about where living representatives of the species, if they still existed in the wild, might yet be found. Graves speculated that they might be found in a remote area of the Eastern Cordillera of the Colombian Andes, possibly within a few hundred kilometres of Bogotá, or maybe in the Central Cordillera. This was informed guesswork and, rather forlornly, Graves also raised the spectre that the bird might already be extinct—any number of bird species in South America exist in extremely isolated and restricted ranges, and that of the Bogotá Sunangel may have been lost to habitat destruction in the intervening decades. One thing was for sure: the Bogotá Sunangel was a lost hummingbird.

Or was it?

In 2011, just a couple of years after the DNA work that confirmed the validity of the Bogotá Sunangel, a striking bird started to appear at hummingbird feeders in the montane forests of the Reserva Rogitama, in the Eastern Cordillera of the Colombian Andes, precisely the region that Graves had posited might hold an undiscovered relic population of Bogotá Sunangels. Better still, the bird in question looked the part—a dark steely blue, with a long, forked tail. In a press release at the time, Roberto Chavarro of Reserva Rogitama said, "I made some photos and videos that I sent to the reserve's friends to get some help with identification. The first response was by [Colombian birder] Diego Calderón, who expressed his almost total confidence that the photos were the presumed extinct Bogotá Sunangel."

Chavarro believed there to be three individual birds in the area. He added,

> We had agreed to keep this big news confidential until the identity of the bird was advanced; however, the rush of some photographs published on the internet without our authorisation forces us to share early this exciting news.
>
> For Reserva Rogitama, this news is a great honour and a big prize, a compensation for the constant work that started in 1982 with the environmental restoration of this land. Basically, we have changed these cattle pastures into a refuge for wildlife in the last 29 years. In 1982 we used to see only a few birds, but nowadays we have recorded 121 species.

This all sounded like such good news and, at the time with my personal interest in hummingbirds piqued, I was thrilled to learn such a mythical bird had come back from the dead. I began to lay plans to visit Rogitama at the earliest opportunity. In the months that followed, those plans unravelled. It appeared that there was only one Bogotá Sunangel in the Reserva Rogitama, not three individuals. That bird was captured and examined in the hand and, after its release, the bird was no longer considered to be a Bogotá Sunangel—the observers felt that plumage features of the bird suggested it was a hybrid, with Long-tailed Sylph and Tyrian Metaltail suggested as the most likely parents.

The story took a new twist in 2018 with the publication of another paper, in the journal *Zootaxa*, subjecting both the 1909 Bogotá Sunangel and the 2011 Rogitama hybrid to further laboratory scrutiny. The authors' conclusions were not good news for the original Bogotá Sunangel. It had DNA that appeared identical to that of the Rogitama bird, but also DNA that suggested the birds both had Long-tailed sylphs as their mothers. The earlier DNA analysis of the 1909 Bogotá Sunangel had used comparative DNA from only one individual Long-tailed Sylph—this new study had used a much wider geographical dataset of Long-tailed Sylphs to compare with the 1909 and 2011 birds. Both seemed to be hybrids after all.

In 2019 BirdLife International, significant contributors to the accurate data that underpin the International Union for Conservation of Nature (IUCN) Red List of Threatened Species, hammered in what appeared to be the final nail in the Bogotá Sunangel's coffin. They said,

> One day the Bogotá Sunangel is a species in its own right, the next it is struck off the record. Following careful examination, scientists have now agreed that it is in fact a hybrid of two other species. You might call that an identity crisis and feel bad for the bird being shunted out of the species list, but really this is a positive outcome. Lacking observations of the bird meant that if it were indeed a species, it was probably extinct. However, [this news means] that this is one fewer species lost to us— we'll call that good news.

Positive news of a kind, but it had been preceded by genuinely positive news from Colombia in 2015 of another lost hummingbird that had been rediscovered in the remote and rarely visited mountainous páramo habitat of the Sierra Nevada de Santa Marta in the north of the country. Blue-bearded Helmetcrest was first described from the region in 1880—an outrageously attractive hummingbird that surmounted a body of buff and chocolate brown with a head that the entire English species name was devoted to describing. An extensive, dark-mocha area around each eye was surrounded by a snow-white neck collar and a swept-back white Mohican above. Below the bill were glittering, sapphire throat feathers that hung over the bird's upper breast, again framed delicately in snow white—this was the blue beard.

Between 1880 and 1946 the bird was collected in small numbers, and a little over sixty specimens reside in museum collections around the world to this day. However, after 1946 the bird dropped off the map, and wasn't seen again. Surveys specifically looking for it in

1999–2003 failed to find any helmetcrests. This looked like another potentially lost hummingbird until, on March 4, 2015, Carlos Julio Rojas and Christian Vasquez found the first bird to be seen for sixty-nine years. Rojas recalled, "I saw the flash of a bird screeching past me, and saw it perch on a bush nearby. I managed to take a quick photo of it before it flew off. I then reviewed the photo on the camera screen and immediately recognized the strikingly patterned hummingbird as the long-lost Blue-bearded Helmetcrest—I was ecstatic!"

Once the news broke, it captured the imagination of many a birder, myself included. In the years that followed, the very most dedicated birders from Colombia and further afield attempted to make the long trek into the Blue-bearded Helmetcrest's home in the Sierra Madre Mountains. Nothing about seeing one was easy. There is no road access to the area, so one must walk or ride in, carrying all of one's equipment and food. The weather up on the páramo can change in a heartbeat, and is often inclement. There is also the matter of the Kogi to take into account. The Kogi are the indigenous people on whose land the helmetcrests are—if one is lucky—to be found, and they restrict the access of outsiders to land they consider sacred.

A deeply insular and religious people famed for their reverence for the natural world, the Kogi view outsiders with justifiable suspicion—we have, after all, a pretty dismal track record of caring for the environment. They refer to themselves as the "Elder Brothers" of humanity, believing they are the guardians of all life on earth. Historian and documentary filmmaker Alan Ereira spent time with the Kogi in the late 1980s, allowed into their guarded society as they had determined that he could carry their message out to the wider world. That message was one of warning to us all—we needed to radically change our way of life, to be less exploitative of the natural world, if we were to avoid an ecological catastrophe.

This seems, now, like a remarkably prescient observation. The Kogi had been observing environmental changes in their mountain homeland during the 1980s, and they were worried. Ereira explained that the Kogi considered the world to be one singular, living entity, which they as people were entrusted to care for. Their entire way of life was said to be concerned with nurturing the world's flora and fauna. While they might not have chosen such a formal description of themselves, they were, in effect, an ecological community.

It is painfully ironic, then, that Rojas and Vasquez rediscovered the Blue-bearded Helmetcrest when they were surveying the extent of the damage done to the fragile páramo landscape by the Kogi setting fires to generate tender, short-lived grass pasture on which to feed the cattle they depend upon for food and commerce. The effect of these fires on the delicate páramo flora is all too predictable—they are indiscriminate, wiping out native flowering plants, lichens and, worst of all for the hummingbirds, the towering *frailejones*, thick-trunked perennial shrubs with glaucous crowns of leaves, whose butter-yellow daisy-like flowers the helmetcrests feed from.

When I thought about the Blue-bearded Helmetcrests, I could feel a sense of impending doom. The biodiversity of the area is unique, as the Santa Marta range predates the rest of the South American Andes by some one hundred million years. Accordingly, the highest areas of the Sierra Nevada de Santa Marta were declared a national park in 1964, and, in 1979, the park was designated a United Nations Educational, Scientific and Cultural Organization (UNESCO) Biosphere Reserve.

One might think that these titles would afford some protection to the area, but actually enforcing any sort of restriction on the burning activities of the Kogi would be almost impossible given the remoteness of the area and, besides, with their famous mistrust of outsiders, would be just as likely to entrench their position as to change it. It felt to me that the hummingbirds were living on borrowed time in a fragment of high-altitude habitat that was only going to get smaller and more embattled. While seeing them might be a bittersweet and poignant experience, it was one I dearly wanted for myself. The birder in me longed to see the rarest of the rare, and the romantic simply yearned to see a formerly lost and now found hummingbird.

I visited the eastern side of the Santa Marta mountain range in 2016. At the time, the logistics of visiting the Blue-bearded Helmetcrest's remote homeland in the western range was inscrutable for a British birder like me. Instead, we drove from Barranquilla, heading east across the mouth of the Magdalena River, home to the thriving feral population of hippopotamuses that, in the wake of the killing in 1993 of notorious Medellín drug cartel boss Pablo Escobar, escaped from his private menagerie in the grounds of his Hacienda Napoles home after a few days of not being fed. The chain-link fences that had surrounded their pool proved no barrier to a herd of hungry hippos and, once they found the nearby river, they were all set for a life of freedom and breeding. Local biologists are concerned that the population begat by the original four hippos, in ideal habitat and without any natural predators, will continue to grow exponentially, with potentially adverse effects on the local ecosystems. They are now estimated to number in excess of sixty animals, and some pioneering hippos have been seen as far as ninety miles away from Hacienda Napoles.

The suggestion of culling the animals has not gone down well with locals, though fishermen on the river are justifiably cautious about going anywhere near them in open water. Capturing and re-locating them may be unfeasible now that the river horse has bolted, while local biologists have understandable reservations about trying to castrate the bull hippos—a procedure that would be both expensive and fraught with danger.

While not a fan of invasive alien species of any kind, I was still hopeful I might catch a glimpse of a hippo in the Magdalena River, but it was not to be—for now, the hippo population has not spread that far north. Instead, I harboured realistic hopes of seeing some endemic hummingbirds in the mountains, albeit nothing as outrageously rare as the Blue-bearded Helmetcrest. My destination was the El Dorado Reserva Natural, a one thousand-hectare nature reserve operated by Colombia's foremost bird conservation organisation, Fundación ProAves.

El Dorado is justly named, being a treasure trove of biodiversity. Spanning an altitudinal range on the mountain slopes between 950 and 2,600 metres would guarantee a wide range of bird species anywhere in South America, a continent so mountainous that some hummingbirds migrate up and downhill depending on the seasons. However, here in the Santa Marta range were conditions quite unique in Colombia, let alone South America. Rather like the sky islands I had visited in the Sonoran Desert of Arizona, the ancient Santa Marta Mountains were isolated from the rest of the Andes that run down the spine of the continent, conditions that allowed evolution to run rampant. More curiously still, their flanks flow down to almost the very edge of the Caribbean—they are the world's highest coastal mountain range, and boast a montane climate quite unlike any other.

What I could anticipate during my stay here were a suite of regular Colombian species and a significant number of endemics, bird species found not only exclusively in Colombia, but nowhere else except in the Santa Marta Mountains and the surrounding coastal areas. Throw in some more species that were found only in this corner of Colombia or across the border in neighbouring Venezuela, and I could expect a potent mix—in the jargon of birders, perhaps twenty-five endemics and twenty-two near-endemics.

There were, inevitably, some hummingbirds amongst their number. In and around the El Dorado Reserve, these included such mouthwatering delights as Santa Marta Blossomcrown, White-tailed Starfrontlet, Black-backed Thornbill and, lastly, smallest but far from least, Santa Marta Woodstar. Each could be expected at different elevations on the mountain—the blossomcrown somewhat lower down, the starfrontlet and woodstar at the height of the El Dorado Lodge in which I would be staying, at around 1,700 metres, and the thornbill, if I was lucky, higher still.

The blossomcrown proved to be extraordinarily frustrating. Some hummingbirds resolutely refuse to come to feeders and must be sought at their favoured nectar sources, flowering plants of one kind or another. The road up to El Dorado is notoriously poor—not only a rough unmade track, but one that during the wet season doubles up as a river. Normal four-wheel-drive vehicles cannot cope with the rigours of scrambling over large exposed boulders, so a small cadre of local drivers with modified and heavy-duty four-wheel-drive vehicles exists to carry birders up to El Dorado, and higher still beyond the lodge to the end of the road at 2,700 metres, at which point the road completely gives up masquerading as anything other than a dried-out watercourse.

It was from one such vehicle that I stepped, slightly shaken, but with no idea of the wrenching, bucking ride that lay ahead, hoping to find my blossomcrown. We had stopped at a small isolated hamlet on the side of the single-track road. Opposite the handful of wood and corrugated iron single-storey homes was a narrow strip of cultivated land, bordered by large flowering shrubs. This was our blossomcrown stakeout, a site where the birds were, if not regular visitors, then at least as reliable as might be hoped.

An hour passed, a pleasant time in which I enjoyed close views of my first Santa Marta Woodstar—a female bird that announced her presence with the sonorous hum of her wings. Woodstars are amongst the very smallest of hummingbirds, with compact, barrel-shaped bodies, short stubby tails, and wings that appear too small to carry them. Those wings beat incredibly quickly, even for a hummingbird, at around seventy-five beats per second, creating a hum that is more insect-like buzz than the usual tone of a hummingbird hovering. Powering this tiny marvel is a heart that is beating twenty times per second, or 1,200 beats per minute—to put that into perspective, our human hearts have an average resting heartbeat of around eighty beats per minute.

Feeding at a shrub with long, trumpet-shaped orange flowers, she had beauty to match her astonishing vital statistics—a metallic, Prussian-blue back, a white breast, and a deep cinnamon belly. Her rump sported a fetching white band, and a racy white stripe ran from above her eye to the nape of her neck. Unlike many hummingbirds that feed as fast as they can and then depart for cover as rapidly as they came, once she had found her nectar source, she took her time to investigate it thoroughly, sinking her short black bill and head deep inside every flower, one after another, systematically working her way around the bush. I could have watched her for hours, my own heart rate elevated though not to hummingbird standards, but I still had the elusive blossomcrown on my mind. I would see more woodstars higher up the mountain, but this threatened to be the only spot at which I might see a blossomcrown.

I regularly tore my eyes away from her, scanning the hedgerow and surrounding trees with my binoculars, hoping against hope to see the metallic tones of a blossomcrown. I had lost myself in photographs of the male bird before leaving for Colombia, and could see in my mind's eye exactly what he would look like, with patinated bronze mantle and a coppery orange forecrown, like a hummingbird of Sparta.

Having such a vivid mental search picture was not helping. When one of my companions, at the opposite end of the hamlet, shouted that he had seen a blossomcrown, I threw caution to the wind and ran, camera and binoculars bouncing around me. I arrived just in time to see the silhouette of a Santa Marta Blossomcrown vanishing over the treetops above us. I was too late and, despite waiting a while longer, the bird did not return.

If I was feeling chastened by that experience, the days that followed at the El Dorado lodge did much to numb the pain. The view from the deck outside the lodge was almost too much to bear— mountains smothered with trees and wreathed in pearly striations of cloud stretched away to the horizon, running parallel with the turquoise Caribbean coast on the horizon some thirty miles away and far below me. The view around the deck itself was a more vibrant affair, with dozens of hummingbirds jostling over the feeders from dawn to dusk.

Jade-green and azure-blue Lesser Violetears flashed and simmered around me, making up a large proportion of the birds on show at any one time, occasionally squaring up to one another midair, hovering beak to beak, their round blue ear coverts at right angles to their heads in a threatening display. Darker and larger were the Lazuline Sabrewings, their bodies predominantly a deep, intense indigo blue, with green hints like spilt oil on tarmac. They were less confident than the violetears, making sporadic smash and grab visits to the feeders, a dark streak at the edge of vision that hurtled past from dense cover to feeder and back again in the blink of an eye.

Sure enough, both male and female Santa Marta Woodstars made occasional appearances, but it was two other endemic hummingbirds that stole the show. I had expected to see White-tailed Starfrontlets here at the lodge, as it is justly famous as a place at which to see them. Starfrontlets are always special—never numerous, whatever species they belong to, they are elegant birds with fine, straight, long bills and a shyness that is engaging but not completely frustrating for their admirers.

One such bird lurked in the undergrowth to the side of the feeders that ringed the El Dorado deck. His body appeared dark, but his tail and lower body were snow white, giving him away against the surrounding lush foliage. It was only by finding a window in the leaves that I could see the whole bird, and then, when a shaft of sunlight struck him in the heart of the vegetation, he lit up—his belly glittering emerald green, and his throat and forecrown flashing sapphire blue. It was as if he was made of gemstones for that fleeting, serendipitous moment.

More brazen was the other endemic hummingbird I'd secretly hoped but not expected to see on this mountainside—a male Black-backed Thornbill. If I was to see one at all, it ought to be at the very highest elevations, but here was a bird down at the lodge, spending every day sitting in the top of one of the tall trees that fringed the sides of the deck, making regular forays down to the feeders. Each visit would be a prolonged one, with time spent sitting in the bushes beside the feeders watching the other hummingbirds with something that looked very much like disdain. Not for him the territorial squabbling and fighting over food sources. He appeared coal black from head to toe, and it was only when he turned his head to precisely the right angle to the observer that his large, leaf-shaped gorget abruptly blazed into life, a rippling metallic shield that could appear anything from citrine yellow to lime green.

My time in the Santa Marta Mountains then was nothing if not productive where hummingbirds were concerned, and I came away with my thirst for them slaked . . . but a lingering hunger remained for the chimera that lurked in the distance away to the west. I was desperate to see the long-lost Blue-bearded Helmetcrest.

Planning a return to Colombia, I corresponded with Diego Calderón, he of Bogotá Sunangel soundbite fame. I had met Diego and spent a couple of days looking for hummingbirds together in the Bogotá area before my first Santa Marta visit, and I liked him enormously. An affable, friendly man with silver-shot dark hair, he was tremendous company to go birding with, and had set up Colombia's first bird-guiding company. Importantly for an expedition of the complexity and sensitivity involved in visiting the remote homeland of the Kogi, he was also extraordinarily well connected with all the right people in Colombia.

Back in April 2004, when he was a student at the University of Antioquia doing ornithological fieldwork in the jungle area of Perija, he was kidnapped by the Fuerzas Armadas Revolucionarias de Colombia (FARC), the Fidel Castro–trained and armed militia group that had fought a prolonged and bitter civil war against the Colombian army. This made Diego the second person I had met who had the dubious distinction of being a former FARC hostage, as British orchid hunter Tom Hart Dyke was also held by FARC fighters for a period of some nine months in 2000.

When Diego was taken hostage he had been looking to fill in some gaps in the biological knowledge of the mountainous area of Perija that straddles the Colombian border with Venezuela and, in particular, he had been looking for a hummingbird, the Perija Metaltail, that had gone unreported there for decades. Diego was clearly a man who relished the challenge of searching for lost hummingbirds.

He recalled, "For FARC we were either military or paramilitary intelligence. We had GPS equipment, cameras, binoculars, maps, and field notebooks that had coordinates and names in Latin."

During the three months he was held hostage, Diego used his time to identify and record on any scrap of paper he could scrounge the names of the birds he saw pass by. In November 2016 a peace agreement was signed between the Colombian government and FARC, bringing to an end a civil war that had rumbled on in the country for some fifty years. In August 2018, Diego joined ten former FARC combatants and fifty scientists on a United Nations–backed reconciliation expedition into the Colombian jungle near Anori in northeastern Antioquia. The former FARC combatants served both as research assistants and guides in the country they knew so intimately from their years in the field beyond the law.

The expedition was a resounding success, not only showing the nation and the watching world that Colombia was moving on and was becoming a safer, more harmonious place than we had been led to believe, but also scientifically—the team found fourteen species new to science. Granted, the ten plants, two beetles, and single individuals of lizard and tree mouse did not include a new hummingbird, but the message for me was clear. Diego was an adventurous birder with a big heart, and if I could entrust anyone to take me to see a Blue-bearded Helmetcrest, Diego was the one.

We laid our plans carefully—all the necessary arrangements were in place, and Diego had organised horses, camping equipment, and local men to accompany us deep into the mountains on a nine-day expedition. For months, I could think of little else and, as the day of departure drew nearer, my excitement mounted steadily. Then, three days before I was due to leave for Colombia, disaster struck. Diego had gone silent in the past fortnight and, while I was mildly concerned, I was not unduly worried. I knew he had been in Uganda recently, and was maybe simply travelling home. Finally, a message from him explained everything:

I finally got out of hospital yesterday after some tough days . . . December 24th and 25th I spent in the intensive care unit as all my levels went down and that fucking African malaria wanted to really, really kill me. I saw the light at the end of the tunnel, mate, believe me.

The thing is I, undoubtedly, cannot do the trip with you to the páramo of the Sierra Nevada. If it was a normal trip to, let's say around 2,000 metres above sea level and going in cars, I could, but this more demanding trip now I'm coming out from this episode of severe, reloaded African malaria . . . it's a nonsense for me, the doctor says, and I agree. I can't do the trip.

While I was, of course, relieved to hear that Diego had survived this severe and sudden illness, this was nevertheless terrible news on the very cusp of my arriving in Colombia. Two mythical hummingbirds remained lost to me: the Bogotá Sunangel, stolen by science; and the Blue-bearded Helmetcrest, at the eleventh hour by sheer bad luck. I needed a hummingbird to save the day.

Colombia, with over 1,900 bird species recorded, is home to the largest number of bird species of any country in the world. Amongst those many birds was one more lost hummingbird, one that I had perhaps overlooked in my desire to be one of only a few dozen birders who had set eyes upon the Blue-bearded Helmetcrest in the four years since its rediscovery. Dusky Starfrontlet, also known as Glittering Starfrontlet, is a hummingbird with a split personality reflected by its two English names. On the one hand, it is a dark-plumaged bird that loves to lurk in the shadows of elfin forest, but when it does deign to come out into the open, its plumage flames like the polished *kozane* scale armour of the samurai. It also had the distinction of being lost to the world's gaze for over half a century.

Melbourne Armstrong Carriker Jr. was a man who, from his first collecting trip in Costa Rica in 1901 to his death in Colombia in 1965, was the natural history equivalent of cinema's Indiana Jones. Posterity records him as best known for his astonishing contribution to our knowledge of *Mallophaga*, or bird lice—in his lifetime

Bee Hummingbird
Mellisuga helenae
(Jon Dunn)

Snowcap
Microchera albocoronata
(Jon Dunn)

White-necked Jacobin
Florisuga mellivora
(Jon Dunn)

Crowned Woodnymph
Thalurania colombica
(Jon Dunn)

Long-tailed Sylph
Aglaiocercus kingii
(Jon Dunn)

Santa Marta Woodstar
Chaetocercus astreans
(Jon Dunn)

White-tailed Starfrontlet
Coeligena phalerata
(Jon Dunn)

Black-backed Thornbill
Ramphomicron dorsale
(Jon Dunn)

Collared Inca
Coeligena torquata
(Jon Dunn)

Dusky Starfrontlet
Coeligena orina
(Jon Dunn)

Sword-billed Hummingbird
Ensifera ensifera
(Jon Dunn)
(left)

White-bellied Woodstar
Chaetocercus mulsant
(Jon Dunn)
(below)

Gould's Jewelfront
Heliodoxa aurescens
(Jon Dunn)

Velvet-purple Coronet
Boissonneaua jardini
(Jon Dunn)

Golden-tailed Sapphire
Chrysuronia oenone
(Jon Dunn)
(above)

Rufous-crested Coquette
Lophornis delattrei
(Jon Dunn)
(right)

Marvellous Spatuletail
Loddigesia mirabilis
(Jon Dunn)
(right)

Marvellous Spatuletail
Loddigesia mirabilis
(Jon Dunn)
(below)

Sparkling Violetear
Colibri coruscans
(Jon Dunn)

White-tipped Sicklebill
Eutoxeres aquila
(Jon Dunn)

The Nazca hummingbird
geoglyph
(Jon Dunn)
(above)

Festive Coquette
Lophornis chalybeus
(Jon Dunn)
(right)

Sr. Jonas D'Abronzo caring for injured
White-chinned Sapphire
Hylocharis cyanus
(Jon Dunn)

Saw-billed Hermit
Ramphodon naevius
(Jon Dunn)

Swallow-tailed Hummingbird
Eupetomena macroura
(Jon Dunn)

Amethyst Woodstar
Calliphlox amethystine
(Jon Dunn)

Black Jacobin
Florisuga fusca
(Jon Dunn)
(above)

Black-throated Mango
Anthracothorax nigricollis
(Jon Dunn)
(right)

Male Juan Fernández Firecrown
Sephanoides fernandensis
(Jon Dunn)

Female Juan Fernández Firecrown
Sephanoides fernandensis
(Jon Dunn)

An abandoned Juan
Fernández Firecrown nest
(Jon Dunn)
(above)

Green-backed Firecrown
Sephanoides sephaniodes
(Jon Dunn)
(right)

he described two new families, four new subfamilies, fifty-three new genera and subgenera, and a frankly bewildering total of almost nine hundred new species and subspecies of bird lice—but Carriker was an intrepid character whose collecting trips across the Americas from northern Canada to Bolivia were prolific and varied, both in their scale and their output. When not collecting bird lice, birds, or mammals for major institutions like the Carnegie Museum or the American Museum of Natural History, he spent time working as, variously, an electrician, a fruit farmer, and a carpenter. To the year of his death, aged eighty-six years, he was still collecting new material and publishing scientific papers.

On December 17, 1951, Carriker was collecting birds in the Andean Cordillera Occidental, high above the town of Urrao, on the eastern slopes of the Páramo de Frontino. He took, that day, a hummingbird that would prove new to science, an immature male Dusky Starfrontlet. Two years later Alexander Wetmore, the ornithologist who had, in 1947, considered Brother Nicéforo María's mysterious blue hummingbird to be a new species despite the prevailing view of his peers at the time that it was most likely a hybrid, formally described Carriker's bird as a new species. Yet from this point onwards, nobody saw a Dusky Starfrontlet again. The intervening decades were, of course, particularly bloody and turbulent ones for Colombia, significant discouragement for anyone hoping to see a Dusky Starfrontlet for themselves in the wild.

Matters took a further discouraging turn in 1988, when Robert Bleiweiss, an American ornithologist, examined Carriker's type specimen of Dusky Starfrontlet. His first observation was that the bird had been mistakenly aged as an adult bird by Wetmore—the specimen had corrugations on the bill sheath that were only found on immature birds. Bleiweiss, evidently, had a keen eye for detail. That discerning eye also noted that the specimen had some bronzy tones on the uppertail coverts and belly—features not mentioned by Wetmore in his description of the bird, but consistent with immature birds of another hummingbird species, Golden-bellied Starfrontlet.

Bleiweiss concluded that on the basis of his observations, and lacking any further information taken from adult birds, it would be best to consider Dusky Starfrontlet no more than a subspecies of Golden-bellied Starfrontlet. It was an understandably cautious and reasoned approach, but one that offered a tantalising glimmer of hope, should anyone be able to find any adult birds at the location Carricker originally took his specimen in 1951.

In 2004, an expedition was launched hoping to do just that, featuring ornithologists from ProAves, the Colombian bird conservation organisation, and the University of Copenhagen. On August 9, they "secured"—an academic euphemism for collected and euthanized— an adult female bird, and observed six further individuals in the area. A fortnight later, an independent second expedition from the University of Antioquia in Colombia collected three further specimens, two males and a female, on Farallones de Citara, a mountain seventy kilometers away to the south. Their combined conclusion, having now obtained adult birds to compare with adult Golden-bellied Starfrontlets, was that they were indeed separate species after all. Wetmore, though he had incorrectly aged the bird in hand, had on this occasion been right all along—Dusky Starfrontlet was indeed a new species to science, if one that was destined to be lost for over fifty years before its rediscovery.

This good news emerged in a paper published in 2005, albeit with a significant caveat—Dusky Starfrontlet was known from only two locations, and the Páramo de Frontino was known to be rich with deposits of high-grade gold, zinc, and copper. It looked as if all that glittered was not hummingbirds, and mining companies were showing an interest in the area. The authors noted that, for the time being, political instability in the region had deterred serious mining activity.

This was a bland statement that highlights a paradox that applies time and again in South America. While political or drug-related instability has a devastating impact on the lives of everyday people in the areas affected, it also helps to suppress economic development and exploitation of natural resources. That suppression usually means that the biodiversity of those areas is considerably less impacted than if the hand of man has had free play.

Fifteen years later, with time suddenly on my hands, and a lost hummingbird to try to see at short notice, I needed to make plans, and quickly. In the intervening years Dusky Starfrontlet had been discovered at a further three sites in Colombia, but had also the dubious distinction of being officially listed as Critically Endangered on the IUCN Red List—a classification that suggested less than 250 birds remained in the world. In 2005 the American Bird Conservancy helped ProAves to establish an eighteen-hundred-acre reserve at the original Páramo de Frontino site. The Reserva Natural de las Aves Colibrí del Sol celebrates the Spanish name for Dusky Starfrontlet—*colibrí del sol*, or hummingbird of the sun, a name that I hoped would make perfect sense if and when I finally caught a glimpse of the bird.

My initial plan, however, was to base myself at the Montezuma Ecolodge, 250 kilometres due south of the ProAves Reserve, and closer to Bogotá. Dusky Starfrontlets were now known to occur there, and my correspondence with the lodge was clear—I was coming, hoping to see the starfrontlets as a matter of some urgency. Everything, once more, seemed to be in order, but as Rob Williams, a British birder who shared my passion for hummingbirds, was to remark wryly, "Colombia has a habit of not working out, in my experience."

Those sage words were ringing in my ears the morning after I arrived back in Colombia, and had made my way to Montezuma. I had got up well before dawn and, at 5 a.m. in the company of another guest at the lodge and our respective local guides, had squeezed into a silver Shogun four-wheel drive—not as heavy-duty as the Santa Marta vehicles, but still a substantial mechanical workhorse. The journey up to the summit of the Montezuma road was slow—road being a euphemism for another unmade and heavily eroded track. Here and there we picked our way past recent landslides of fresh red earth. Yesennia, the guide accompanying Ben, an American bio-acoustic engineer hoping to record the rainforest dawn chorus, explained that these landslides were a regular feature of the Andean primary forest, helping to maintain a succession of new growth and habitat.

"Of course," she added, "it helps that the army have a base on the mountaintop. They keep the road open for us."

Having dropped off Yesennia and Ben further down the road, my guide Fernando, our driver Duverney, and I arrived at the very gates of the army base as an opalescent dawn was breaking over the Andes. Some fifty metres above us, leaning on the parapet in front of a fortified pillbox, a Colombian army soldier stared fixedly at us, his face in deep shadow. I felt intimidated, but my companions seemed at ease. I turned my attention to the handful of hummingbird feeders arranged in a small clearing on the brink of the hilltop. Before us, stretching to the horizon, was a succession of heavily wooded mountainsides—the habitat looked excellent for hummingbirds. Sure enough, the feeders were busy with hungry Tourmaline Sunangels and Collared Incas—the former green but for their rubellite-pink throats, and the latter appearing, in the cool morning light, entirely black and white. This was an illusion, for when the rising sun caught them, their black plumage was revealed to be a velvety atramentous green. Four or five of each species were contesting the feeders, driving one another off and sparring amongst themselves too, the incas towering high into the blue sky above us, bill to bill, tails fanned and screaming defiance.

"There! Look, Jon! At the feeder!"

Fernando was agitated, pointing towards one of the feeders. Could this be it, so quickly, a Dusky Starfrontlet? Surely it couldn't be that easy?

"It's a hybrid! Quick, get a photo!"

I was too slow, the camera not ready for this sudden drama. The bird fed quickly, and then flew off over the rim of the mountaintop, lost to view in the vastness of trees below.

"Did you see? It had the tail of Buff-tailed Coronet, but the head of an Empress Brilliant. That's a rarity!"

I confessed that while I did see those features, I'd failed to take a photograph. The encounter was all too fleeting—but it felt like a propitious omen, nonetheless. I asked Fernando how often the starfrontlets came to the feeders. He looked a little awkward. "The last ones were seen here in November, just twice. They're probably somewhere in the area, but you would need to be very lucky to see one here. If you want to definitely see one, you need to go to Urrao . . ."

I told Fernando that the correspondence I'd had with the lodge staff had implied, heavily, that the starfrontlets would be present. His expression grew more pained still. "They probably did not know how important it was to you to see it. Perhaps they thought you'd be happy with all the other hummingbirds here?"

I did not want to make Fernando feel any more uncomfortable than he already clearly did by the circumstances, but inside my spirits were plunging. Colombia's lost hummingbirds continued to play with my emotions. A little time passed, in which Fernando gamely tried to attract a starfrontlet by playing a recording of its call. The sound seemed laughably feeble in the immensity of the greenery around us, and no birds were forthcoming. All the meantime, the soldier at the gates above us continued to glower threateningly.

"Jon . . . I have an idea. I've a *parcero*, a friend who might be able to help. He's a bird guide too. I could call him and see if he's interested in helping you in Urrao?"

I didn't have to think twice, and clutched at this lifeline. A series of phone calls ensued and, eventually, we had confirmation that Arnulfo was indeed prepared to help, and that the ProAves Lodge on the Colibrí del Sol Reserve could provide both overnight accommodation and horses to make the steep climb to the páramo more straightforward. There was just the small logistical problem of how to get there in what remained of the day. Duverney consulted Google Maps on his phone. There was no easy or quick way of doing this.

"There are buses," he mused, "but they will be very, very slow. It's maybe an eight, nine hour drive by car, so the buses will be slower."

Hiring a car for myself was out of the question in this remote location. Arnulfo was only able to help the following day—after that, he had other guiding commitments to honour. It sounded as if I could not get to Urrao by nightfall, and that meant the star-frontlet remained out of reach. Duverney and Fernando sat on the grass beside the Shogun, speaking quietly between themselves, and then Duverney wandered up the short track towards the army camp, making still another phone call. The impassive soldier continued to lean on the parapet, watching us, and with the timely appearance of two Swallow-tailed Kites overhead I dared to raise my binoculars in their general direction, but instead took a covert look at him. I felt a little foolish when I realised he was an artfully posed jacket on a wooden frame, with an army cap pulled down low to shade the security camera that made up his face. Duverney returned to us, the phone call finished.

"I can take you, if you'd like. We'll pick up Arnulfo on the way."

This was an incredibly generous offer, and I knew it. Duverney would be almost certainly sacrificing the following day's work for me, not to mention the time and effort involved in driving three hundred kilometres, some of which would be on unpaved roads and all of it sinuously twisty as the route followed the contours of the many mountains and hills that lay ahead of us. This was no time, however, for apologetic modesty. I readily agreed, and we climbed into the Shogun for a breakneck descent to the lodge and then onwards towards Urrao.

Duverney proved a superb driver, if an unsettling one—on the unpaved roads he drifted the heavy Shogun around corners, allowing it to slide on the loose gravel and mud, and did not discriminate for downhill sections—all were taken at the same pace, with the brakes getting a punishing workout. We collected Arnulfo from the roadside after an hour, a cheerful and immensely likeable man in his early thirties, and continued to push on north, stopping only for a short lunch on the roadside overlooking the isolated peak of Cerro Batero, a rocky finger rising from the surrounding tree-clad and heavily corrugated landscape. A large metal crucifix was fixed on top. I wondered how it had been placed there, and learned that, if one really wanted to, there were a series of metal ladders and rungs driven into the rockfaces that one could climb to ascend the 1,800-metre-high pinnacle and touch the Cross.

I really didn't want to.

While we ate, Arnulfo was constantly scanning for birds and, to Fernando's visible delight, he found a species Fernando had never seen before, a Yellow-headed Brushfinch. I, meanwhile, found it hard to ignore the clouds of small blue butterflies that rose from the grass at our feet. I was reminded, irresistibly, of Vladimir Nabokov. At the same time in the mid-twentieth century that Melbourne Armstrong Carriker Jr. was searching for bird lice new to science in South America and, along the way, discovering the first ever Dusky Starfrontlet, the author of *Lolita* was, unbeknown to many, devoting days on end to the search for new species of South American *Lycaenidae*, or blue butterflies.

Nabokov had no formal scientific training, and in his lifetime found himself set against the implacability of the scientific community, which closed ranks against him to dismiss his butterfly work as of lesser worth than their own. His 1945 paper "Notes on Neotropical Plebejinae" was groundbreaking in its analysis of the taxonomy of blue butterflies, but largely ignored at the time by the scientific establishment. It was not until the 1990s that a team of scientists went to South America to study the blues Nabokov mentioned in his paper and discovered that, in fact, Nabokov's taxonomical approach was significantly more accurate than that which had prevailed even after his death. There are now species of blue butterfly in Peru and Chile that bear, in tribute to Nabokov, the names Lolita, Kinbote, and Pnin, but I always felt sorry for him that, while lauded as a writer, he never knew in his lifetime the respect he deserved for his butterfly work. He was a man who said he loved the fusion of poetry and science, who could not separate the aesthetic pleasure of seeing a particular butterfly from the scientific pleasure of being able to conclusively identify it.

I knew exactly how he felt.

After night had fallen, and on the last stretch of twisting mountain road to Urrao, the Shogun's altimeter fluctuating around the 2,200-metre mark, I wondered if Nabokov had ever felt quite as uneasy on his butterfly-collecting trips as the inhabitants of our vehicle did when the Shogun's beleaguered brakes finally stopped working altogether. We crawled the last thirty kilometres to Urrao at a snail's pace, Duverney patiently using engine braking to trim our speed for corners and on descents. Nonetheless, we still came to a landslide more quickly than any of us would have cared to and, for a short while, we drove pressed against the raw earth on one side of us and, below, on my side of the car, a black nothingness—the landslide had taken half of the road away with it. Far, far beneath us the white fluorescent lights of scattered homes painted a constellation on the valley floor. Nobody said a word.

Before dawn the following morning, a taxi carried Arnulfo and me from Urrao out to a cattle corral some way out of town. From here, we would have to hike up to the ProAves lodge and, once there, we could continue the rest of the way up to the páramo on horseback. Carrying 15 kilograms of camera gear on my back, I was feeling the effects of the altitude as we pressed on in moonlight through cattle pastures and then, as the day broke, through dense woodland beside a boulder-strewn and rushing river. The lodge stood at 2,850 metres above sea level—quite a difference from my Shetland home, which is, essentially, at sea level. I found myself unexpectedly breathless or, as my Shetland friends would have said, *peckin'*.

Some hours later, we crossed the river, jumping from water-worn boulder to boulder, and reached the compact, mustard-yellow lodge, set a little way above the river and nestling in a cleft between mountain slopes. It was impossible to miss the hummingbirds upon our arrival—five feeders were suspended, in a row, beneath a warped wooden stave smothered with grey lichen, the ends turned upwards like a Japanese temple roof. As many as twenty hummingbirds at any one time were thronging in worship at the feeders. There were more Tourmaline Sunangels and Buff-tailed Coronets, but some new faces too—buzzing White-bellied Woodstars, Mountain Velvetbreasts with elegantly curved bills, permanently squabbling Lesser and Sparkling Violetears, and the villain of the Bogotá Sunangel's piece, Long-tailed Sylphs, their outlandishly elongated green tail feathers like bolts of neon as they wove their way through the crowds of hovering, chattering birds.

We decided to rest for a while, hoping our first Dusky Starfrontlet would come readily to us. Once again, I was caught napping. Arnulfo saw a male bird and called to alert me to it—but I was unsighted by a feeder between me and the bird and, by the time I got to my feet, it had gone. I was feeling frustrated, and ready to head for higher pastures new. To fuel us, we ate a simple breakfast of rice, a small piece of bacon, and a thin, slightly charred *arepa*, or maize cake, and then it was time to take to the horses for the climb to the edge of the páramo.

If I had had some reservations about this, it being over twenty-five years since I had last ridden a horse, they were cast aside in the wake of the considerable effort it had taken to carry my heavy camera gear this far already. The climb from the lodge to our final destination would take us another 750 metres above sea level, and I was grateful to Tall Horse every step of the way. I did not like to ask Jair, the lodge's solemn horseman, cook, and steward if Tall Horse had a name, but felt he needed to be called something if we were to have an understanding. He was tall, and a horse, and the name would have to serve.

Only once did I see a hummingbird on the ascent, a brief flash of a Tourmaline Sunangel, and it was not until we finally stopped climbing at two hummingbird feeders suspended in a small clearing beneath tall, shady trees on a steep slope that I began to see more birds. They were, of course, Tourmaline Sunangels and Collared Incas, my familiars from the top of the Montezuma road the previous day. In other circumstances, wonderful birds, but not what I was hoping for. After waiting patiently with me for a while, Arnulfo shouldered a hessian sack containing fresh sugar water, and indicated he was going to refill feeders at a higher elevation still.

I was now alone in the same location that, some seventy years previously, Melbourne Armstrong Carriker had first laid eyes upon a Dusky Starfrontlet. I tried to imagine how that must have felt, that jolting realisation that here was something he did not recognise. One as well-travelled as he in Colombia by that stage in his life would have known, instantly, that this was something special.

In the event, I did not have to rely upon my imagination for long, as something dark flew across the small clearing in front of me and, from sound alone, I knew this was a very different hummingbird, one that I had not seen before. It sounded almost clattery, as if those fast-beating wings were striking one another at every other stroke. If hummingbirds were engines, this was the powerful sound of a V8, full of potency and promise. The bird vanished low into the undergrowth at the side of the clearing and instantly attracted the attention of one of the resident Tourmaline Sunangels. These feisty little birds had spent the past twenty minutes fighting whenever they paused from feeding. This behaviour seemed to go beyond merely defending a food source—they seemed to loathe the very sight of one another. This new interloper, sequestered deep in the tangles of vegetation where I could not see him, had not escaped the sunangel's vigilant attention. He darted in to challenge the intruder. A flurry of movement could be heard inside the bushes, and a chastened sunangel sped out into the open, perching on the opposite side of the clearing. Whatever was in the bush had seen him off.

Innately, I knew what I would see if only I could find a window in the leaves without disturbing the bird within. This, surely, was my Dusky Starfrontlet. I moved painstakingly slowly around the clearing, changing the angles until, at last, I could see a dark bird perched low above the ground. I raised my binoculars to my eyes, and there it was. Black as tar, a long, straight, thin bill, and a glittering obsidian eye that stared watchfully back at me. He cocked his head slightly, and his throat lit up cobalt blue, while his forecrown blazed golden green. A small shift on his perch, and the whole bird was alight—his breast and belly made up of many dozens of iridescent, coruscating scales of lime green. He looked otherworldly, like some enamelled hummingbird god fallen to earth. I hardly dared breathe.

I lost track of time. He probably sat there for only a minute or two, but those minutes became elastic, and the moment felt infinite. When he flew, time snapped back into the now, and I was released. This bird was so loaded with romance, longing, and history, seeing it was quite unlike watching any hummingbird that had gone before for me.

I remained at the side of the clearing, all the effort, all the dashed plans, time, and expense involved in bringing myself here, to a remote Andean mountainside in the northwest of Colombia, all of it suddenly seeming irrelevant and trifling. Arnulfo found me still sitting there, and he must have known, in an instant, something had changed. Probably my broad smile gave it away.

"You have seen it, the Dusky Starfrontlet?" he asked. I told him I had, though simply confirming the sighting did the experience no justice whatsoever. I described how I had heard the bird before I saw it. Arnulfo nodded enthusiastically.

"Si, muy fuerte!" he agreed, very strong. Very strong summed up the experience for me. It had the potency of powerful drugs—I felt wobbly on my feet, and it wasn't just the altitude.

We remained on the mountainside for several hours, seeing the male bird again several times, even fly-catching on one occasion and joined, just once, by a more muted female bird that came to perch in the same place the male had initially chosen, from which to survey his lofty fastness. Nothing could break the euphoric spell they cast, not even a Sword-billed Hummingbird that came to hover, briefly, above me, his preposterously long bill magnificent but no substitute for the starfrontlets' glamour.

Returning to our horses, we made a slow descent back down to the lodge, the horses' hooves slipping on the loose stones of the narrow, steep path they carefully picked their way along. I leaned back in my saddle, half concentrating on pushing overhanging branches away from my face, but preoccupied still. It was only when we reached the lodge and I had dismounted, walking around the path that led to the feeders, that I was jolted fully back into the present. On the path at my feet lay a hummingbird, a male Tourmaline Sunangel. He was motionless, and I picked him up. One tiny eyelid appeared to flutter, infinitesimally. Seen up close, either in a photo or, as I was now able to, a few inches from my face, hummingbird eyelids have tiny but distinct serrations, as if the bird has applied heavy mascara. I could see this clearly now as he lay on the palm of my hand. This was the first time I'd actually touched a hummingbird, but I could not say for sure if he was alive or dead. I took him to one of the feeders, and dipped his bill into one of the wells over which the birds usually hovered to feed from. His throat feathers pulsed, and his eye opened fully, briefly, before closing again. He was still alive, just.

Hummingbirds need to feed regularly throughout the waking day but, as I had seen, many of them spar and fight with one another, Tourmaline Sunangels perhaps more than most. I surmised he may have been stunned in an impact with another bird and, once his energy was unreplenished, had been unable to take to the air once more. I fed him again, and this time his wing pulsed against my thumb. I opened my hand, hoping he would fly away, but only one wing flapped, and I had to cup my hands quickly to save him from dropping to the floor.

My fear was that the other wing would prove to be broken by the impact of whatever mishap had befallen him before I found him. Closer examination suggested that might not be the case—the wing in question lay neatly at his side, but was being stopped from beating by his own foot clasped tightly around the long, curved primary feathers. A hummingbird foot is an incredibly delicate thing, and it took us some time to tease the toes apart and free the wing. We took turns to feed him, leaving him between feeds resting on a nest of tissue on a table just inside the door of the lodge. One moment he was there and then, suddenly, he was gone, back on the wing and among his own once more.

As dusk fell, I sat watching the feeders. The level of activity was peaking as all the hummingbirds in the immediate area came to top up their energy levels before the cold night ahead. I paid particular attention to the sunangels, and wondered which one was my bird. I felt a proprietary sense toward him. The lost *colibrís del sol* had given me an experience approaching the transcendental that day, and it felt somehow fitting that I should have given a little something back to one of their kin.

It was only when we had returned to Urrao that I heard the sobering news. A guide, Alfonso Rodriguez, had been murdered just outside of the town, a few miles from where we had been, and only the day before we arrived. He had been shot by unknown gunmen in front of his guests as they returned from the páramo. This was, apparently, the sixth murder in the Antioquia department since the turn of the New Year. The date was January 12th.

It was a stark reminder that, for all Colombia has moved forwards and put its dark past behind it, the shadows of that past still bleed into the present. I loved the country unreservedly, not just for its hummingbirds but for the warmth of its people and, yes, its contradictions too. On that long, eventful drive from Montezuma to Urrao, we had passed many homes with barbed wire strung around their boundaries, a reminder that security was not a given here—yet many of those householders had painstakingly painted the barbed wire in cheerful colours to match their homes beyond, homes that were festooned with hanging baskets dripping with bright flowers. When I thanked Fernando and Duverney for helping me to see a Dusky Starfrontlet, I asked them why they had gone to so much trouble on my behalf. They looked embarrassed and a little confused.

"It's the Colombian way. We like to help people, and we want visitors to know what a good country Colombia is. We knew it was important for you to see this bird, so we did what we could to help."

Bogotá's airport is named El Dorado and, as I made my way back there, the unexpected kindness and the extent of the generosity of my Colombian friends reminded me of the myth behind the legendary lost city of gold, El Dorado. The myth had, for centuries, assumed an extraordinary potency for Europeans, speaking volumes about their lust for wealth and power, and the way in which they viewed South America as simply a resource to be exploited as thoroughly as possible.

The Spanish conquistador Jiménez de Quesada mounted two expeditions to Colombia, hoping to find the incalculable wealth of El Dorado. Of the first expedition, in 1537, only one hundred and sixty-six conquistadors returned from the nine hundred who had set out. Never a man to be daunted, in 1569 de Quesada was back, this time with a larger force behind him. Of those two thousand men, only thirty survived to tell the tale. It is suggested that de Quesada was the inspiration for Cervantes' Don Quixote. What is certain is that during his quixotic explorations, de Quesada encountered the fine and intricately worked gold produced in the Colombian kingdom of the Muisca.

European explorers heard enough firsthand accounts of the Muisca to fuel their greed for centuries. The initiation ceremony for the Muisca king was said to involve him naked, coated from head to toe in gold dust, borne on a raft into the middle of a sacred lake, there to cast a host of golden offerings into the waters. In 1537 de Quesada found Lake Guatavita, the site of this periodic ritual. For centuries attempts were made to drain the lake to uncover the riches beneath its surface, with mixed success, but nonetheless significant quantities of gold were recovered.

Prussian naturalist and explorer Alexander von Humboldt, better known for his contributions to science than his unabashed avarice, calculated in 1801 that the lake might hold as much as $300 million worth of gold. Europeans only saw the monetary value of what might lie beneath those inscrutable waters, or in some unfound city of gold—but they missed the point.

The Muisca placed value in gold not for its material value, but instead for its spiritual power and connection with their deities. Thus, it was highly sought-after and intricately worked by Muisca craftsmen; and desired for baser reasons by a succession of Europeans.

I felt there were some parallels here in terms of cultural misunderstanding. I preferred not to dwell on the thought that I had come to Colombia consumed with a lust to find, not gold, but hummingbirds—though I could console myself with the knowledge that I took away only the experience and some photos, and left only footprints. However, I could not think of a British birder or a driver who would unthinkingly drive for almost eleven hours in challenging terrain just to help a visitor they had met only a short while earlier that day. That sort of generosity of spirit seemed rare and precious to me, but appeared to be just a matter of course for these kind young Colombians. I left Colombia with more than my longed-for lost hummingbird—I carried away a new appreciation for this wonderful, complex country and its people.

CHAPTER SIX

THE FEATHER TRADE

~

Ecuador, various locations. The Equator.

*C*OLOMBIA HAD BEEN AN INTOXICATING INTRODUCTION TO THE abundance of hummingbirds of South America. I had learned firsthand how some species had evolved to exist solely in glorious isolation within tiny home ranges, and I had enjoyed my first taste of the sheer diversity of species that might be encountered within relatively small areas.

To experience the ultimate expression of this cornucopia, I planned to move south down the spine of the Andes, passing from Colombia into Ecuador. Once in Ecuador, I would join a group of others as consumed with the hummingbird passion as I am. A tour, led by the coauthor of the definitive *Birds of Ecuador* field guide, Paul Greenfield, would spend eight days exploring the north of Ecuador on both the eastern and western Andean slopes, focusing particularly on finding as many hummingbird species as possible. My decision to do so was an easy one—while some birders are a little contemptuous or wary of joining organised tours, for a country as richly blessed with hummingbirds as Ecuador, I could think of no better or more effective way to immerse myself in a plethora of hummingbirds. I was also curious to meet other people for whom hummingbirds had come to exert such magnetism.

I hoped I would encounter scores of species new to me, but above all there were two species of hummingbird I particularly yearned to see. One of these, the Velvet-purple Coronet, was simply on the basis of sheer aesthetic wonder—it is regularly mooted as one of the most beautiful of all the hummingbird family and, as far as I was presently concerned, therefore of all the birds in the world. The other, Gould's Jewelfront, commemorated one of Victorian London's most obsessed hummingbird fanatics, John Gould. He only saw his first living hummingbird in Philadelphia in 1857, at the age of fifty-two, but by this point in his life Gould had been under the hummingbird spell for a great many years, and they had come to define him—quite a statement for a character who was known worldwide, in his own lifetime, as "The Bird Man."

Gould started his working life as a gardener, but at the age of twenty became self-employed in London as a taxidermist—a decision that, given the nascent British upper- and middle-class enthusiasm at the time for displaying stuffed birds and mammals in their homes, would provide him with a steady stream of income. Gould was evidently skilled at his fledgling trade for, just three years later, he was appointed as the first curator and preservist at the museum of the Zoological Society of London, the precursors of London Zoo. His new position meant that Gould, suddenly, found a steady stream of collections of bird specimens from all around the world passing across his desk. Many of these were strikingly beautiful compared with the relatively subdued species found closer to home in Europe—birds-of-paradise from New Guinea, parrots from Australia, and hummingbirds from South America. Gould, displaying the same entrepreneurial spirit that had seen him take the brave leap from gardener to self-employed taxidermist, recognised a commercial opportunity.

Over the course of twenty months in 1831–1832, Gould compiled *A Century of Birds from the Himalaya Mountains*, featuring eighty colour plates executed by his wife, Elizabeth, a talented natural history artist. Taxidermy seems to have brought them together for, like Gould, Elizabeth's younger brother Charles was a taxidermist in London. Legend had it that when Gould shared his idea for this first publication with his wife, Elizabeth was not convinced of the venture's viability. When she asked him who would undertake the considerable and important work of preparing the illustrations, Gould was said to have replied to her, with a brusque practicality that was to become his trademark, "Why you, of course."

Further works followed in the years to come—Gould became a prolific author of fifteen natural history folios in forty-nine separate volumes, including forty-one works on birds, using, in addition to Elizabeth, a team of artists to illustrate his publications, including Edward Lear, whom Gould was said to have discovered sketching parrots in the grounds of the newly created Zoological Gardens in Regents Park. Lear, the twentieth child of a failed businessman, was asthmatic, epileptic, and crushed by shyness—it is perhaps no wonder that his planned monthly publication of a parrot monograph was not the commercial success he hoped it would be. Such ventures were better left to the astute and confidently businesslike kinds of men like John Gould.

Gould used Lear extensively as an artist in the production of the books *The Birds of Europe* and *Family of Toucans* but, in 1836, Lear made his excuses to his employer, citing his failing vision for his inability to provide further illustrations: "[My eyesight has become] so sadly worse, that no bird under an ostrich should I soon be able to see to do."

Given that Lear continued to paint birds and landscapes in later years, this may have only been partly the reason why he stepped back from assisting Gould. The latter's reputation amongst his contemporaries was a mixed one—whilst esteemed as a taxidermist and an ornithologist in his own right, Gould was also renowned for his manners, or perceived lack thereof. Those, such as Lear, who encountered Gould in a business context remembered him with mixed emotions. Lear would, in later life, describe Gould as egotistical, possessed of both good intentions and offensive manners. *Family of Toucans* provides a case in point—in the second edition of the book, Gould removed Lear's signature from all the plates he had prepared.

Elizabeth died in 1841, leaving Gould caring for their six young children, but this burden of care does not seem to have hindered his output in any way—indeed, Gould appears to have been driven to fresh heights by his responsibility. Writing to his friend William Jardine only a few weeks after Elizabeth's death, Gould was characteristically more concerned about the practical implications of her passing rather than the emotional distress it must have caused their family: "The loss of my very efficient helpmate will necessarily involve me in considerable trouble with respect to the drawings and although I am happy to say I have artists in training who are fully competent for every thing that can be wished they require from me more perfect sketches [and] constant supervision while each drawing is in progress."

Gould's publications continued to appear apace in the years that followed and, in the meantime, Gould had a new hobby that combined both his interest in birds generally and his omnipresent eye for a moneymaking opportunity. Gould had started to collect, with monomaniacal zeal, hummingbirds.

These were not, of course, living birds—they were dead specimens, their tiny bodies dried over a stove and then packed in camphor to preserve them before shipping overseas. The late Elizabeth Gould's letters home reveal that she had recognised something of the hard-eyed, unsentimental nature of the collector in her husband during the time they spent together in Australia researching *The Birds of Australia*. She was concerned about the sheer volume of bird specimens her husband was collecting, noting, "He has already shown himself a great enemy to the feathered tribe . . ."

Gould's hummingbird collection was, at first, a purely personal source of pleasure and satisfaction, typical of many gentleman collectors of the day. When nurseryman and fellow hummingbird collector George Loddiges died, in 1846, Gould allowed himself free rein—in the introduction to his *Monograph of the Trochilidae, or Family of Humming-birds* Gould admits, "It was not until after Mr Loddiges' decease that I determined upon forming the collection I myself possess, which now far surpasses every other, both in the number of species and examples."

True to Elizabeth's observation, Gould was gathering a collection of hummingbirds that, in its scope, proved him to be an unsurpassed enemy to their kind. By the time of his death in 1861 Gould had amassed a staggering collection of 1,500 mounted and 3,800 unmounted hummingbird specimens. His daughter Lizzie recalled, "The drawing room when I first remember it was very pretty, but as father's collection of hummingbirds grew larger . . . it became almost too full to move about. The housemaid was not allowed in it with broom or duster except on rare occasions, so in time it looked anything but pretty."

Owning such a vast collection was, of course, not enough for Gould. He knew all too well that such a colourful family of birds had commercial possibilities he could exploit—not least because he was fully aware of other collectors who desired them keenly. The *Family of Humming-Birds* monograph, published in instalments between 1849 and 1861, would follow Gould's tried and tested formula of selling to subscribers. In 1851 Gould recognised the marketing potential of the Great Exhibition of the Works of Industry of All Nations championed by Prince Albert. This was the first of a popular series of themed World's Fairs held in the nineteenth century, showcasing international exhibits of, for the most part, contemporary industrial technology and design and, to a lesser extent, culture and the arts.

Gould displayed pages of *Family of Humming-Birds* in the Crystal Palace in Hyde Park, rather tenuously claiming himself to be an inventor on the basis of the incorporation of gold leaf on the plates to confer iridescence to the hummingbirds' plumage. French naturalist and author Jean-Baptiste Audebert had, however, used much the same technique in his hummingbird folio published half a century beforehand—a fact that Gould, in his desire to be included in the Great Exhibition, appears to have conveniently forgotten. That technique had been further developed by a young hummingbird enthusiast and artist in the United States, William Baily, who was incorporating gold leaf, gelatin, and pigments ground in honey to recreate on paper the lustrous colour and iridescence of the birds' plumage. Gould corresponded extensively with Baily about his artistic innovations, but typically afforded him no credit whatsoever for them in his book.

Capitalising on the Great Exhibition's popularity and foot flow, Gould had a temporary building erected in the Zoological Gardens in Regents Park, where he displayed his by now considerable collection of hummingbird specimens, mounted in lifelike poses in twenty-four custom-built, revolving cases that were specially lit to enhance the iridescence of the birds' feathers. Visitors to the Zoological Gardens were asked to pay "sixpence extra" in order to gain admission to "MR GOULD'S Humming Birds."

Another Victorian, George Jennings, is remembered as the inventor of the first flushing public toilets—his invention was installed in the Retiring Rooms of the Crystal Palace and, during the six months of the Great Exhibition, 827,280 visitors paid one penny to use them, giving rise to the euphemism "To spend a penny." Gould's stuffed hummingbird display spawned no such euphemisms, but it was certainly a commercial success—over 75,000 visitors attended his pavilion in Regents Park, including Charles Dickens and Queen Victoria. Gould, while he had not made quite as much money at the door as Jennings, could still have felt reasonably flushed with success—the bottom line of his exhibit was healthy, and he would have gained many more new subscribers for *Family of Humming-Birds*.

It was Queen Victoria to whom Gould dedicated the publication, though in a letter written in 1850 he had boasted, "Humbolt [Alexander von Humboldt] has promised to get me the Queen of Prussia as a subscriber to the Humming Birds and I have already obtained the Queen of Saxony, the Princess of Wied and several other noble ladies for whom the work is specially adapted."

Blissfully unaware of Gould's coldhearted commercial pragmatism, Queen Victoria, having visited his hummingbird display in Regents Park, and greatly taken with the jewel-like birds she had found there, recorded in her diary, "It is impossible to imagine anything so lovely as these little humming birds, their variety, and the extraordinary brilliancy of their colours."

Charles Dickens, meanwhile, wrote of Gould's hummingbirds as "stars of the morning" and "tresses of the day star." Having met Gould, he provides us with a little more insight into the man himself and hummingbird collectors as a whole. Gould, Dickens recounts, began his collection "with a little case of the most beautiful and curious, picked out of the odd groups of glass domes in curiosity shops," and thereafter,

> Sometimes bought a specimen for a dozen pence, and sometimes for as many guineas. They have come from the South American Continent and the Antilles; sometimes in packing-cases, sometimes in a letter containing a single bird.
>
> The fortunate possessors of the rarer species are known to the naturalists of all countries. Those who have secured a specimen considered unique, are looked upon with the same sort of admiring envy that gathers round the owner of a genuine Correggio.

Prominent Victorian critic and scholar John Ruskin also paid the exhibit a visit and, afterwards, lamented that he had studied mineralogy rather than ornithology.

"Had I devoted myself to birds," he said, "I might have produced something myself worth doing.

"If only I could have seen a humming-bird fly, it would have been an epoch in my life."

None of this hyperbole could have hurt the sales of Gould's books, providing him with further funds to expand his collection. Dickens, while effulgent in his praise of both the birds and John Gould himself, was at pains to stress that hummingbirds were God's creation. He exhorted, "Wondrous provision of the Creator! Study the useful and ornamental inventions of the civilised world; but study, too, the work of the Divine hand in these little birds."

This statement, echoed directly in *The Old Curiosity Shop* when notary Mr. Witherden cites "the mountainous Alps on the one hand, or a humming-bird on the other" as amongst the "noblest acts of God," was to have considerable ironic resonance just a few years later when Charles Darwin published *On the Origin of Species*, laying down the principles of evolution as he understood them, to the consternation of many God-fearing scholars of the day for whom Divine creation was a matter of immutable fact. It was Gould who, in 1837 whilst working for the Zoological Society of London, was asked to identify the bird specimens Darwin had brought back from the Galapagos Islands and, to Darwin's consternation, determined that what Darwin had thought to be merely a selection of blackbirds, "gross bills," and finches were, in fact, "A series of ground Finches which are so peculiar [as to form] an entirely new group, containing 12 species."

The speciation demonstrated by these finches was to be one of the central showpieces of Darwin's evolutionary theory; unfortunately, Darwin had not been scrupulous in his labelling when collecting in the Galapagos, and could not be sure to which specific island each finch owed its origin. Having been alerted by Gould to the finches' importance, Darwin had to rely upon further specimens gathered at the time, with accurate data, by Captain FitzRoy and the crew of the HMS *Beagle* for the case study in his pivotal book. Unlike Gould, happy to gloss over the contribution artists had made to his own publications, Darwin credited Gould's contribution in *On the Origin of Species*.

If Darwin initially stumbled in his evaluation of the finches that would, latterly, become synonymous with his reputation, one of his foremost scholarly detractors, the Duke of Argyll, made a particularly egregious hummingbird error in his *Reign of Law*, a book written to partly refute Darwin's theory of evolution—the duke, whilst not denying evolution happened, argued that God himself was the architect of the process. The duke was unequivocal about certain immutable laws of nature as defined by the Almighty, one of which was "no Bird can ever fly backwards." Hummingbirds, he conceded, *appeared* to do so, but this was simply an error of both reasoning and observation on the part of the onlooker: "A bird can allow itself to fall backwards by merely slowing the action of its wings so as to allow its weight to overcome their sustaining power. A Humming Bird . . . in short . . . is falling downwards, not flying backwards."

In 2017, for an exhibition entitled *Visual Voyages: Images of Latin American Nature from Columbus to Darwin*, the Huntingdon Library, Art Museum and Botanical Gardens in California commissioned two replica cases of Gould's hummingbird exhibition. Taxidermist Allis Markham commissioned a wood carver to recreate the bases of each cabinet, and learned to weld in order to make the frames of the cases herself. Her specimens were provided by the Moore Laboratory of Zoology from the extensive collections of American ornithologist, poet, businessman, and philanthropist Robert Moore. Even in the present day, a static display of dead hummingbirds still has the power to stop visitors in their tracks and inspire awe, just as it did over 150 years ago.

Gould finally saw his first living hummingbird, a Ruby-throated Hummingbird, on May 21, 1857, in Bartram's Garden in Philadelphia, after he had travelled with his son to the United States. In the days to follow, in Washington, DC, he saw many more. He recalled, "For some time a single Humming-Bird was my constant companion during days of toil by road and rail; and I ultimately succeeded in bringing a living pair within the confines of the British Isles, and a single individual to London, where it lived for two days, when, from the want of proper food or the change in climate, it died."

Gould imprisoned his first captive hummingbird in a small gauze bag, with a slender piece of whale bone providing a little space within the bag for the prisoner to move. He wore it suspended from a button on his coat, an ornament on display like an animate pocket watch. It is worth noting that Gould, having seen living hummingbirds, remarked upon them appearing like compact pieces of machinery "acted upon by a powerful spring."

I would like to believe that, after so many years collecting so many dead hummingbirds, when Gould finally set eyes on a living example of their kind he may have realised that dead specimens, whilst still beautiful, were a pale shadow of their living counterparts. Given that he was still using his extensive network of contacts and collectors in the Americas to add more specimens to his collection in the decades that followed, I suspect that his desire to bring living birds back to Britain owed much to their moneymaking possibilities. The manner in which he outwardly displayed his living hummingbird in public whilst travelling some 1,500 miles in the United States suggests a man who was acquisitive and who viewed nature as a commodity to be exhibited, exploited, and used. The Gouldian leopard did not change its spots.

Nor was Gould the first Englishman to attempt to import living hummingbirds to Britain. The earliest known account, related by John Latham in 1801, is of a short-lived but nevertheless somewhat more successful attempt than that made by Gould half a century later. Latham wrote,

A young gentleman, a few days before he set sail from Jamaica to England, was fortunate enough to meet with a female Humming Bird, when cutting off the twig, he brought all together on board the ship.

The female became sufficiently tame, so as to suffer itself to be fed with honey, and during the passage hatched two young ones; however, the mother did not survive long, but the young were brought to England,

and continued alive for some time in the possession of Lady Hamond. Sir H. Englefield, Baronet, and Colonel Sloane, both witnesses of the circumstance, informed me that these little creatures readily took honey from the lips of Lady Hamond, with their bills.

One of them did not live long, but the other survived at least two months from the time of its arrival.

From Georgian ladies enjoying the novelty of feeding hummingbirds from their pursed lips to Edwardian playboys wanting to ostentatiously flaunt their wealth, the desire to see living hummingbirds in Britain did not go away. Edwardian textile heir Sir George Bullough spent a small fortune in the early twentieth century turning the Hebridean island of Rum into the ultimate aristocratic retreat, with a bespoke red sandstone castle featuring an immense steam organ originally commissioned by Queen Victoria, capable of simulating a forty-piece orchestra and, in the castle grounds, a heated aviary designed to house birds-of-paradise from Papua New Guinea and hummingbirds from the Americas.

History does not record whether Bullough was successful in importing either family of birds, but in the middle of the twentieth century other British exhibitors were keen to have living hummingbirds to show their paying guests. Guyana, formerly British Guiana before the country gained independence in 1966, was a popular hunting ground for zoos hoping to display some South American fauna to the paying public.

Gerald Durrell collected there in 1950, bringing back a variety of animals and birds to offer for sale to the British zoo community. He wrote, in his typically engaging and thoughtful style, of his efforts to look after captured hummingbirds whilst there. Once a fortnight a hunter would bring him a cage containing five or six birds that Durrell would patiently teach to feed from small glass pots containing a mixture of honey and water, mixed with a small amount of Bovril and Mellin's Food, a soluble baby formula. Unsurprisingly, given the yeasty additives, Durrell noted that this cocktail tended to turn sour very quickly in the heat of the tropics. Within two days of coming into his care, he recorded that each batch of hummingbirds would have become so tame they would even perch on his fingers when he refreshed the drinkers in their cages.

Durrell went on to fundamentally change the zoo format, founding a zoo on the island of Jersey that had conservation at its heart, dedicated to breeding programmes of endangered species for release back to the wild, developing the skills and tools to conserve species in the wild, training others in animal husbandry and conservation practice, and communicating critical conservation messages to visitors. The visitors were, whilst important, subsidiary to the main objective, which was conservation. After Durrell's death in 1995, Sir David Attenborough described him as, "A renegade who was right. He was truly a man before his time."

Attenborough too had collected hummingbirds, a revelation that came as a surprise to me, born in the 1970s and used to thinking of the great man as, first and foremost, a presenter and communicator of wildlife and conservation documentaries on the television. Early in his career at the BBC, Attenborough collaborated with London Zoo to pioneer a new format for television—the *Zoo Quest* series documented animal-collecting expeditions to various countries worldwide, with Attenborough presenting in front of camera in the field. The first expedition was to Sierra Leone; the next to British Guiana.

There, one evening, a young local boy, blowpipe over one shoulder, shyly approached Attenborough and handed him a cloth bag. Inside, Attenborough found several hummingbirds, each stunned in flight by a wax-tipped dart fired from the boy's blowpipe. Amongst them was a male Tufted Coquette—these are an ostentatious species with a spiky blood-orange arrangement of feathers on their heads that look like David Bowie's hair during the Ziggy Stardust phase of his career. This was the hummingbird that Attenborough had hoped to see more than any other whilst in British Guiana, and he felt a mixture of delight and dismay—the latter emotion because he did not have the necessary feeding equipment with him to allow the birds to be retained in captivity. He improvised hummingbird feeders from lengths of bamboo, but they were crude devices that leaked sugar water prodigiously and were not fit for purpose. With a heavy heart, the following morning, he released the birds—they flew strongly away into the forest and, with them he said, a weight lifted from his mind.

Gould, collecting hummingbirds a century before Attenborough, also noted approvingly the use of blunt darts and blowpipes to capture birds without damage to their feathers.

> Many really absurd statements have been made as to the means by which these birds are obtained for our cabinets. It is most frequently asserted that they are shot with water or with sand.
>
> Now, so far as I am aware, these devices are never resorted to, but they are usually procured in the usual way, with Nos. 10 and 11 shot, these being the sizes best suited for the purpose. If smaller shot be used the plumage is very frequently so cut and damaged that the specimen is rendered of little or no value.
>
> By far the greater number fall to the clay ball of the blowpipe, which the Indians, and in some instances even Europeans, use with perfect certainty of aim.

Once again with Gould, we see the collector's preoccupation with possessing the perfect specimen for his collection. Similar gauge shot was employed by butterfly collectors in the tropics—the first example of the largest butterfly species in the world, Queen Alexandra's Birdwing, was shot from the treetops above him in New Guinea by Albert Meek. The specimen, presented to zoologist Walter Rothschild in 1906, exists to this day in the British Natural History Museum, replete with holes in its twenty-centimetre-wide wings from the shotgun pellets that brought it eddying down to earth, as helpless as Icarus. Inevitably, demand soared for less damaged specimens of this great rarity. As author John Fowles, himself a secret collector of orchids dug from the wild in France and Greece, once scathingly observed, "All natural history collectors in the end collect the same thing: the death of the living."

With a particular irony, given how many hummingbirds must have fallen to the shotguns of European collectors who were not adept in the art of using a blowpipe, one of the most lauded shotguns ever made is known as the Hummingbird Gun. Created over a period of years in the 1990s by engraver Rashid El Hadi for gunmaker Westley Richards, the finished shotgun was achingly beautiful, even to the eyes of a naturalist opposed to the killing of animals for sport. Hummingbirds, cunningly wrought in yellow, white, and rose gold, fly above and around meticulously rendered flowers, framed by detailed, flowing feathers.

A strange twist in the tale was to follow in the years after the Hummingbird Gun's completion, a case of art imitating life. With echoes of the Harlequin Hummingbird, the fake bird that for years fooled the ornithological establishment, a pair of Westley Richards shotguns appeared for sale in September 2014 at the Illinois auctioneer Rock Island Auction. Whilst considerably less detailed than El Hadi's design, the engraving on these guns bore striking similarities—hummingbirds in flight over flowers, framed by feathers. In 2019 the guns surfaced again at an auction house, their identity now a little more embellished. The auctioneer, Morphy Auctions of Pennsylvania, listed them as an incredibly rare pair of Westley Richards, known as "The Hummingbird Guns," with their engraving and gold inlay inspired by the artwork of Martin Johnson Heade.

Heade was a nineteenth-century American artist and hummingbird obsessive whose hummingbird and orchid artwork had enjoyed a renaissance of popularity in the United States in the latter half of the twentieth century. In his lifetime he was unusual insofar as, when many European and American visitors to South America collected as many bird specimens as they could carry home with them in trunks and packing cases, he took home only artwork he had created from observations in life. "The Hummingbird Guns" eventually sold for $135,300—the semirelief hummingbird decoration elevating the guns from mere antiques to works of art sought after by collectors of a different kind.

Yet, just like the Harlequin Hummingbird, all was not as it seemed. The provenance of the guns had been revealed by Simon Clode, the director of Westley Richards, in the wake of the first auction. Speaking shortly after their sale, Clode described them as an audacious copy of the original Hummingbird Gun.

In the same manner that the "made-up" Harlequin Hummingbird became a sufficient embarrassment for the British Museum that it was expunged from its collection, I wondered if the current owner of "The Hummingbird Guns" was aware of their dubious provenance. Perhaps they simply did not care—the hummingbird artwork being attractive enough to render the guns a notable feature of their collection.

Back in the closing years of the nineteenth and the dawn of the twentieth century, the zenith of the hummingbird-collecting mania was reached. By this stage, hummingbirds were being harvested not so much for the cabinets of curiosity in the studies and parlours of Victorian and Edwardian homes as for the insatiable appetite for feathers for the fashion industry—specifically, to adorn increasingly elaborate hats.

The feather industry, in the 1880s, was big business. A worldwide network of collectors, like Gould's blowpipe-wielding Indians, supplied local middlemen who, in turn, exported vast shipments of feathers to the global centres of plumage commerce in London, Paris, and New York. Here, those feathers were auctioned, and bought by dealers whose workforces prepared the feathers for use in what came, in time, to be known as murderous millinery. The *plumassiers* in the Faubourg Saint-Martin district of Paris and the feather foundries of New York's Lower East Side had their equivalents in London, sweatshops where poorly paid women and children cleaned, picked, and prepared feathers in a miasma of feather dust and mercury salts, the latter toxic chemical widely used as a preservative at the time.

The demand for feathers was insatiable, from high-society ladies to the very women who, paid a pittance for their labour, worked in those terrible conditions in the feather factories of London's East End. For the working-class women, a feathered hat was a means of expressing some dignity and pride in an otherwise degrading and brutal workplace. Some would band together in savings clubs, incrementally adding their shillings together until they could afford a particularly fine set of hat feathers. While new feathers were always in demand in novel colours or forms, in 1887, the year of Queen Victoria's Golden Jubilee, *Harper's Magazine* recommended recycling older stuffed birds on one's hat, each arranged in new positions with an "appealing expression" on its face. Hummingbirds, with their flashing, bejewelled gorgets and metallic hues of every colour of the rainbow, were perennially popular, and were seen as a relatively cheap fix for a tired hat. They were displayed in trays at London markets, priced from tuppence a bird, "So cheap that even the ragged girl from the neighbouring slums could decorate her battered hat, like any fine lady, with some bright-winged bird of the tropics," as one commentator in *The Times* observed. An American monthly journal, *Our Dumb Animals*, related in 1875 that, "Lady Burdett Coutts certifies from personal knowledge that one Parisian milliner uses 40,000 hummingbirds every season."

The English and French markets for murderous millinery had their equivalents in New York—George Bird Grinnell, an American anthropologist and founder of the Audubon Society, the United States' equivalent to the Royal Society for the Protection of Birds (RSPB), noted dismally in 1886, "The headgear of women is made up in as large degree as ever before of the various parts of small birds. Thousands and millions of birds are displayed in every conceivable shape on their hats and bonnets."

Just like the present day, fashions changed from season to season. What was *chic* in spring would be *de trop* by autumn, and utterly *passé* by the following spring. *Harper's Bazaar*, just one of the many fashion magazines that chronicled what was hot and what was not at the time, tells us that, for example, in winter 1881 pheasants and grebes were *de rigeur*, worn either as entire birds' breasts displayed on bonnets and dresses, or as small bonnets comprised entirely of their finest feathers; spring brought a phase of wearing grey birds on medium poke bonnets, mainly doves; summer was a time of flamboyance, with the feathers of ostriches and egrets worn as pompoms or long aigrettes; and when autumn came around, it was the turn of the small birds to be worn in profusion upon turbans, large round hats, and the sides of bonnets—kingfishers, parakeets, and hummingbirds.

Hummingbirds never really went out of fashion, so compelling, varied, and unlike the plumage of any other birds were they. The French pioneered a variation on the theme, using either entire birds or constituent body parts—whole heads were popular—as decorations on hat pins, brooches, and earrings, featured in contemporary industry journal *The Millinery Trade Review* as "The Latest Parisian Fancy Feather Novelties." Hummingbird feathers were also used to make artificial insects to adorn hats—imaginative milliners finding myriad uses for the most iridescent and unusual feathers of all.

The records of auction houses and contemporary observations made at the time reveal the extent of the trade, and what it meant specifically for hummingbirds—they were just one component of a vast industry that included feathers from the very smallest to the very largest of bird species, from hummingbird to ostrich. A correspondent to *The Auk*, the journal of the American Ornithologists' Union (AOU), recounted a visit to a plumage sale on March 21, 1888, at the London Commercial Sales Rooms in Mincing Lane. There he found, amongst tens of thousands of other birds offered for sale, twelve thousand hummingbirds. The anonymous correspondent goes on to relate the particulars of another London auction, held the previous year, where "there were sold 6,000 birds-of-paradise, 5,000 Impeyan Pheasants [and] 400,000 Hummingbirds." The scale of the slaughter was scarcely credible, and it continued apace for decades. As *The Auk*'s correspondent lamented, "The traffic, if much longer sustained, cannot fail to have a marked effect in depopulating the countries supplying these sales of their bird life. What a bloody Moloch is fashion!"

By the early twentieth century, with the trade showing little sign of abating—eight sales in London alone between 1904 and 1911 accounted for 152,000 hummingbirds—the effect of this plunder was becoming all too apparent. Speaking in 1908 to a House of Lords Select Committee, Lord Strathmore, formerly governor of a number of overseas territories including Fiji, Ceylon, and Trinidad, bore witness to the scale of the loss: "The activities of plumage hunters have cut the number of hummingbird species in Trinidad from nineteen to five."

American ornithologist Robert Ridgway, meanwhile, took a somewhat more pragmatic view of the situation. Like John Gould, Ridgway was a hummingbird fanatic and, while he deplored their collection for "purely ornamental purposes," he viewed the feather trade also as a useful source of new species. He gleefully said, "Though demand [for the feather trade] has vastly added to their destruction it has, as a fortunate recompense, enabled naturalists to become better acquainted with them, the immense numbers in milliners' and taxidermists' stocks frequently yielding species which otherwise would scarcely have become known to science."

In both Britain and the United States, however, the tide of public opinion had started to turn against murderous millinery. George Grinnell, in the States, formed the Audubon Society in 1886 as a response to the industrialised slaughter of birds he was bearing witness to at the time. The society, naturally, took its name from John Audubon, father of American ornithology. The organisation's initial impact was limited, as recorded with some satisfaction in *The Millinery Trade Review* in autumn 1889:

The humane efforts of the Audubon Society seem to have been ineffectual in staying the capture of birds for millinery ornament, and birds this season are extremely popular.

Notable effects in bonnet trimming are triplets of canary-birds and the little white Java nun, and clusters of South American humming-birds, and the birds-of-paradise are made to do much more than ordinary duty on the millinery of the season.

Nevertheless, the Audubon Society continued to find traction and, in 1895, the Massachusetts Audubon Society was founded by Boston socialites Harriet Hemenway and Minna Hall, encouraging other women to join them in "a society for the protection of birds." They were reacting directly to the burgeoning feather trade. In Britain, they had their counterparts in Etta Lemon and Emily Williamson.

In 1889, appalled by the use of animals in fashion, Lemon founded the Fur, Fin and Feather Folk Society—within a year the society had nearly five thousand members. That same year Williamson founded the Society for the Protection of Birds (SPB) and, in 1891, the two societies merged under the name of the latter. Driven by the dedication and zeal of Lemon and Williamson, and cohorts of other determined women, and in the face of stiff opposition from men and women alike, the SPB grew in influence and popularity, gaining a royal charter in 1904 to become the RSPB as we know it to this day.

Lemon worked ceaselessly to protect birds and, in particular, to undermine the feather trade. She was one of the architects and proponents of the Plumage Bill, proposed to Parliament in 1908, and designed to limit the importation of feathers into Britain—a bill that ran out of time in the Commons in 1908 and, when next read in 1913, was set aside, apparently for "trade interests." During the First World War the feather trade declined, not least as feathers were listed amongst luxury items whose import was banned for the duration of the war—a restriction that Lemon, with a number of cosignatories including H. G. Wells and Thomas Hardy, implored the president of the Board of Trade, Sir Auckland Geddes, to continue after the war ended until such time as the Plumage Bill could be passed into law. When men, perhaps with vested interests in the trade, continued to prevaricate and obfuscate, Virginia Woolf wrote a scathing short essay in July 1920, entitled "The Plumage Bill" and concluded, "The Plumage Bill is for all practical purposes dead. But what do men care?"

When the Importation of Plumage (Prohibition) Act was finally passed into British law in 1921, the culmination of decades of hard work by Lemon, Williamson, and their many supporters, the egrets of Europe, the birds-of-paradise of New Guinea, and the humming-birds of South America could finally rest a little easier. Though not entirely—in 1932, twenty-five thousand hummingbirds were killed in the Brazilian state of Pará and exported to Italy, where they were used to adorn chocolate boxes. To this day, in Brazil, the imported Italian custom of eating small passerine, or perching birds, hum-mingbirds included, has endured in the region surrounding the city of Caxias do Sul, where *passarinhos com polenta*, or little birds with cornmeal, is a lingering legacy of the Italian immigrants who settled in the region in the nineteenth century.

As lately as the 1980s, hummingbirds were still to be found in some zoos and aviaries in Britain—imported birds, for the most part, from South America. I spoke to British birders who had fond mem-ories of the Tropical House at the Wildfowl and Wetlands Trust's flagship reserve, Slimbridge—in the early 1980s this steamy paradise provided a welcome winter refuge for visitors to the reserve who had spent hours in the bitter cold watching wild Bewick's Swans gather-ing outside, hungry migrants from Siberia. The Tropical House held captive wildfowl that hailed from warmer climes—Hottentot Teals and African Pygmy Geese, and some other birds to lend a further note of the exotic—bleeding-heart doves and hummingbirds.

I had only the faintest recollection of the old Tropical House. My father took me to Slimbridge once as a boy, but my abiding memory was not of hummingbirds seen in the foggy, warm embrace of that long-lost building—I remembered standing, consumed with embar-rassment, as my dad pretended to other visitors that he knew the identity of various ducks on the surrounding saltmarshes. I could see the looks the other adults were covertly exchanging, and for the first time I realised my father's fallibility. As even a fledgling birder, I knew that getting birds' identities right was important amongst our tribe. The names of birds *mattered*.

Over a century before I came to that epiphany, another realised that the names given to birds and, in particular, hummingbirds was no trifling matter. John Gould, as part of his marketing for *Family of Humming-Birds*, enthusiastically embraced some of the existing English species' names for known species, and bestowed upon many of the new species he was introducing to his subscribers names that implied incomparable glory and exoticism compared to any other family of birds. Only some of the birds-of-paradise, with names that celebrated royal patrons, could come close to them. In his monograph Gould introduced his readers to hummingbirds that took their names from an intoxicating variety of sources.

From mineralogy came a glittering array of precious gemstones— beryls, emeralds, rubies, sapphires, topazes, and tourmalines— while metallurgy supplied components of bronze, copper, and gold. The skies above gave comets, rainbows, sunbeams, and stars, while the heavens gave us sunangels and Lucifer himself. Mythology provided nymphs and sylphs; and some names appeared to reference a more martial theme—lancebills, sabrewings, sicklebills, and a personal favourite, the Sword-billed Hummingbird. Flowers appear sparingly—there are blossomcrowns, hyacinths, and violets in the hummingbirds' garden. Adjectives announce many of them—they glitter, they glow, they shine, and they sparkle. While no hummingbird bore quite such an overtly royal name as the King of Saxony Bird-of-Paradise, heraldic themes were nonetheless present in some names—hummingbirds have, amongst their number, coronets and trainbearers. Relatively few bear the names of specific individuals, though rather more do in their scientific names. The French naturalist Jules Bourcier commemorated his daughter Francia and his wife Aline, as well as an intriguing number of the wives and daughters of other people, in the scientific names of hummingbirds he described for the first time.

Amongst the precious few hummingbirds to commemorate a naturalist in their English names was one of the species I particularly wanted to see for myself in Ecuador—Gould's Jewelfront. It was with John Gould and the hummingbird that carried his name for posterity in mind that I met the rest of my hummingbird-hunting companions early one morning in the reception area of the Hotel Quito. The hotel had an air of faded 1960s style that spoke of past glories. It felt as if a member of the Rat Pack could stroll through the lobby at any moment, an impression reinforced by the sound of Frank Sinatra playing as background music and the slightly surreal sight of a succession of unfeasibly groomed young women languidly striking poses for photographers all around us—the hotel was hosting the hotly contested Ecuadorian heats of Miss World, a competition I had thought long consigned to the footnotes of the mid-twentieth century. Surrounded by the contestants, half a dozen American and one British birder dressed in various shades of olive-green and sun-bleached khaki stood out. The contestants, to a woman, gave us a conspicuously wide berth.

Paul Greenfield, our tour leader for the days that were to come, is an avuncular and genial American who has lived in Ecuador for some thirty years, studying and painting the country's birdlife. We wasted little time with introductions, keen to leave the city and strike into the Andes. We passed through the suburbs of Quito, past houses behind high walls topped with long shards of broken glass and electric fences, with yellow warning signs hanging on the wires warning of *peligro de muerte*, danger of death, a visible manifestation of a fear and insecurity in the city that otherwise went unspoken. Many walls were adorned with graffiti—Quito's night artists had a particular fondness it seemed for faces and executed them with particular flair and panache. On the edge of the city we passed a long blue wall with a large, stylised hummingbird painted upon it—the bird came and went in the blink of an eye, like the real thing. A little further on, there were words stencilled at eye level, with a heart on their side, forming an arrow pointing to the green smudge of open countryside that lay at the end of the road: *Sigue tu corazón & disfruta el viaje.* Follow your heart & enjoy the journey.

That felt like the very best advice as we shortly encountered our first Ecuadorian hummingbirds in the first of several roadside stops—a quick succession of many Sparkling Violetears, a buzzing White-bellied Woodstar, sinuous Black-tailed Trainbearers and, much drabber than all of them, but dramatic for its sheer size alone, a Giant Hummingbird seen just outside Pifo, at an elevation of some 8,500 feet above sea level. Compared to the tiny woodstar in particular, the Giant Hummingbird amply deserved its name—while still recognisably a hummingbird, and hovering periodically as such, its flight seemed more laboured than that of its smaller counterparts, and its plumage was dull—shades of olive green and soft, earthy grey, with a smudged, indistinct white rump. This was a hummingbird that had taken the same approach to its wardrobe as we had earlier that morning, favouring camouflaged tones over bright colours that advertised its presence. It is the largest hummingbird in the world, but the "giant" prefix it enjoys, is somewhat misleading, as the bird itself was still no larger than the starlings that were ubiquitous back home in Shetland. In Bolivia, they are known prosaically as *burro q'enti*—a *burro* being an inelegant, earthen beast of burden, a donkey.

If the largest hummingbird species in the world was, if one was honest, a little underwhelming, the days that followed provided ample consolation whilst we explored the eastern Andean slopes. The dark, moss-dripping trees of Guango harboured a posse of Tourmaline Sunangels, combative Chestnut-breasted Coronets, Tyrian Metaltails that gleamed like sharpened blades, and the neon brilliance of Long-tailed Sylphs, their slender streamer tails searing through the gloom like the taillights of speeding cars in manga cartoons. The air around us seemed to crackle with their collective electricity.

At heavily forested Sumaco the trees boiled with birdlife of all kinds. Roving flocks of tanagers moved through the canopy, their fleeting appearances cause for intense activity on the forest floor as we scrambled to sift through them, giving names to colourful forms that appeared from nowhere high overhead, paused, fed, and vanished as swiftly and mysteriously as they had come. Paradise, Magpie, Blue-necked, Golden-eared, Swallow, Summer, and Scarlet, a host of varied and enticing tanagers. One of our number said thoughtfully, "I could get into tanagers . . ."

I knew how she felt—they had chutzpah to spare—but it was here at Sumaco that hummingbirds new to me began to mount up at an irrepressible pace. The feeders on the edges of the wooden deck of our lodge were busy with Wire-crested Thornbills, the males of which quickly endeared themselves to me with green upperparts the colour of weathered bronze supplanted by a spiky Mohican crest, with two long, needle-fine feathers like antennae that quivered at right angles to their crown. If that were not enough, each bird sported a thick white stripe wrapped around his rump like a race car decal, and long, pointed steel-blue tail feathers, each with a hint of snow-white shaft at the base.

It was, however, the feeding station that had been set up a short walk away in the forest itself that delivered, spectacularly, an overwhelming deluge of hummingbirds. Booted Racket-tails with rich buff pom-pom legwarmer feathers flew, like dragonflies, around the perimeter of the small clearing in which the feeders were hanging, their long delicate tails tipped with petrol-blue discs that gleamed in the broken sunlight that streamed through the overarching trees in pale golden shafts. Black-throated and Violet-fronted Brilliants were more substantial arrivals at the feeders, while a dark, brooding presence that perched deep in cover at the back of the clearing made sporadic forays into our midst—my first Napo Sabrewing, a large, powerful hummingbird clad in dark coniferous-green plumage that shifted hue and gleamed in the changing ambient light, with an extensive midnight-blue throat that sent occasional bursts of clear sapphire blue towards me from the gloom.

It was while watching the sabrewing that a smaller hummingbird appeared at the forest edge, perching on an exposed twig to closely examine the hummingbird activity at the feeders before deigning to feed for himself. At first glance, he was predominantly a rich, emerald green, his chest emblazoned with an apricot shield that encircled him in a pectoral band. Looking more closely, I could see a hint of turquoise on his pulsating throat, and an intense amethyst blaze on his forecrown. Illustrations of Gould's Jewelfront in field guides did him scant justice—in the flesh, he was mesmerising.

Found sparingly across an extensive range that spans the edge of Venezuela in the north to the northwest of Brazil in the south, Gould's Jewelfront was first described by John Gould himself on October 13, 1846, in a paper he presented to the Zoological Society of London, amidst seventeen further new species he was pleased to announce, proudly noting that the species in question were all to be found in his own collection of hummingbirds.

Gould gave the bird in question the scientific name *Trochilus aurescens*. When his popular monograph *Family of Humming-Birds* was published in the years that followed, even Gould, no stranger to self-promotion and the commercial possibilities afforded by marketing, did not have the temerity to claim the English name for his own—he called it the Banded Ruby. That the genus it resides within has subsequently changed from *Trochilus* to *Helidoxus* matters not to the birds themselves, but Gould would, presumably, be pleased to find that after devoting so much of his life to the study of hummingbirds, one of them had, in time, come to bear his surname in its English species name for perpetuity.

Another hummingbird, known colloquially as Gould's Inca, divides opinion amongst taxonomists—some considering it a subspecies of Collared Inca, and others elevating it to full specific species status in its own right. Gould, one of the earliest examples of what birders now refer to as a "splitter," or one who prefers more full species rather than the conservative approach of subspecies existing beneath the umbrella of overarching species, would doubtless approve of the inca that bears his name too. Gould might, however, have preferred that another species altogether bore his name for, amongst the seventeen species he announced that autumn day in 1846, was one that he considered to be "without exception the most gorgeous species of the *Trochilidae* yet discovered. It is somewhat larger than *T.pella* [the Crimson Topaz], which fine species it far exceeds in the brilliancy of its colouring, and from which it is distinguished by the fiery lustre of its body and the purplish colouring of its tail feathers."

This was *Trochilus pyra*, what would come to be known in English as the Fiery Topaz. John Gould, judging by his language, had a bad case of hummingbird love for the species—but his name, in time, came to be affixed to the jewelfront that he described, rather coldly, later on in his paper. Faced by the bird that bore his name, I felt a little pang of sadness for Gould—even the English name, jewelfront, was a touch hyperbolic for the bird in question. Granted, it was an attractive hummingbird and, as I had wanted particularly to see one, I found it captivating, but in terms of sheer brilliance, Gould's Jewelfront faced stiff competition from hummingbirds more beautiful still—one of which, Velvet-purple Coronet, was assuming mythical proportions in my mind as the days passed, and no bird was forthcoming.

The following day began with a walk along a pre-Incan irrigation ledge that traces the contours of the northeastern flanks of the Pichincha Volcano in the Yanacocha Reserve, a one thousand-hectare nature reserve encompassing high Andean forest and páramo habitats, a short distance outside Quito. Our target, though one that Paul warned us we were extremely unlikely to actually see, was *el zamarrito pechinegro* or Black-breasted Puffleg. When it was adopted as the official "emblematic bird" of Quito in 2005, former local politician and founding member of Aves y Conservación (BirdLife in Ecuador), Juan Manuel Carrión, said, "[We must] make the species visible, to attract attention in a symbolic way and for the city to have a natural emblem embodied in a bird; as well as encouraging municipal participation in efforts to preserve it."

This is a hummingbird endemic to a small area of the Ecuadorian Andes and, even there, one that appears to be teetering on the very brink of extinction. Known to exist at only two sites, it appears to have been extirpated from much of its former historical range, the victim of habitat destruction—trees felled for lumber and firewood and, on the flatter ridgetops in this steeply corrugated landscape, land cleared for agriculture. That former range was never a large one, but now the estimated 250 birds remaining in the world cling on, precariously, in increasingly trying circumstances. The human pressures upon their habitat have not gone away—nearly half of rural households in the vicinity are said to still rely upon wood and charcoal for cooking and heating, while climate change may yet render the remaining pockets of habitat less suitable for the birds. Rising temperatures may change the ecology of the mountainsides, pushing the flowering species the birds depend upon higher up the mountains until, eventually, there is nowhere left for plants or birds to go.

Hummingbirds are sensitive to change. While some species are generalists, found over large ranges that span countries and many hundreds or even thousands of miles, many of their kind have evolved to prosper in the local conditions of a much smaller area. A bleak example of their general sensitivity came from the controlled environment of Biosphere 2, an experiment conducted in the Arizona desert in the early 1990s. Here a three-acre sealed world within a world was created, housed beneath geodesic domes and glass pyramids. This world was to contain a variety of habitats, from forest to desert, mangrove swamp to coral reef; many thousands of plant and animal species, including Amazilia Hummingbirds, an Ecuadorian and Peruvian species chosen as they were generalist pollinators; and eight so-called Biospherians. The latter were eight carefully selected men and women who would spend the next two years living sealed off from Biosphere 1, the outer world, in a place without pollution, producing their own food, and living in harmony with the environment around them. It sounded gloriously utopian.

The hummingbirds were among the first to die, along with the honeybees. Nematodes and mites attacked the Biospherians' struggling crops, while ants and cockroaches began to proliferate. Carbon dioxide levels soared, while oxygen levels plummeted. The Biospherians ran short of breathable air, food, and clean water, while the ecological balance around them ran horribly out of kilter. As a parable for humanity's clumsiness when we attempt to manage our environment, Biosphere 2 had a clear message. When I heard of hummingbirds in decline in the wild, those poor Amazilia Hummingbirds, early victims in the Biosphere 2 experiment, came unbidden to mind.

Black-breasted Pufflegs, judging by the numbers of collected historic specimens held in museums worldwide, were once more numerous than they are now and appear to be particularly sensitive to disturbance—not a helpful trait for a hummingbird in a changing world. A conservation project has started in Ecuador, hoping to make some steps towards reversing that inexorable decline. Using camera traps to study the feeding activity of the pufflegs and other local hummingbirds, scientists have studied the interactions between birds and flowers, determining which species of hummingbird rely most heavily upon which species of plant. Tatiana Santander, of Aves y Conservación, said, "The cameras were used to record activity at the flowers . . . Then we used software to analyse the information and determine the network of plant-hummingbird interactions."

The outcome of this has been reassuringly practical—a nursery, overseen by six women from the local community of Alambi, has been set up to propagate thirty-two species of native plants identified as most hummingbird-friendly. To date, in 2020, over 4,500 plants have been grown—to restore and enrich degraded former forest habitats on the slopes of Pichincha. There is some modest cause for hope for the pufflegs.

By hummingbird standards, Black-breasted Pufflegs are quite subdued, lacking the extravagant plumage of other pufflegs. All share the feature that lend them their name—voluminous white bloomers at the base of their legs—but the Black-breasted Pufflegs are uncharacteristically muted in appearance. The males are particularly dark, befittingly so for a hummingbird that has assumed such a reputation for lurking in the shadows and rarely deigning to show itself, a scaly, deep bottle-green bird with a midnight black breast and a royal-purple gorget. Between 1950 and 1993 only one confirmed sighting was made, of three individuals seen in 1980. Latterly it has become a little easier to encounter, but only insofar as birders know they stand the faintest chance of crossing paths with a bird on the slopes of Pichincha. They are achingly rare, and Paul was right to manage our expectations.

The trail that wound its way around Pichincha was an easy one to follow, being almost level, albeit at an altitude of some 10,500 feet above sea level. In the cool sunshine of early morning we made good progress, interrupted only by a confiding pair of Plate-billed Mountain-Toucans, their appearance the very definition of exoticism—a heady combination of powder-blue underparts, coppery upperparts, scarlet undertail, and a claret eye surrounded by blue, yellow, and green eyeshadow. The yellow "plate" on their large black bills that lent this extraordinary toucan its name was quite redundant in the midst of such an explosion of colours.

The toucans were only temporarily distracting—the view across the Andes was spectacular from our lofty vantage point, a series of peaks stretching away from us into the distance. On the southern horizon, an ashen column marked the smouldering location of another volcano, Tungurahua, a stirring giant that has been threatening to erupt properly for years now. Our arrival coincided with a period when the volcano was enjoying one of its occasional sullen episodes, like a moody teenager on the cusp of a door-slamming meltdown.

Some way along the trail we finally arrived at a feeding station and found ourselves surrounded by pufflegs. Not the Black-breasted birds I yearned for, but still new for me and utterly beguiling. Sapphire-vented Pufflegs were most numerous, with a dozen birds visible at any one time, irresistible palettes of shimmering emerald green, with sapphire-blue counterpoints beneath their tails and on their forecrowns, and a wash of gold on their necks and forewings. Two considerably scarcer Golden-breasted Pufflegs came and went amongst their Sapphire-vented brethren—lacking any blue, and with a richer suffusion of gold about their bodies, they seemed to be carved from animate peridot that flashed from hundreds of facets in the sunlight.

The memory of those pufflegs was still seared in my mind's eye late that afternoon. I needed only to close my eyes and there they were. They had outshone all the other hummingbirds at the Yanacocha feeders, Great Sapphirewings and Gorgeted Sunangels reduced to a mere supporting cast. We had now crossed the Andes to the Pacific-facing western slopes, basing ourselves in the Mindo Valley. In the intervening páramo, at fourteen thousand feet above sea level, we had found truly montane hummingbirds—Blue-mantled Thornbills and a solitary female Ecuadorian Hillstar. The latter species has been found at altitudes of up to seventeen thousand feet, a feat of hummingbird endurance I could scarcely grasp as I struggled for breath and tried, in vain, to get a better view of her in the misty conditions that prevailed that high up. She was better adapted to the altitude than I—at night, she could enter into a state of controlled torpor, slowing her heartbeat down from around one thousand beats per minute to a mere one hundred beats per minute. That might still sound like a fast heartbeat but, to a hummingbird, it was barely ticking over, just enough to sustain her in a state of near hibernation until the morning and a chance to look for food once more.

Our brief stay in her realm behind us, we had arrived at the Septimo Paraiso Lodge with less than an hour of dwindling daylight remaining. Of all the countries I was to visit during the course of my journey, Ecuador boasted ecolodges of a luxurious standard the likes of which I encountered nowhere else. Septimo Paraiso was an exceptional example, boasting swimming pools, swathes of polished wood, and soft amber lighting in the refined public areas. Ecuador recognised, earlier than neighbouring nations, the potential for eco-tourism as an important aspect of the rural economy, and the investment made in lodges such as this reflected the income they generate locally. The scale of this lodge, and others we stayed at in the Ecuadorian countryside, suggested that they must be locally significant employers too.

While my companions took to their rooms to freshen up, I walked to the lodge's hummingbird feeding station, set in an enclosed amphitheatre of surrounding trees and bushes outside the main entrance to the complex, to sit quietly with whatever birds I might find there.

The feeders were busy when I arrived, thronged with hummingbirds making the most of the last opportunity to top up their batteries before the night ahead. Purple-bibbed Whitetips jostled with Booted Racket-tails and Violet-tailed Sylphs, while in the quickening dusk the shadowy forms of Brown Incas and White-whiskered Hermits lurked. Some minutes later, as if a switch had been thrown, they were all gone, with just the occasional buzz of wings somewhere unseen in the gloom betraying them as they melted away into the swelling darkness. I sat, reflecting on the day just gone, in the warm, humid evening air, the lights of the lodge twinkling through the branches of the trees that framed the clearing.

A deep, throbbing hum of wingbeats rose in the darkness nearby, growing louder as an unseen bird approached me, the tone of his flight unfamiliar to me. The sound grew louder still, and then I could feel the downdraft of a hummingbird sweeping slowly past my cheek. I turned my head to face him, and there, hovering inches from my face, was a hummingbird the likes of which I had never seen before, a bird that appeared at first black as night and then, as he rotated deliberately to look me in the eye, clad in an impossibly rich and overpowering imperial purple that, as traces of golden light from the lodge struck his breast, exploded into myriad sparks of palatinate life, each feather coruscating and glittering. Time seemed to slow down, the air thick and oily as black butter while we shared some sort of communion. He moved from side to side in front of me, unmistakably taking my measure. I had never had a hummingbird approach me like this before. This was my first Velvet-purple Coronet, and I was in love.

Later that evening, when our small party gathered for dinner and Paul was working through the checklist of birds we had seen that day, I enjoyed some modest bragging rights—for now, I was the only one of the guests to have seen this exquisite hummingbird. So close and intimate, and so longed for was my encounter that I was euphoric, though I did not want to make too big a deal of this—it always feels slightly awkward for a birder to have seen something others have missed. Paul reassured the rest of the group there would almost certainly be Velvet-purple Coronets for all to see the following day.

In the morning after breakfast, I returned to the hummingbird feeding station with two of the group, Pam and John. They both badly wanted to see a Velvet-purple Coronet. The clearing was, however, no longer the hive of activity I had described to them the previous evening. All of the hummingbird feeders had vanished. In the centre of the clearing was a pile of large leaves, beneath which the missing feeders had been concealed. To one side of the clearing, a cut spray of red flowers had been carefully bound to a carbon fibre tripod, surrounded by a battery of further tripods, each surmounted by a flashgun. Two Belgian photographers sat nearby, watching the flower intently in their camera viewfinders, waiting for a hummingbird to visit their carefully staged set. All around us, agitated hummingbirds chattered and buzzed at the fringes of the vegetation. Pam was incensed, "This just isn't right! See how unhappy those hummers are? They just want to feed. They're used to having the feeders!"

I could see her point all too clearly. By providing feeding stations for any wildlife, be it birds or mammals, we create an artificially enriched food source, a place of easy pickings and, with it, some dependency from the wild visitors. The hummingbirds in the bushes all around us sounded distressed, and while no longer able to feed, they were expending energy looking for the missing feeders they knew should be present. I spoke to the photographers.

"Guys, do you mind if we put the feeders back up, please? I think the birds aren't happy . . . it's early in the morning and they want to feed."

One of them ignored me completely; the other looked up from his camera to reply tersely, "Yes, we do mind. We are here to take photos. This place is not just for birdwatchers, it is for us too. You can come back later when we are finished."

Pam, furious, marched wordlessly from the clearing back towards the lodge. A few minutes later one of the staff joined us in the clearing and, tossing the leaves that covered them to one side, she began to hang the feeders back in their usual positions.

"Hey! What are you doing?" demanded the younger of the two photographers. "We're trying to take photos!"

The lodge worker was apologetic, but firm in her reply. "I am sorry, but you cannot take the feeders down. You can take photos here, as much as you like, but you cannot stop the birds feeding while you do it. It is not allowed."

Harsh words followed from the Belgians, directed at the implacable staff member and us alike, while they angrily dismantled their camera gear. They stormed back towards the lodge and, in the calm that followed, dozens of hummingbirds swarmed around the feeders. I was left reflecting upon what had just happened. I had, hitherto, thought that watching and photographing hummingbirds was at heart a benign pastime and, by placing local economic benefit in those birds, had the happy side effect of helping to ensure that the birds were valued by those in the areas we visited, making a case for their habitats to be cherished and preserved. For some, however, it seemed hummingbirds were to this day still a commodity to be consumed and manipulated for their own ends, regardless of the birds' welfare.

CHAPTER SEVEN

MARVELLOUS SPATULETAIL

~

Peru, Bongará. 5° S

*I*F HUMMINGBIRDS WERE ONE OF THE BRIGHTEST STARS IN THE firmament of pre-Columbia oral mythology across the Americas, more contemporary writers held them in high regard too. In *Love in the Time of Cholera*, Gabriel Garcia Marquez's love-stricken heroine, Fermina Daza, returns from her honeymoon in Paris with six trunks stuffed full of vintage clothes, amongst them one filled with ostrich plumes, peacock crests, pheasant skins and, inevitably, hummingbirds.

She is said to be resistant to the changing demands of fashion; her husband, meanwhile, views her purchases with dismay, swearing that they are corpses' clothing. Marquez, writing almost a century after the feather trade in hummingbirds ceased, was aware of their potency and their dark place in the history of murderous millinery.

The writer D. H. Lawrence saw something dark in them too. His poem "Humming-Bird" is amongst my favourites of any genre, my love for hummingbirds notwithstanding, and part of my affection for it stems from Lawrence's refusal to fetishise them as blameless innocents. Describing some ancient, primeval hummingbird, he muses,

> *Probably he was big*
> *As mosses, and little lizards, they say, were once big.*
> *Probably he was a jabbing, terrifying monster.*
> *We look at him through the wrong end of the long telescope*
>   *of time,*
> *Luckily for us.*

Virginia Woolf also used hummingbirds to allude to a more ancient time in her last novel, *Between the Acts*—she wrote of a time when the earth was a riot of flowers from which quivering hummingbirds fed. Imagining the primal hummingbird to be a jabbing, terrifying monster may be something of an exaggeration, but Lawrence is not really so far off the mark. Despite what we might like to project upon nature, it is neither entirely good nor bad, and hummingbirds are, in real life, not the angelic sweet beings some infer them to be. Hummingbirds fight amongst themselves, ferociously, and sometimes to the death.

Alejandro Rico-Guevara, an evolutionary biologist at the University of California, Berkeley, has been studying hummingbirds for years. While the general consensus amongst biologists is that hummingbird bills have evolved, over countless millennia, to shapes that allow them to efficiently extract nectar from particular shapes and sizes of flowers, Rico-Guevara has been paying attention to those tropical species that have weaponised bills—beaks that are straighter and stronger, with sharper tips and even, in some cases, sporting tooth-like serrations.

Using high-speed cameras that recorded, in slow motion, the birds feeding and feuding, Rico-Guevara and his team observed male birds fighting in hitherto unprecedented detail. Feathers flew as they stabbed and bit at one another in midair, or tugged one another away from a cherished nectar source. They damaged or even plucked the feathers from their rivals. It appears as if these birds have accepted an evolutionary trade-off, where the ability to defend a food source and drive off potential sexual rivals is given some priority over simply having the perfect bill for maximising the ability to feed themselves.

Lawrence, however, was not paying such detailed attention to the specifics of hummingbird biology. For him, hummingbirds were metaphors—they represent change and, perhaps, serve as a warning to us—he infers we are fortunate to live in tame times, and his poem reminds us that we have never been the masters of nature, for all we might think we are. We are warned not to be complacent about our place in the world—a message that I feel resonates with increasing clarity with every fresh, horrific revelation about the insults we continue to heap upon the world's wild places and its very atmosphere, and the bitter harvest we are reaping from our actions.

If Lawrence chose to represent hummingbirds as darkly metaphorical, Chilean poet Pablo Neruda was more unabashed in his appreciation of their aesthetic charms. His "Ode to the Hummingbird" is constructed of fragmentary lines, each a considered, polished gem that combines, like the lustrous, scaled feathers of a hummingbird's body, to form the whole.

If I preferred the increasingly topical metaphorical thrust of Lawrence's hummingbird-inspired poetry, I had to admire the richly evocative language of Neruda's work—his poem blazes with precious metals and jewels, fire and the cosmos. Reading "Ode to the Hummingbird," I concluded that Neruda, surely, had seen many hummingbirds by the time he came to write it, and there he had the advantage over Lawrence. Lawrence, abandoning England after the First World War on what he described as his "savage pilgrimage," travelled to the United States and Mexico, and he would have encountered hummingbirds for himself there. Neruda, ranging more widely through South America, would have seen many more species, in many more thrilling colours and forms than Lawrence in the relatively hummingbird-impoverished regions of the USA and Mexico. It was little wonder that Neruda's paean to their kind was so focused upon their appearance.

No poet, surely, no matter how imaginative or in thrall to hummingbirds, could have dreamed of a bird quite as outrageous as one that dwelt in a small area of the Peruvian Andes. Found only in the Rio Utcubamba Valley, some seven hundred kilometres north of Lima, Marvellous Spatuletail has, from the very moment of its discovery, been a mythically rare and sought-after hummingbird, one that collectors and, latterly, birders have yearned to find.

The very first bird, a male, was taken somewhere in the vicinity of Chachapoyas in 1835 by Andrew Mathews, a collector in the employ of George Loddiges. Loddiges was the British nurseryman whose network of collectors throughout the world's tropics supplied the plants that fed the insatiable appetite of Victorians suffering from the affliction known as orchidelerium—a feverish compulsion to amass collections of exotic orchids in the purpose-built, dripping and steaming hothouses of their otherwise cool, temperate homes. Loddiges, we know, had a compulsion too—an obsession with hummingbirds that manifested itself in building a collection of stuffed specimens of as many species as he could gather. That other obsessive Victorian hummingbird collector, author, and entrepreneur John Gould, described himself and Loddiges as imbued with a kindred spirit where these "living gems" were concerned—a bleak accolade, given that the birds they both amassed were long-dead.

Loddiges' small army of orchid collectors in the Americas were under instruction to bring back any hummingbirds they could find. Many of these would have been specimens he was already familiar with, but every now and then one of his collectors would send back something unusual. One wonders what Loddiges would have felt the day he examined the cargo from a boat that had docked at the wharves in the East End of London and, amongst the orchid specimens destined for his market gardens, opened the small package that contained a hummingbird the likes of which he had never seen before. His heart must have raced as he gingerly lifted the small body from the surrounding material to examine it closely.

The bird was clearly a male, judging by the shining turquoise gorget and amethyst crown, and the extravagant tail feathers—and what tail feathers they were! The bird had only four tail feathers in total—two of which were merely long, narrow, and dark blue. The other two feathers were extraordinary. Each was over twice the length of the bird's body, being around twelve centimetres long apiece. The shaft of each was reduced to a thin, flexible spine, at the very end of which was a circular area of midnight-violet feather—the spatule itself. Loddiges would have known, instantly, that this was something very special indeed.

Some years later, in 1840, German botanist Richard Schomburgk visited London and, whilst there, took the opportunity to mingle amongst the natural history society circles of the day. He recalled, "Amongst the many private collections which I had the opportunity of visiting, there was one that particularly engaged the whole of my attention: it was the beautiful, really fairy-like collection of hummingbirds, the property of Loddiges, containing all the species of this interesting family at present known, and considerably richer in them than is the British Museum."

John Audubon, meanwhile, credited Loddiges in his *Birds of America* for providing the male specimens of Anna's Hummingbird from which he produced his painting of the species. He described Loddiges' collection of hummingbirds as "unrivalled." Schomburgk and Audubon were not exaggerating—after all, in 1840, Loddiges' collection contained the one and only known example of Marvellous Spatuletail. None had been found in the years that followed.

Seven years later, in 1847, the spatuletail was formally described by Jules Bourcier, a French naturalist with a particular zeal for hummingbirds. He named many new hummingbird species, several of which rejoiced in scientific names that honoured his daughter,

Francia; to this day, the Andean Emerald *Amazilia franciae* bears her name. Loddiges' unique Peruvian hummingbird was, however, so remarkable that Bourcier chose to include *mirabilis*, or marvellous, in the binomial. For a short while, the bird was known as *Trochilus mirabilis*, or Loddiges' Spatuletail.

Then, in 1850, a nephew of Napoleon Bonaparte imparted further colour to this increasingly kaleidoscopic hummingbird's tale. Prince Charles Lucien Bonaparte, in addition to being a notable taxonomist, shared the family tradition of a keen interest in politics, although his avowed republican stance did not endear him to his cousin, Louis, at the time ruling France as Napoleon III—in 1849 he was summarily exiled from France by Louis for his part in the unsuccessful republican defence of Rome against forty thousand French troops sent there earlier in the year by Louis. In 1850, having spent some time in the United Kingdom, Charles reaffirmed his republican credentials by formally describing the Wilson's Bird-of-Paradise *Cicinnurus respublica* in his *Conspectus generum avium*—a subtle insult that apparently went overlooked by his cousin, for in that year Louis allowed him to return to Paris.

When Charles was not making covert republican digs at his more illustrious cousin in *Conspectus generum avium*, he was turning his considerable taxonomic expertise to making sense of the deluge of new species that were being described from all around the world. The nineteenth century was a glorious time for global exploration and discovery. Of *Trochilus mirabilis*, Loddiges' Spatuletail, Charles decided it was sufficiently different to all other hummingbirds to warrant placing it in a genus all its own—*Loddigesia*, honouring George Loddiges who had, by this time, died at the age of sixty in 1846. His was an untimely death, one that took him before he had the pleasure of seeing the unique hummingbird in his collection immortalise his name, first in the initial English name bestowed upon it and, latterly, in the scientific name *Loddigesia mirabilis*—Loddiges' marvel, the Marvellous Spatuletail.

In the years after the spatuletail's discovery, and before Loddiges' death, for one as increasingly consumed with the zeal for humming-bird collecting as John Gould, not having his own specimen of the spatuletail must have been a bitter pill to swallow. For all Gould states that he and Loddiges were kindred spirits in their love for hummingbirds, the very nature of collecting would suggest that there must have been an element of competition and one-upmanship at play. Gentlemen naturalists would open up their collections for the viewing pleasure of their peers, and for the use of scholars like Audubon—but also for the satisfaction of showing off a little. How satisfying would it be to possess something that few others in the world had seen, and that nobody else possessed?

Gould's feelings about the spatuletail are hinted at, politely, in his monumental hummingbird book, *A Monograph of the Trochilidae, or Family of Humming-Birds*. Writing after Loddiges' death, he laments,

> For more than twenty long years have I been sending the most earnest entreaties, accompanied with drawings, to my correspondents in Peru and Ecuador for additional examples of that truly wonderful bird the *Loddigesia mirabilis*. These entreaties have been backed by the offers of large sums of money to any person who would procure them; but up to the present moment no second example has been obtained.
>
> That it may be a nocturnal bird has sometimes suggested itself to my mind, and that this may be the reason why it has not since been seen.

Gould's yearning for a specimen or two to call his own is clear—he was prepared to pay handsomely for examples for his collection. At one point he was offering, in his desperation, the sum of £50 for a pristine example of the bird—the equivalent, in today's money, of around £7,000. Given that a second example of the Marvellous Spatuletail was not forthcoming until 1880, despite that considerable financial inducement, and given the increasing tempo of collecting in

South America at the time, one comes to the conclusion that, even then, Marvellous Spatuletail was, whilst not nocturnal, simply never a particularly common or widespread species.

The twentieth century was not kind to the Marvellous Spatuletail. Once the initial fervour for exploration and specimen collecting during the previous century had worn off somewhat, South America seemed to be left to its own devices to a certain extent by the world's naturalists. A century of spasmodic political upheaval globally and locally would not have helped matters, insofar as anyone paid much attention to the small area of Peru in which, in time, we came to know the spatuletails were restricted. As the century progressed, economic factors began to impact heavily on the Rio Utcubamba Valley—forested hillsides were cleared to make way for coffee plantations, a habitat within which the spatuletails could not flourish. Marvellous Spatuletails need humid forest edges and botanically diverse scrubby areas in which to feed and breed. Coffee plantations are neither humid forests nor botanically diverse; and nor are marijuana fields, but these were proliferating in the area too.

To make matters worse, anecdotal evidence suggested that a tradition of hunting the male birds using slingshots existed amongst young local men in the area—apart from the sporting challenge this was said to represent, the birds' hearts and tail feathers were considered to be a potent aphrodisiac. Recalling a visit to the local town of Pomacochas in 1999, American birder Richard Garrigues said, "The feathers and heart are dried, then ground into a powder and surreptitiously slipped into the drink of the young woman that the hunter desires. The belief is that, once this is imbibed, the woman will fall in love with the young man."

Garrigues went to the Mercado Modelo in nearby Chiclayo, a market notorious, like the Mercado Sonora in Mexico City, for providing everything witchdoctors might require to practice their dark craft—myriad herbs, whale bones, snake skins, hallucinogenic cacti, and hummingbird hearts. There he asked several stallholders if they could supply him with *el corazón del colibrí mariposa*, or the heart of the butterfly hummingbird—a beautiful synonym by which the Marvellous Spatuletail is locally known. They all knew what he was asking about, and one of them offered him a thumbnail-sized dried heart in a small glass vial. That this local tradition had gone unnoticed by outsiders until comparatively recently suggests that, like the *chuparosas* in Mexico, hummingbirds elsewhere in the Americas may be under hunting pressures to this day that we know nothing about. One does not have to look hard online to find many accounts of hummingbirds being used in Andean traditional medicine— drinking their blood is said to cure epilepsy, heart problems, and *susto*, or shock.

At the same time Garrigues was uncovering this dismal aphrodisiac tradition, BirdLife International continued to regularly update the conservation status of Marvellous Spatuletail for the International Union for Conservation of Nature (IUCN) Red List of Threatened Species. The species charted a miserable downward trajectory, from a status of merely Threatened in 1988, to Vulnerable in 1996, and then to its current status of Endangered in 2000. Beyond that, there is only Critically Endangered left before the IUCN's final status on their scale—Extinct in the Wild.

Endangered is not a good place for a hummingbird to find itself. BirdLife estimates that the entire population of Marvellous Spatuletails numbers between 250 and 999 mature individuals. While hunting may be playing a part in their decline—adult males are said to be outnumbered by females and immature males at a disproportionate ratio of five to one—habitat loss seems to be driving them towards the brink. BirdLife concluded that the species, at the current rates of Amazonian deforestation, will lose over 50 percent of its suitable habitat in the space of three generations which, for Marvellous Spatuletail, equates to a mere twelve years.

This was a hummingbird I badly wanted to see. Which birder would not, given how outlandishly beautiful the birds were said to be? I had seen photos of them, and these had whetted my appetite; and then a BBC documentary aired showing the male birds lekking, displaying to a female. With David Attenborough providing a commentary, I had watched spellbound as a male spatuletail first, from a perch, wafted his preposterous tail feathers around himself, encircling his body with a halo of his own manufacture; and then, having taken to the air to hover in front of his prospective mate, curved his long spatule-feathers to frame his body within a lyre shape, dipping and rearing his head enticingly at the female, allowing his iridescent turquoise gorget and violet crown to shimmer and blaze to their full effect. Dancing in a theatre of lichen-encrusted branches, his was a performance that not only endeared him to a mate—he stole my heart too.

If I was honest with myself, there was also a selfish element of wanting to see a Marvellous Spatuletail in case they subsequently became extinct. Whilst I knew that efforts were being made on the ground in the Rio Utcubamba to support local landowners to preserve remaining habitat for the hummingbirds, and to restore degraded habitat to make it suitable for the birds once more, I feared for their future. I had seen and heard so little on my travels to date that gave me confidence that such piecemeal efforts, while welcome, could do more than delay the inevitable decline of such a localised and imperilled bird. I thought ruefully of the pressures faced by the Blue-bearded Helmetcrests and Dusky Starfrontlets in Colombia, and the Black-breasted Pufflegs in Ecuador, and found few straws of comfort to clutch.

While this was preying on my mind when my plane touched down in Tarapoto in the north of Peru, my overwhelming emotion was a sense of keen anticipation. As the plane doors were flung open, a wave of hot, humid air rolled through the interior, rich with the scent of aviation fuel and promise. Somewhere out there, in the hills far beyond the waving palm trees that fringed the shimmering runway, were my Marvellous Spatuletails. What lay between us were some days in the company of local birder Henry Gonzales Pinedo and our driver, Victor, crisscrossing the lush forests that blanketed the area, searching for other less rare but nonetheless wonderful hummingbirds.

The drive out of Tarapoto, in the late afternoon, to our lodgings for the night at the Pumarinri Lodge perched high on the banks above the fast-flowing, chocolate-brown Huallaga River, was a short but slow journey. Heavy rain had preceded my arrival, and the road was badly affected by landslides. Every few miles we came across vast mounds of red earth and boulders larger than cars laid slumped across the tarmac, the earth on the road churned to calf-deep liquid mud through which our minibus surged while the local *trimovils*, or mototaxis, picked a more cautious path. These three-wheeled motor-bikes—with a small, covered seating area sufficient for three passengers comfortably or, in some cases, many more crammed together in a jumble of limbs and luggage—were ubiquitous on Peru's roads. Passing in a haze of blue exhaust fumes, all were brightly painted in primary colours, and many had been pimped by their owners to reflect their personalities and tastes. Some bore graphics that declared an appreciation of heavy metal music, Che Guevara, or improbably busty bikini-clad women. A very few appeared to suggest an interest in the area's birdlife, with paintings of tanagers and parrots on the canopies that shielded their passengers from the worst of the elements.

Nearing Pumarinri, we came to the village of Shapaja. Here, the mototaxis pulled to the side of the road to allow their passengers to buy food from roadside cafés, which they ate sitting in the back of the vehicles, the mototaxis crammed tightly together allowing animated conversations to spill three or four mototaxis deep along the road. We wove our way through the village, Victor carefully avoiding large sheets of tarpaulin spread on the tarmac, each covered in a thin layer of garnet-red coffee cherries spread out to dry in the sun.

Leaving Shapaja as the light began to bleed from the sky, we paused beside the river to watch Hoatzins coming to roost in the trees that overhung the eddying water. These large, bronze-winged and punk-crested primitive birds are famous for having chicks that bear claws on their wings—a bridge to an ancient time when the boundaries between birds and the dinosaurs that begat them were more blurred and indistinct. With night falling rapidly, in the humid half-light it was easy to imagine myself in another more innocent world, a place in which humankind was still just a nervous glimmer in the eyes of those early small mammals that crept furtively in the undergrowth.

I wondered about the early evolution of hummingbirds, the point at which hovering became technically feasible, when those astonishing metallic feathers began to bloom on their bodies, the journey that led some species to develop outlandish, exaggerated tails and crests. While I asked myself the question of when, the hummingbirds' ancestral story was more a case of where.

The Hoatzins, shuffling awkwardly through the treetops before me, are only found in South America—a range only a little more restricted than that of all the hummingbirds, found throughout the Americas yet nowhere else in the world. Fossils of both, however, have been found in Europe. Gerald Mayr, a palaeontologist at the Senckenberg Research Institute in Germany, found himself confronted in 2004 by two fossilised birds found in Frauenweiler, a village in southern Germany. The birds were small—just four centimetres long—with bills two and a half times the length of their skulls, and wing bones that looked just like the short, stocky humerus typical of modern-day hummingbirds.

Mayr knew just what they were—these birds, some thirty million years old, were D. H. Lawrence's "jabbing, terrifying monsters"— they were hummingbirds. Recognising them did not diminish the unexpected nature of their discovery, a shock that Mayr reflected in the scientific name he gave them, *Eurotrochilus inexpectatus*, or unexpected European hummingbird. The surprise lay not only in their location, an ocean away from the only other fossilised hummingbirds that had, to date, been found in South America—more surprising still was the age of the fossils, for those South American hummingbird fossils were relative youngsters, dating to just one million years ago. In the years that followed, further hummingbird fossils were unearthed in Germany, Poland, and France. In the meantime, the hummingbird history books were being rewritten.

Tens of millions of years ago, primal hummingbirds darted and hovered through the forests and hills of Europe. At some point, they made the long journey to the Americas. How, and when that journey was made, we don't know. Presumably they made the journey across the land bridge that formerly existed between Siberia and Alaska—it seems unfeasible that those first pioneering hummingbirds could have flown across the Atlantic. It felt fitting to me now that my hummingbird story had begun in Alaska, as surely that was where our modern-day hummingbirds' story began too, when they left their European ancestors behind them to make a new life in the new world.

My journey continued the following morning, leaving Pumarinri while it was still dark. Our target, once daylight broke, would be a hummingbird that celebrated a German ornithologist, Maria Koepcke, who, prior to her tragic death in the infamous LANSA Flight 508 aircraft crash in Amazonia on Christmas Eve in 1971, had contributed so much to our understanding of Peru's birdlife that she had become known as the "Mother of Peruvian Ornithology." She was unusual, at the time, for her success and hard-earned reputation in a field of science that was largely dominated by men. Her death, at just forty-seven years of age, robbed South American ornithology of one of its brightest stars.

Her teenage daughter, Julianne, was the sole survivor of the plane crash that stole the life of her mother and those of ninety other passengers and crew—struck by lightning, the plane caught fire and, in violent turbulence, came apart midair. Julianne, still strapped into her seat, fell some ten thousand feet into the dense jungle below. Nine days later, having followed a stream through the jungle, she was finally found by local woodcutters and brought by canoe to safety, nursing a broken collarbone, a badly wounded arm, an eye injury, concussion, and innumerable insect larvae infesting her body.

The woodcutters poured petrol on her skin to address the latter—she later recalled that she alone removed thirty maggots, and was very proud of herself. Her remarkable tale of survival was made into a documentary, *Wings of Hope*, by Werner Herzog—the filmmaker was in Peru in late December 1971, and was also meant to be on Flight 508 but, at the very last minute, cancelled his reservation.

Fate had intervened for him and, while Julianne had fallen from the skies, Herzog fell hard for the forests of Peru. In 1971 he was there scouting locations for *Aguirre, the Wrath of God*. *Fitzcarraldo*, a film about obsession, which involved, without the benefit of computer-generated special effects, the transportation of a three-hundred-tonne ship over a mountain, was also shot in Peru. Herzog's screenplays for both films feature hummingbirds—clouds of them whir into flight through dense clouds of Amazonian steam, hover above treetops, and dive towards his protagonists from roiling fog. Herzog plainly has some affection for their ability to anchor a scene in the South American present he wishes to portray. Herzog's unique approach to filmmaking is, perhaps, typified by *Into the Abyss*, an investigation of a triple murder and its consequences. Who else but Herzog would make a death row documentary that opens with a chaplain relating an anecdote about squirrels to illustrate the fragility of life, and closes with a former death row prison officer talking about hummingbirds? Fred Allen, captain of the "Death House Team" that executed Karla Faye Tucker in 1998, the first woman to be executed in Texas since Chipita Rodriguez in 1863, asks what Herzog would later go on to describe as the ultimate question. Allen sounds almost pensive as he reflects upon what he did, and looks towards the future—he says he's going to watch the hummingbirds, and he wonders why there are so many of them. And his voice trails off.

There, again in Herzog's oeuvre, we find hummingbirds.

Back in Peru, I was anxious to see the hummingbird that bore Maria Koepcke's name. Koepcke's Hermit is something of a debutante in the world of hummingbirds, having only been discovered as lately as 1977. It is shy and unobtrusive, as so many of the hermit tribe typically are, and is to be found only in a narrow corridor that runs along the eastern foothills of the Peruvian Andes. Having devoted her working life to Peru's birds, Maria Koepcke would surely have felt honoured had she known her contribution to science would live for perpetuity in association with this hermit.

A narrow, muddy path led uphill from the wooden roadside gates that announced we had arrived at the Aconabikh Koepcke's Hermit reserve. Persistent rain fell and dripped heavily from the leaves we brushed our way past. A covered wooden viewing platform in a small clearing was a welcome sight, not least when I realised that the clearing in question had a series of hummingbird feeders hung around the margins. While the rain continued to fall heavily, there was not a lot of activity at the feeders. A young boy, wearing a Barcelona football shirt and a bored expression on his face, sat playing idly with a machete almost as tall as himself. He visibly brightened at our arrival, and launched into a flood of questions about what brought us to Aconabikh. I fielded them easily enough, skirting around the more obvious question that hung, unsaid, in the waterlogged air—why was such a young boy armed with such a lethal machete?

The rain stopped and, without a word, the feeders' custodian set off into the trees, heading uphill, machete resting casually on his shoulder. His departure coincided with the arrival of a swarm of hummingbirds—suddenly, the feeders were a flurry of activity as birds that had sat, hungrily, in the sheltering vegetation during the deluge seized their opportunity to refuel. Chief amongst them were Golden-tailed Sapphires, hummingbirds that looked as if they had been dipped in rainbows. Their crowns were deep indigo blue, fading into turquoise on the napes of their necks; this merged into the emerald green of their backs, and that gave way in turn to a golden yellow rump that blazed, on their tails, into deep rich copper. Mirroring their plumage, sunshine replaced the recent rain and set myriad small rainbows glancing off the steaming leaves at the clearing's edge. The moment, suddenly, had a filmic, magical quality worthy of Herzog.

Gould's Jewelfronts, so elusive in Ecuador, proved to be common-place here, allowing better opportunities to appreciate them than I had enjoyed hitherto. While renowned for their beauty, they could not, I felt, hold a candle to the glorious sapphires that swirled pris-matically around us. I was lost to them, barely sparing a glance for the other hummingbirds that came and went—Fork-tailed Wood-nymphs and White-necked Jacobins did their best to catch my at-tention, but to no avail. Henry, however, broke the spell.

"There! The Koepcke's!"

He was pointing at the far side of the clearing where, hovering at a partially concealed feeder, I could see the unmistakeable elongated, elegant leaf-litter-brown form of a hermit, all tapering tail and long, slender bill. The bird fed, fleetingly, and then dived back into deep cover, threading its way through the surrounding vegetation with needle-like precision. I could not, in all honesty, have said that this was definitely a Koepcke's—the moment had been too transitory, too ephemeral for that. I had barely had time to register the bird's pres-ence, let alone lift my binoculars to appreciate any field marks that distinguished it from any other hermit. Nevertheless, the familiar euphoria was bubbling under the surface. This had happened so soon after our arrival, and surely that augured well.

The hours that followed were, for anyone familiar with the ways of hermits, entirely typical. The bird returned, regularly, to feed from the hummingbird feeders and also the surrounding spires of frosted pink and white *Etlingera* torch ginger flowers. Each visit was over almost as soon as it began, a smash-and-grab nectar raid. I soon gave up trying to take a satisfactory photo of a Koepcke's Hermit—the technical frustration of framing and focusing on such a slippery hummingbird was getting in the way of simply appreciating the bird for what it was—a subtle confection of cinnamon and bronze, with snow-white counterpoints around the eyes and in the two elongated central tail feathers.

The days that followed settled into a familiar rhythm as we worked our way slowly towards the fabled Marvellous Spatuletail

Reserve at Huembo Lodge. We would start early in the morning, before first light, with the implacable Victor loading our gear into the minibus before we set off through the Peruvian forests towards a new site for the coming day, each day being marked by the finding of yet another totemic, remarkable hummingbird. I lost myself to the spiky, orange headdresses of Rufous-crested Coquettes; the sombre, midnight-blue majesty of Royal Sunangels; and many more hermits too. Great-billed, Black-throated, White-bearded, Green and Reddish hermits came and went, but none came close to the enigmatic Koepcke's in my affections.

I also came to learn more about my Peruvian companions. Henry, I judged, was a few years younger than me, Victor a little younger still. One day, over lunch, I asked Henry what it was like growing up here in Peru. Had he always been interested in birds? My hobby had been viewed with deep suspicion and scorn by my peers at school, and I wondered what Henry's experience had been like in a country with even less historic interest in natural history. He paused before answering, chewing for a little while, gathering his thoughts.

"I grew up near Tarapoto. It was impossible to go into the country at the time to look for birds. The Sendero Luminoso ruled our lives in those days."

The Sendero Luminoso, or Shining Path, are a revolutionary Communist organisation that, from 1980 onwards, waged a sporadic and brutal guerrilla war against the Peruvian government. During the 1980s and 1990s the organisation was at the zenith of its power, and accounted for over thirty-five thousand deaths in the country. Shaking his head for emphasis, Henry continued, "They used to fight with the army, and with other rebels too. At home, we could hear the AK47s chattering nearby. *Tok-tok-tok!* My family, we used to lie on the ground underneath our beds while the gunshots were audible."

I had not expected the conversation to take this turn. I felt a little foolish to have thought that Henry's fledgling interest in birds might have been difficult to nurture due to the disapproval of his peers when, in fact, he was growing up in one of the most troubled times in Peru's recent history. I apologised for having been so ignorant of the realities of his everyday life at the time, and joked feebly that this made my childhood bullying episodes seem rather tame. Henry looked at Victor, and they both burst into laughter.

"Ay, Jon! You don't know how lucky you were," Henry said. "On Sundays, the Sendero Luminoso would execute people in the street outside our house. They would line up the men accused of being involved with drugs or robberies. And they would shoot them, in the back of the neck, one by one."

Henry mimed how this was done, holding two fingers to the nape of his neck, his hand bouncing away with the recoil of the shot.

"They did that on Sundays. They'd leave the bodies in the road, so the kids would walk past them on their way to school on Monday morning."

The conversation petered out, none of us sure what to say. Victor broke the awkward silence. "It's much better now though. There's been no fighting for years. At least, not around here. There are still some places in the country it's better not to go to . . . Sometimes we meet birders from overseas, and they say they're going to explore Peru on their own. They've hired a car, and they'd like to see what they can find for themselves.

"Mostly, that's okay. But there are some places we wouldn't go, us Peruvians, so when a foreigner goes there, they can get into trouble. A lot of trouble. There's still a lot of problems with drugs in some areas. A foreign birder, looking at a map—they can't know where's safe and where's dangerous."

Henry's sobering account of growing up as a fledgling birder in Peru under the Sendero Luminoso, and Victor's more contemporary warning of the present dangers in parts of the country, were chilling, to say the least. The Shining Path was infamous amongst birders for the murder of two British birders, in Peru for the birding trip of a lifetime in 1990. Mike Entwistle and Tim Andrews had, apparently, failed to appreciate the value of local advice not to travel into a particular area of the mountains. While neither man's body was ever recovered, we understand that they were surprised by a group of Shining Path guerrillas, who attempted to lead them away at gunpoint. One of the pair tried to run from their captors and was gunned down in cold blood. The remaining birder was then encouraged to confess to being either a Central Intelligence Agency (CIA) or Drug Enforcement Agency (DEA) agent. Presumably, as had been the case when my friend Diego Calderón was seized by FARC guerrillas in Colombia, the pair's notebooks and maps would have heightened the rebels' suspicion about their activities in the area. Diego was fortunate to have been released. The surviving Briton back then in Peru was, at some point, summarily executed.

Shortly after we had finished eating, with our conversation haunting me, I received an urgent and immediate warning all of my own from Henry. Wandering around the outbuildings of a small farm, looking for White-bearded Hermits in the surrounding waterlogged swamps, I found myself approached by an animal the size and heft of a modest badger, its coat predominantly a glossy black with a fetching ginger bib. Having noticed me, it walked confidently towards me from across the farmyard, hissing loudly to itself like an unhappy tyre deflating, peeling back its long prehensile snout to reveal a set of sharp white teeth. Henry was quick to react.

"Jon! Be careful! They can be dangerous!"

This, it transpired, was my first coatimundi, a territorial, semidomesticated animal that was displeased to find me near to its home. Henry proceeded to explain that in rural Peru they are often kept as pets.

"My first pet was a coati. My mother got it for me, when it was young. They can be good pets, very affectionate with the people they know. But they are very bad for the environment, they eat anything they can find."

Leaving the coati in peace, we got back in the minibus to keep travelling towards my Marvellous Spatuletail, still a day's drive away from us through the mountains. I had plenty to think about to keep me occupied in the meantime, but found myself returning time and again to reflect upon Henry's childhood. I could not stop wondering how confused and scared that long-ago coati and his young owner would have been when the gunshots rang out within earshot of their home.

The following afternoon we drove into the centre of the small rural town of Florida Pomacochas. The town square announced that we were in spatuletail country now, with a small concrete relief work of a male bird at the roadside. It was encouraging to see this reflection of civic hummingbird pride. Nikki Waldron, a researcher for the BBC when they filmed the spatuletail's courtship display nearby for the first time in 2009, recalled, "It's a poor area. The kids, instead of playing with Nintendos, they'd shoot hummingbirds with catapults. But now they've realised they can make a bit of money from tourists, it's completely changed the culture. If any of the kids get caught with a slingshot they get teased by the other kids."

I hoped that this cultural shift had continued to this day, despite what I had heard about the birds still being hunted for their hearts and tail feathers. The local fortunes of the bird were, perhaps, beginning to change for the better. One local man has led the charge in this regard—Santos Montenegro. In 2000, he noticed a group of four foreign birders in the countryside near the town and, curious about what they were doing, introduced himself and asked what they were looking for. One of them showed Montenegro an illustration of a Marvellous Spatuletail and explained they had been looking for this mythical hummingbird in the area for the past five days.

Montenegro shrugged. He told them, to their surprise, that at his *chacra*, or farm, there were plenty of Marvellous Spatuletails. When, the following day, they accompanied Montenegro to his chacra, they found he was not exaggerating—the birds were there, and readily photographed. They gave him 200 soles—around $50—for his trouble.

Montenegro was astonished. He had, hitherto, no idea that a hummingbird could be worth that much money to a birder. The encounter completely changed his way of looking at birds—he started birding, just for the sake of learning more about the birds he'd previously paid scant attention to. In no time, he came to enjoy a reputation as the man with the key to the Marvellous Spatuletail—while he was now looking for birds, birders now came looking for him.

Montenegro's life came to be defined by the Marvellous Spatuletail. Visiting birders gave him a pair of old binoculars and a bird book, and it was he who showed the BBC film crew where to see the lekking male birds that had so entranced me in the documentary. He is now highly sought-after as a bird guide for visiting birders and film crews alike, and works for Asociacion Ecosistemas Andinos (ECOAN), a Peruvian not-for-profit nongovernmental organization (NGO) dedicated to the conservation of endangered species and threatened Andean ecosystems. ECOAN works with local communities to protect the habitat of those endangered species, with the objective of improving the use and exploitation of natural resources, and of restoring degraded areas.

One such area is the grounds of the Huembo Lodge, set in the mountains at seven thousand feet, a little way outside of Pomacochas. The land is owned by the local community and managed for conservation in partnership with ECOAN. With the support of the American Birding Association, ECOAN have set about restoring a formerly heavily farmed area of a little over one hundred acres, planting trees and improving the habitat for all birds, but particularly with the Marvellous Spatuletail in mind. Santos Montenegro, the former farmer turned conservationist, is the manager of the Huembo Lodge, and it was here that I hoped to see my Marvellous Spatuletail.

I had worked hard for some of the hummingbirds I had encountered to date, but Marvellous Spatuletail was a joyous exception. Not for me the frustration the species had induced in poor John Gould. A narrow path led along the contour of the steep hillside away from the bluff on which the Huembo Lodge itself was set and, in a tiny sheltered clearing minutes away from the lodge, a small hummingbird feeding station had been established. The clearing was buzzing with

Sparkling Violetears, a bold and confident hummingbird clad head to toe in metallic grass-green and cerulean-blue feathers as glossy as fish scales. They seethed around the feeders, occasionally confronting one another with their blue ear coverts extended in a threatening display. They guarded the feeders zealously, driving away other hummingbirds that dared to visit—I had brief glimpses of Long-tailed Sylphs, Bronzy Incas, White-bellied Hummingbirds, and Andean Emeralds, and then . . . something different flew across the clearing. That first glimpse was over before it began, an encounter insufficient to say whether I had seen a bird or an insect—something that might have been a dragonfly, it was so small and slender compared to the other hummingbirds. A moment later, it was back, and now perched on a thin branch a few feet away from me, hidden from the zealous violetears, but wonderfully framed for me.

A searing bolt of turquoise, the colour of Caribbean water over white coral sand, shone from its throat above a tiny white body bisected by an inky-black stripe. Beneath him hung two midnight-purple discs, seeming unattached from the bird itself, so thin were the filaments of feather spine that supported them. He sat, looking curiously at the other hummingbirds in flight across the clearing, his crown giving searing shafts of violet as the light caught the feathers at just the right angle. This was what the female birds saw when he displayed to them, these arresting blazes of blue and purple. His tail feathers shivered, and then he was in flight, a delicate arrow that threaded his way through the crowds to a feeder where he hovered, tremulously, and fed for an instant before vanishing high over the canopy of the surrounding trees.

The entire encounter was over in a matter of minutes. I took a deep breath. I was shaking, and I found my jaw was hanging open—hitherto, I had always assumed that this was just a figure of speech, but here on a remote Peruvian hillside I discovered for myself that one bird, at least, was literally as well as figuratively jaw-dropping.

Some ten minutes later, he was back again, and for the remaining hours of the day followed the same pattern. More often than not, he would be driven away from the feeders by the Sparkling Violetears. Henry, sitting beside me whilst I watched the spatuletail, told me about the early days of the Huembo Reserve.

"When the feeders went up, and the hummingbirds came to know they were here, one of the local men noticed that the violetears kept chasing away the spatuletail. Some years ago he caught all of the violetears, and let them go ten miles away. He was sick of the violetears chasing off the spatuletail whenever it tried to feed, and he wanted to provide the visitors with better views of the bird they had come all this way to see."

Henry paused for comic effect.

"But they came back, in just two months' time, and they brought friends with them! Now there are more of them than ever before."

That evening, the lodge's power having been turned off for the night, I lay in my bed in the dark under a heavy blanket and listened to the sound of rain drumming on the roof above me and hurrying down the gutters outside. I felt overwhelmed with happiness, a joy so pure and unadulterated it caught me by surprise. I wondered when I had last had that feeling. Perhaps as a child at my grandmother's farmhouse in Cornwall, on the first day of my summer holiday there. I had the Marvellous Spatuletail to thank for recapturing that memory and sensation.

The following morning I took myself back to the clearing at dawn, and for the first hours of the day had the hummingbirds all to myself. The male spatuletail returned shortly after the sun had risen and, after an initial bout of feeding, settled himself within the dense vegetation nearby, sitting motionless there for half an hour. I wondered what he was waiting for—a female, perhaps, or the presence of a rival—but then he was gone again as unobtrusively as he had come in the first watery-green light of daybreak. He left, in his wake, a potent mix of elation and melancholy. Of all the hummingbirds I had seen, none had seemed as fragile and delicate as he. ECOAN's work in the area was admirable, and there seemed to be local pride in the rare hummingbird in their midst that drew birders from all around the world to visit the region, but I had that familiar nagging fear that, on the whole, an endangered hummingbird's fortunes rested on a knife-edge, and were being weighed against the competing economic pressures of mankind. Were the ecotourism to dry up, what would happen to the Marvellous Spatuletail and the habitat upon which it depended?

Later that morning, Henry took us back into Pomacochas and, after we had navigated the rutted backstreets, up into the foothills behind the town. We trailed behind us a barking comet tail of maddened, deliriously excited street dogs, apparently unused to motor vehicles heading up this dead-end track. Henry leaned out of his window, swearing at them and exhorting them to go home, while Victor made the minibus swoop and dive like a drunken swallow, swerving to avoid them as they darted to bite the tyres, apparently timing his manoeuvres to the beat of the omnipresent music that played on the stereo. Victor seemed to be fond of disco, so our dog dance was performed to the strains of the Spanish disco classic, "Yes Sir, I Can Boogie." Looking in the rearview mirror, I caught Victor smiling to himself as he flung us rhythmically back and forth across the track, confirming my suspicions.

We were met at the end of the track by a taciturn farmer who, with the merest of pleasantries, led us through a series of rough grassy fields to a small ridge that overlooked the pastures. Here, on a short length of hedgerow that also held a tethered brown cow, he had hung a number of homemade hummingbird drinkers, made from plastic bottles. Amongst them was a pair of proprietary feeders.

"I gave him those," Henry said, indicating them. "I'm trying to encourage him to diversify his farm. He knows that people come to the area to see the spatuletails, so if he starts to earn some money from people visiting his land, maybe he will plant some more trees, return some of the land to how it used to be."

The farmer tended to the feeders, removing each one in turn from the hedgerow, and bringing it up onto the ridge where, squatting beside us on the bare earth, he enclosed the feeder in a black plastic bag, scraping off the wild bees that swarmed across their surfaces. Removing the feeder, he then crushed the bees inside the bag. Feeders cleaned, he refilled them with sugar water and hung them back in the trees. For the remainder of our stay he sat silently beside us, waiting for bees to come to a tub of sugar water between his feet, seizing them between thumb and forefinger and popping them. I felt badly conflicted, wanting to encourage his hummingbird tourism initiative but wishing he would not kill the peripheral wildlife so overtly.

We stood there for a while, the grassy tang of cow dung heavy in the humid air. The feeders were a pale shadow of those at Huembo, with barely any activity—just a handful of Chestnut-breasted Coronets and some White-bellied Hummingbirds. I sensed that we were there as much to support the farmer's initiative as to realistically hope to see any more spatuletails.

Later, driving away from Pomacochas, we stopped at a more successful example of local enterprise. A roadside petrol station and shop, with swathes of green bananas heaped outside the doors, seemed like an unlikely place at which to find another hummingbird I had longed to see for years, but thanks to the owner's teenage son this had become the most reliable place in the area to see White-tipped Sicklebills.

Sicklebills are similar to hermits, insofar as they are shy and skulking plainly marked hummingbirds that eschew brilliant, bejewelled plumage in favour of streaky shades of olive green and bronze. There the similarities end, for sicklebills have a bill that, as their name suggests, is so abruptly curved as to appear almost deformed. That bill is, of course, no mere ornamentation—evolution has equipped the birds with a beak that fits, exactly, into the acutely curved structure of a heliconia flower. Heliconias are found throughout the tropical Americas, their waxy red and yellow bracts and flowers hanging in heavy, pendulous strings from beneath an overarching canopy of long, banana-like leaves. Those flowers hold ample reserves of nectar, but are so deep and structurally complex that they exclude all but the most determined and most adaptable pollinators. Some humming-birds fit the bill, so to speak, and none better than sicklebills.

The garage owner's son had planted an extensive grove of heli-conias on a terrace carved from the hillside overlooking the road, and had invested in some plastic chairs for his paying guests. What brings those guests are the sicklebills—presumably delighted to have found such an ample source of nectar, for heliconias are often found sparingly scattered through the jungle in the wild. The approved method for seeing a sicklebill is usually to find a heliconia in the wild and wait, hoping that it is on a sicklebill's trapline and will, eventually, be paid a visit by the bird in question. That may be the approved method, but in Costa Rica, Colombia, and Ecuador it had never worked for me. Neither of the sicklebill species, Buff-tailed or White-tipped, are particularly rare, but personally they had both come to assume a mythical, chimaera quality, a simultaneously gro-tesque and compelling wraith that existed only in the pages of my field guides.

There was a sense of some anticlimax when, within minutes of settling down inside the heliconia grove, a White-tipped Sicklebill ap-peared and promptly landed on the flowers of a plant before us. Un-like the Green Hermits that also attended the heliconias, it preferred not to hover and, instead, clung to the brightly coloured bracts of the flowers, burying its bill deep inside the plant, its forehead dusted with lemony-yellow pollen. With the best will in the world, it was no beauty, or at least not in the conventional hummingbird sense. I was, however, enchanted by it—I loved the dramatic presentation of coevolution before me, a hummingbird and a plant that had, over aeons, come to fit one another like lock and key.

If coevolution could explain the unique shape of a sicklebill's beak, my final Peruvian hummingbird encounter was to be with a bird that defies, to this day, any unequivocal explanation. Some four hundred kilometres south of Lima, on the floor of the high, arid Nazca Des-ert, are to be found a remarkable array of hundreds of geoglyphs—enormous figurative representations, hundreds of square metres in size, of animals, birds, plants, and humanlike figures. What is known about them is vastly outweighed by what we do not know. Archaeologists estimate they were made in the period between 500 BC and AD 500, and were created by removing the ochre iron-oxide–coated pebbles and gravel that lie liberally scattered across the desert surface, exposing a contrasting pale-white clay soil beneath. That soil contains high amounts of lime that, over time, has reacted with airborne moisture to form a hard, protective crust on the exposed soil, preventing erosion and degradation of the figures.

This much seems fairly clear. Harder to explain is why the figures were created in the first instance by the Nazca people—not least because most of the geoglyphs are only fully visible from the air and, hence, would have gone unseen in their full glory by their makers. What purpose did the lines have? Theories have abounded that they are religious symbols, astronomical calendars, irrigation systems, or even, in the wild claims of Swiss author Erich von Daniken in his popular 1968 book *Chariots of the Gods?*, airfields for flying saucers built on the instructions of ancient extraterrestrial beings.

Quite why ancient aliens would have wanted to land on immense representations of a spider, a llama, a Jaguar, a monkey, or a hummingbird, amongst other creatures, was never made entirely clear by von Daniken. Nonetheless, in the absence of any compelling evidence in favour of any of the other theories to explain the Nazca Lines, we're left with an enduring mystery about which von Daniken, and his supporters, still expound their version of events to this day.

When I set out to see the most dramatic of the hummingbirds in the Americas, I knew that Giant Hummingbird would not be the largest example of their kind I would encounter. To see the largest hummingbird in the world, I would need to travel to the town of Nazca and take to the skies in a light aircraft, to fly over the Nazca Lines and look down upon the most famous hummingbird of all. Alongside the Mono, a monkey geoglyph sporting a magnificently spiral tail, the Colibrí or hummingbird is arguably the most iconic of all the Nazca figures. Almost one hundred metres long, the geoglyph depicts a long-billed hummingbird in flight, wings outstretched and tail spread behind it.

The figure's prominence was surely the reason that it acted as the lodestone for an act of hummingbird iconoclasm. In December 2014 Greenpeace activists walked into the desert and laid down large banners on the desert floor beneath the hummingbird. The message the banners carried was "Time for Change! The future is renewable"—a laudable sentiment, but one that unfortunately involved permanent damage to the delicate desert floor in the telling. One of the Greenpeace activists involved, a German archaeologist named Wolfgang Sadik, who should surely have known better, was given a suspended prison sentence and fined 650,000 soles (around $180,000) for his involvement in the desecration of what was, by this point, a UN World Heritage Site.

Until recently the hummingbird was usually referred to as just that, a generic hummingbird. In 2019 a team of Japanese researchers compared all of the Nazca bird geoglyphs to more than two thousand scientific drawings of Peru's native birds. Masaki Eda of the Hokkaido University Museum said, "Until now, the bird [geoglyphs] have been identified based on general impressions or a few morphological traits present in each figure. We closely noted the shapes and relative sizes of the birds' beaks, heads, necks, bodies, wings, tails and feet and compared them with those of modern birds in Peru."

In the case of the hummingbird, Eda and his colleagues decided that, on the basis of its long, thin beak and elongated tail feathers, the figure in question best matched the morphology of a hermit. With this new perspective in mind, I was looking forward to seeing the hummingbird for myself but, as we walked across the tarmac at the Nazca aerodrome towards the light aircraft that was to carry us over the desert, my unspoken thoughts echoed those of two Japanese tourists walking beside me, who asked our Peruvian pilot, "Is that it? The plane is very small . . ."

The plane in question was indeed very small. I am used to light aircraft, as these serve some of the outer islands in Shetland, and

I have taken many short flights over the sea to Fair Isle in rugged Britten Norman Islander planes. The plane in front of us was distinctly smaller, and decidedly flimsier. Once on board we quickly dispensed with safety announcements by the simple expedient of not having any, and without any further delay were hurtling down the short, bumpy runway and into the sky. We were barely airborne before the terse announcement came through our headsets, breaking through the loud engine roar: "*Ballena*. On the left . . . now. And on the right . . . now."

The plane dipped first one wing, and then the other, banking steeply to allow passengers on both sides to look straight down at the Ballena, or whale. To my astonishment, I found myself staring at a recognisable bull Killer Whale in the middle of the desert floor, the prominent vertical dorsal fin completely unmistakeable. This increased my puzzlement about the origins and meanings of the Nazca Lines still further—the ancient architects of the geoglyphs might have been familiar with hummingbirds or monkeys in the relatively near proximity of their settlements, but a Killer Whale? To have known what one of those marine predators looked like, someone had to have carried that knowledge inland from the ocean.

The plane continued to weave an erratic course over the figures, darting to and fro in parabolic loops, banking over each figure first one way, and then the next. With the morning sun beating on the Perspex windows of the plane, the air inside grew hot and stuffy. The excited chatter from my Japanese co-passengers grew more subdued and sporadic, and then stopped altogether. I was aware that one of them was gagging, trying her very best not to be sick. I concentrated on the geoglyphs below us and, in between them, the faraway horizon.

"*Perro . . . Mono . . . Colibrí . . .*"

The names were announced one after another. Dog . . . Monkey . . . Hummingbird . . . as abruptly as a real hummingbird appearing at a flower, suddenly there below us on the dry desert floor was the famous Nazca hummingbird. Already imbued with the unexpected strength of feelings the Marvellous Spatuletail had engendered within me, seeing this immense ancient representation of a hummingbird felt surprisingly emotional. I certainly could not decipher what the figure's purpose was, but the fact that centuries ago the native people of the Nazca Desert had felt a hummingbird had sufficient significance to warrant the creation of this immense representation of it felt . . . significant in itself.

Seeing the hummingbird with my own eyes, I could not bring myself to agree with Masaki Eda and his colleagues. The bird's bill seemed way too long for any hermit but just right for a Sword-billed Hummingbird, the likes of which I had seen in Colombia, Ecuador, and here in Peru. Like every theory to date concerning the Nazca Lines, and reflecting some parallels in the murky world of avian taxonomy, there was no consensus to be found here in the desert.

The following morning, with the memory of my flight over the largest hummingbird artwork in the world fresh in my mind, and its image inked indelibly between my shoulder blades, I climbed on board a bus for the long, slow journey back to Lima and my onward flight to new hummingbird stories. To read on the journey I carried a worn copy of *Mama Amazonica*, a collection by contemporary poet Pascale Petit that I had returned to time and again on my journey through South America. I fell asleep as the bus hauled a ponderous path across the shimmering desert, leaving the earthbound Nazca hummingbird anchored behind me, Petit's hummingbird verses floating on the edge of consciousness.

> *Let my mother's dryads and sylphs,*
> *hermits and Incas, her sapphires,*
> *her ruby-topaz moustiques,*
> *practice flying again . . .*

CHAPTER EIGHT

CHASING COQUETTES

~

Brazil, São Paulo. 23° S
Bolivia, Santa Cruz. 17° S

*T*HE GREAT EXPLORER OF SOUTH AMERICA, ALEXANDER VON Humboldt, was from an early age marked out for a career in politics—his mother, Maria Elisabeth, had high hopes for both him and his elder brother, Wilhelm, hiring the very best tutors to educate the young men. With hindsight, her choices in this regard may have been counterproductive, as one of those tutors, Carl Ludwig Willdenow, became one of the great German botanists of the Enlightenment. Given young Alexander's propensity for collecting shells, plants, and insects—a predilection that gave him the affectionate boyhood nickname "the little apothecary"—a career as a naturalist was always a distinct possibility given the tutelage he received.

If von Humboldt set foot in South America having escaped the tedium of working as a cog in a political machine, in years to come another explorer would arrive there who had embraced the cut and thrust of politics with gusto. In 1914, having served as the twenty-sixth president of the United States for two terms between 1901 and 1909, Theodore Roosevelt joined forces with Brazilian explorer Cândido Mariano da Silva Rondon to explore the course of the Rio da Dúvida, or River of Doubt, through the Brazilian Amazon Basin. Roosevelt was an inveterate adventurer and, seeking a fresh challenge after he had tasted electoral defeat in the 1912 presidential election, he did not hesitate to accept the invitation of the Brazilian government to break fresh ground in their country. The expedition was sponsored by the American Museum of Natural History and, amongst the nineteen-strong company of men, there were two naturalists—mammalogist Leo Miller and ornithologist George Cherrie.

Roosevelt was greatly impressed by them both. In his account of the expedition, he recorded that no two better men for such a trip could have been found. His admiration for Cherrie in particular was unabashed. Roosevelt wrote warmly of Cherrie's former involvement in South American politics, recounting how Cherrie had named a new species of ant-thrush after a revolutionary chief Cherrie had supplied weapons to in the course of his rise to power, describing this as, "A delightful touch, in its practical combination of those not normally kindred pursuits, ornithology and gun-running."

Roosevelt is now remembered fondly for his commitment to conservation during his time in office—he oversaw the creation of five national parks, fifty-one bird reserves, and one hundred and fifty national forests and, in all, placed over 230 million acres of land under public protection. His interest in birds was genuine and is recorded in an article in the Audubon Society magazine *Bird-Lore* in March–April 1910. The author of "President Roosevelt's List of Birds Seen in the White House Grounds," Lucy Maynard, recalled,

> I had the opportunity to speak with the President, and I asked him if I might make, from a magazine article of his, a list of the birds he mentioned having seen about the White House.

"Why yes," he answered cordially. "But I'll do better for you than that. I'll make you a list of all the birds I can remember having seen since I have been here."

Within twenty-four hours of that conversation Roosevelt sent Maynard a list of ninety-three species he could recall seeing—one of which, "Hummingbird," we must assume was probably a Ruby-throated Hummingbird. However, for all he knew his birds, and for all his unprecedented steps to protect the United States' wild-life, Roosevelt was also a passionately committed hunter—an eight-month expedition to Africa in 1909 collected a bag of 5,013 mammals; 4,453 birds; 2,322 reptiles and amphibians; and assorted sundry invertebrates, plants, and shells. Unsurprisingly then, in his account of his months in Brazil, once introductions to the expedition members have been made, he commences his description of the equipment they carried into the jungle with them by listing in detail the guns, an exotic medley of revolvers, rifles, and shotguns.

The rest of the party's equipment is afforded a cursory mention. The expedition carried some basic United States Army emergency rations but, for the most part, intended to fend for themselves. In the months that followed, with the expedition subsisting on starvation rations and badly afflicted with malaria and infected wounds, the overprovision of firearms and the lack of essential food and medical supplies may have weighed heavily on Roosevelt's mind, though he makes light of the situation in his account. The brevity with which he recalls the tragic death of Simplicio, one of the Brazilian *cama-radas* or porters, when one of the party's dugout canoes capsized in some rapids approaches the cold-blooded:

> Simplicio must have been pulled under at once and his life beaten out on the boulders beneath the racing torrent. He never rose again, nor did we ever recover his body.
>
> On an expedition such as ours death is one of the accidents that may at any time occur, and narrow escapes from death are too common to be

felt as they would be felt elsewhere. One mourns sincerely, but mourning cannot interfere with labor.

We immediately proceeded with the work of the portage.

The following day, having carried the remaining canoes around the impassable rapids, the party made camp at the riverside and resumed their collecting activities, Roosevelt bemoaning the difficulty of shooting the many small birds they found in the surrounding high tree canopy. Nonetheless, Cherrie managed to acquire four new species for the expedition's collection, among them a hummingbird: "Of the species known as wood-stars, with dainty but not brilliant plumage; its kind is never found except in the deep, dark woods, not coming out into the sunshine. Its crop was filled with ants; when shot, it was feeding at a cluster of long, red flowers."

Hummingbirds did not feature largely in Roosevelt's account of the expedition; not, one suspects, because they were not regularly encountered, for Cherrie took some 2,500 bird specimens for the American Museum of Natural History, but instead because Roosevelt was more interested in the big game he and his colleagues shot. His graphic descriptions of Jaguar hunts make for particularly uncomfortable reading. Accounts of birds are relatively few and far between, still less, observations of hummingbirds. One such, late in the expedition, hints at the hunger the party were contending with.

In this neighbourhood the two naturalists found many birds we had not hitherto met. The most conspicuous was a huge oriole, the size of a small crow . . . There was also a tiny soft-tailed woodpecker, no larger than a kinglet; a queer hummingbird with a slightly flexible bill; and many species of ant-thrush, tanager, manakin and tody.

Kermit [Roosevelt's son], with the small Luger belt-rifle, collected a handsome curassow, nearly as big as a turkey—out of which, after it had been skinned, the cook made a delicious *canja*, the thick Brazilian soup of fowl and rice than which there is nothing better of its kind.

All these birds were new to the collection—no naturalists had previously worked this region—so that the afternoon's work represented nine species new to the collection, six new genera, and a most excellent soup.

While the party was wracked by hunger and the ravages of biting insects, the accidental death of poor Simplicio was not the end of their misfortunes. Another of the Brazilian camaradas was shot in cold blood by one of his colleagues—the party summarily abandoned the murderer, "an inborn lazy shirk with the heart of a ferocious cur in the body of a bullock," in the jungle to fend for himself, almost certainly a death sentence in itself. They caught sight of him three days later, on the banks of the river down which they were once more making slow progress in their dugout canoes. Both Roosevelt and Rondon chose to ignore his entreaties to allow him to rejoin the expedition.

If Roosevelt's account of his time in Brazil underplays both the vicissitudes he and his colleagues faced and the daily work of the naturalists, one recurrent observation is made throughout the approximately one-thousand-mile journey—and that is of the development potential Brazil represents. Given the considerable emphasis Roosevelt had placed in conservation during his presidency in the United States, it is interesting to note that, in addition to the excellent sporting opportunities he found hunting Jaguar, caiman, and tapirs in Brazil, he was moved to repeatedly extol the economic qualities of the land. The following observation is not untypical: "This is a fertile land, pleasant to live in, and any settler who is willing to work can earn his living. There are mines; there is water-power; there is an abundance of rich soil. It offers a fine field for immigration and for agricultural, mining and business development."

These words, written by the former president of the United States in 1914, might very well have been drafted as a manifesto for the president of Brazil a century later, for in 2019, Jair Bolsonaro swept to victory in the country's presidential elections on a wave of populist promises to unlock the economic development potential of the country's natural resources by obliterating existing legislation that protected the environment and indigenous peoples. In an ironic twist, Bolsonaro had publicly proclaimed his admiration for contemporary US president Donald Trump, who had, by that point, made it clear he wished to privatize and exploit the very US national parks that Roosevelt had championed as sanctuaries for wild creatures and the American people.

During Bolsonaro's election campaign, the then Brazilian environment minister, Edson Duarte, warned, "The increase of deforestation will be immediate. I am afraid of a gold rush to see who arrives first. They will know that, if they occupy illegally, the authorities will be complacent and will grant concordance. They will be certain that nobody will bother them."

Bolsonaro even promised to open indigenous lands to economic development, to timber extraction, agriculture, and mining. Some 13 percent of the country was formally recognised as being indigenous lands, and these had hitherto been spared the worst of the ongoing erosion of the Amazon rainforest—a mere 2 percent of rainforest deforestation had occurred within those indigenous boundaries. Bolsonaro did not recognise any such distinction. Speaking of Brazil's indigenous peoples, he was dismissive: "Minorities have to bend down to the majority. Minorities [should] either adapt or simply vanish."

My arrival in Brazil was just a few months after Bolsonaro's inauguration, and the new president was abundantly delivering on his electoral promises to the collective horror of the watching world. Having slashed personnel and funding at Brazil's environmental agency Institute of Environment and Renewable Natural Resources (IBAMA), and with swathes of the Amazon now on fire, Bolsonaro was unrepentant: "I used to be called Captain Chainsaw," he said. "Now I am Nero, setting the Amazon aflame."

By July 2019, satellite imagery showed that more than 3,700 square kilometres of rainforest had been cleared since Bolsonaro's inauguration. By August, the sheer scale of the fires burning in Brazil was becoming clearer, and the world was uniting in its condemnation. Some of those fires were related to the recent deforestation and represented cut vegetation being burned as part of land clearance for cattle ranching. Other fires were alight on existing agricultural land, either to clear encroaching shrub or as part of rotational agriculture. Alarmingly, some of the fires appeared out of control, wildfires in standing forest that had spread from the deliberately started fires nearby. The situation was exacerbated by the effects of previous, selective illegal logging that, by removing high-value timber from virgin forest, had led to the forests in question being drier, more open places with increased flammability; and by climate change that was demonstrably making the dry seasons longer and, hence, the vegetation drier. Globally, the very process of deforestation appears to be affecting water cycles and patterns of precipitation—in a vicious circle, the rain that the forests depend upon is no longer falling on what's left of them in the volumes they require.

On August 10, ranchers in southern Amazonia organised the infamous *Dia do Fogo*, or Day of Fire, a day marked by an explosion of coordinated blazes in the area—over 120 fires in the vicinity of Novo Progresso alone. Their objective, according to one of the ranchers, was to "show the president that we want to work." Bolsonaro was, presumably, emboldened by their actions. Days later, he had the audacity to claim that environmental NGOs were behind the fires.

"On the question of burning in the Amazon, which in my opinion may have been initiated by NGOs because they lost money, what is the intention? To bring problems to Brazil . . ."

In the weeks that followed, Bolsonaro continued to shift the blame for the fires elsewhere, even at one point bizarrely and falsely implicating actor, environmental activist, and philanthropist Leonardo DiCaprio.

"This Leonardo DiCaprio is a cool guy, right? Giving money to torch the Amazon."

The area of Brazil I was visiting was one that had already experienced devastation on a scale that I fervently hoped the Amazonian rainforest would not endure, but watching the news in the weeks before my arrival, I was feeling pessimistic about the latter's prospects. I would not see, for myself, the devastation in Amazonia—but whilst travelling to what remained of Brazil's Atlantic rainforest, I would pass through countryside that had been cleared for agriculture in the past. As an example of what had been lost, the contrast could not have been any starker. Stretching from the northeast of the country down the coast and then inland to Argentina and Paraguay, what remains of the formerly vast Atlantic rainforest is now highly fragmented, a scattered shadow of what it once was—before agricultural expansion and logging tore through it, the forest once covered some one million square kilometres. Less than 7 percent of that now remains, still providing a biodiverse home to a panoply of creatures, some enticing hummingbirds amongst them. The sobering reality of the lost 93 percent of the forest is that within it will have been species of bird, mammal, insect, and plant that have gone forever, before we even knew they were there. South America's tropical forests are crucibles of endemism, with some species inhabiting extraordinarily specific habitat types, or restricted to one or two mountains or valleys alone.

I could not stop thinking about what was lost as I drove east out of São Paulo, heading towards the coastal town of Ubatuba. The landscape I passed through was unremittingly bland, consisting of cleared fields and rough pastures. I wondered what the countryside here had looked like a century ago when Roosevelt had visited Brazil, or in the late nineteenth century when an English noblewoman, Baroness Annie Brassey, visited Rio de Janeiro. Voyaging around the world with her husband on board their yacht *The Sunbeam*, she recorded a visit to the Rua do Ouvidor, a fashionable shopping area, to buy a large number of the more expensive varieties of artificial flowers, each petal consisting of the entire throat or breast of a hummingbird, and the leaves made from the wings of beetles. They are very rare and beautiful, their manufacture being quite a *spécialité* of this city.

The prices asked astonished us greatly; the cost of five sprays, which I had been commissioned to buy, was 29l, and the price of all the others was proportionately high. But then they wear forever. I have had some for nine years, and they are as good now as when they were bought.

She does not record the name of the shop in question—it may well have been *Ao Beija Flor*, At the Hummingbird's. The street on which it was to be found and the surrounding neighbourhood was famed as a place of manufacture and sale of feather flowers, with French florists standing side by side with local shops. The Scottish naturalist John MacGillivray, stopping briefly in Rio de Janeiro in the 1850s, recounted a visit: "The narrow Rua do Ouvidor, filled with shops, many of which equal in the richness and variety of their goods the most splendid establishments of European capitals. Of these the most tempting, and the most dangerous to enter with a well-filled purse, is the famous feather-flower manufactory of Mme. Finot, where the gorgeous plumage of humming-birds and others of the feathered tribe is fabricated into wreaths and bouquets of all kinds."

The manufacture of fake flowers using harvested hummingbirds was a Brazilian speciality, built upon a traditional use of feathers as decorative items amongst the native peoples who lived along the Brazilian coast at the time of the arrival of the Portuguese. One nation, the Tupinambás, established trading connections with the Portuguese and, in due course, indigenous featherwork found its way back to Europe, mirroring the export of Mexican featherwork under the auspices of the Spanish.

The hummingbird feather flowers were pioneered by two nuns, mother superiors Josefa Maria and Maria da Trindade, from the Ursuline convent Our Lady of the Soledade, in Salvador, Bahia. They had adapted techniques used to make cloth flowers, incorporating the considerably more lustrous natural materials readily found in the countryside around them. The nuns used a network of local hunters to supply them with the raw materials they required. John Gould, Victorian hummingbird obsessive, remarked, "The residents of many parts of Brazil employ their slaves in collecting, skinning and preserving [hummingbirds] for European markets . . . They also supply the inmates of the convents with many of the more richly coloured species for the manufacture of artificial feather-flowers."

At first the nuns were said to have made altar pieces, a religious employment of feathers that echoed that of the Spanish icon-makers in Mexico centuries previously; but in time they made bouquets, garlands, and wreaths of feather flowers for sale across the country, the income helping to maintain their convent. French traveller Ferdinand Denis, in 1875, described their products possessing "a subtlety that would drive the most experienced colourist to despair."

The nuns' innovation was enthusiastically adopted in Rio de Janeiro, where artisans responded to advertisements in Parisian fashion magazines, giving French fashion an exotic, tropical twist; back in France, the hummingbird flowers became known as "the Brazilian style," perceived to be a fusion of impeccable French taste with tropical nature. A correspondent in the monthly American magazine *Our Dumb Animals* recounted an episode in 1875 that bore bleak testimony to how realistic these hummingbird flowers were:

A few days ago, while strolling in the woods between Bethlehem and Littleton [New Hampshire] with some fellow-sufferers from hay fever, a beautiful humming-bird attempted to extract sweetness from the artificial flowers on my wife's hat. The bird did not seem to be disturbed by the exclamations of our astonished party, but presented his bill to every flower upon the hat before leaving. I think the manufacturer of the flowers may be congratulated upon possessing a skill capable of deceiving a humming-bird.

The flowers' popularity endured and their reputation grew throughout the course of the nineteenth century, helped in no small part by their exhibition at the various world fairs held throughout Europe in the late nineteenth century, and by the patronage of royalty.

Princess Therese of Bavaria—or, to use her full name, Princess Therese Charlotte Marianne Auguste von Bayern—was by the standards of any day a remarkable woman. Descended from one of Europe's most powerful royal families, she took over the running of the royal household at the age of thirteen upon the death of her mother. At the age of twenty-one she began to travel, first throughout Europe, then North Africa, the Middle East, the United States, and South America. Fluent in twelve languages, she was a skilled naturalist and keen ethnographer who preferred to travel incognito, or at least what passed as incognito for a princess. Arriving in Brazil in 1888, accompanied only by a servant trained in taxidermy, a lady in waiting, and a bodyguard, she explored the lands around the Amazon and Rio Negro, collecting plants, birds, mammals, insects, and mineral specimens and, with the assistance of local translators, ethnological artefacts. So prolific was her collection, on her return to Bavaria it took her over nine years to catalogue and analyse her material.

For all her scientific integrity and curiosity, once Princess Therese found herself in the Rua do Ouvidor, she was swept off her feet by the luxury goods she found displayed there. In *Meine Reise in die Brasilianischen Tropen*, her account of her Brazilian expedition, she enthused about the diamond tiaras and bracelets she found in the Rezende jewellery store, and of the street itself she noted, "Iridescent flowers made from hummingbird feathers, and decorative objects containing beetle wings with a metallic shine are temptingly displayed in the shop windows."

Like Annie Brassey before her, Princess Therese succumbed to the temptation to purchase some hummingbird feather flowers.

Additionally, she bought two rigid fans, one comprising Rose-ate Spoonbill feathers, and the other parrot and tanager feathers. Hummingbirds, while highly prized for artificial flowers, had feathers that were simply too small to make up a satisfactory fan. They were, however, considered to be an excellent centrepiece for a rigid fan, and many produced at the time had an entire, colourful stuffed hummingbird posed coquettishly upon them. On June 6, 1871, Alexandra, the Princess of Wales, stepped out at the Waverley Ball in London dressed as Mary Queen of Scots, her outfit rather incongruously accessorised with a white fan adorned by a Ruby Topaz hummingbird, said to have been a gift made to her earlier that evening by Emperor Pedro II of Brazil. These hummingbird fans exported from Brazil became so fashionable amongst European society ladies that they became known simply as "Brazilians"—a lady of the time saying she was getting a Brazilian having a very different meaning to that of today.

Imitation was said to be the sincerest form of flattery and, if one could not obtain or afford a genuine Brazilian, something similar could be sourced from closer to home. A battered wooden box, found tucked away on a bookshelf in Culzean Castle on the west coast of Scotland, contains an ivory and silk fan believed to have belonged in the nineteenth century to Julia, Marchioness of Ailsa. The silken material of the fan itself is white, and, hand-embroidered upon it, are an array of hummingbirds in flight, recognisable pufflegs and coquettes—the latter species particularly apt if we are to believe the stories that fans were used by society ladies to communicate and flirt with their admirers. Certain movements or poses of the fan held coded messages: *I love you. I am engaged. We are watched. Kiss me.* A pamphlet, *The Language of the Fan*, detailed every nuance of this secret mode of communication. That it was printed by Duvelleroy, one of the leading French fan manufacturers of the day, is perhaps telling—fan language may have been no more than a marketing ploy, as effective in generating sales as the incorporation of hummingbirds, with their air of exoticism, in the fans themselves.

While those nineteenth-century feather fashions are now a thing of the past, and hummingbirds no longer need fear for their lives to feed the demands of haute couture, a recent issue of *Vogue Brasil* returned to the roots of the hummingbird feather industry, featuring an editorial photographed in Salvador, Bahia, the home of the convent that pioneered the creation of feather flowers. One image in particular stands out, a tableaux featuring models in feathered turbans and carrying bejewelled clutch bags with green fanned-feather motifs. Elsewhere in the magazine, either by accident or design, Brazilian model Izabel Goulart is presented as a smouldering-eyed, sultry nun.

Quite what Mother Superiors Josefa Maria and Maria da Trindade would have made of this fashionable tribute is hard to say. Perhaps, given their readiness to exploit the commercial potential of their hummingbird feather flowers, they would have secretly approved.

If all of this colourful history was helping to while away the long drive to Ubatuba, it was not completely distracting me from the countryside through which I passed. It was only in the last few miles before Ubatuba that the road finally began to pass through forested areas—until then, areas of woodland had been few and far between. I had travelled through some of the lost 93 percent of the former Atlantic rainforest, and it was a depressing agricultural sight.

Some way outside of the town, hidden at the end of a long, muddy, and undulating track, lay the home of Senhor Jonas D'Abronzo. Branches whipped and clawed at the sides of my four-wheel-drive hire car as I made my slow ascent from the village of Folha Seca. I was glad I had opted for this rugged vehicle, as anything smaller would surely have struggled with the slippery track. At first the track had threaded its way through scattered roadside dwellings, with children playing in chicken-strewn yards beneath laundry hung on washing lines in the sun, but now I was pressing into dense woodland. I was just beginning to doubt whether I was on the right track when I came upon a pair of metal gates at the side of the track, and a driveway descending towards a small single-storey house tucked deep in the trees. If nothing else, this promised somewhere to turn the car, but the sight of hummingbird feeders hanging from the trees in the garden in front of the house suggested I had found Sr. Jonas' home after all.

A short man with wavy white hair, thick black-framed glasses, and a gentle smile came walking across the lawn to greet me. We had emailed one another before my arrival, so I was not an unexpected guest. I came bearing gifts too—some bunches of bananas for the frugivorous birds that visited his garden and, most importantly of all, bags of sugar for the hummingbirds. Keeping a dozen hummingbird feeders stocked with sugar water was a time- and sugar-consuming job for Sr. Jonas. He told me about how his hummingbird garden had come to pass.

"I've lived here for nearly twenty years. My sister had a house nearby, so I was aware of the hummingbirds before I moved here, but I chose this place because I wanted to be a hermit. It's at the end of a dead-end track, so I thought it would be peaceful and quiet, and I wouldn't see any people. I'd lived in São Paulo before so, when I retired, it was time for a change.

"I put up a couple of hummingbird feeders, just to have the birds around the house. Straightaway, the first coquettes arrived in the garden."

These were Festive Coquettes, a small species of hummingbird that was to be found in a narrow range down the southeast coast of Brazil—a hummingbird that I dearly wanted to see. Before the loss of so much of the Atlantic rainforest, they would have been considerably more commonplace than they presently are. For birders visiting the area, they have long been a sought-after target, as Sr. Jonas was to discover.

"I didn't realise it, at first, but the track leading to my house was known to British and American birdwatchers before I moved here. They would come here hoping to see the coquettes.

"I used to have my gates locked—I didn't know the area so well at the time, and it's a remote place, after all. One day, I was outside and I heard applause from the track above the garden. I walked onto the track, and I found some birders looking into my garden at my feeders. They were applauding because they'd just seen their first ever coquette.

"Now people come here from all over the world."

The pride in his voice was unmistakeable. Despite having moved to Folha Seca to remove himself from society, people had found him, brought to this hidden corner of Brazil by his hummingbirds.

"At first there were just one or two coquettes; there are more now. I wonder how many more might be out there in the trees," he said reflectively. We had walked from my car to the terrace of his small home, and sat there watching the feeders hung around the garden perimeter and from the eaves of the terrace itself. A cache of hummingbird jewels sparkled around us—Glittering-throated and Versicoloured Emeralds, White-chinned Sapphires, and Brazilian Rubies. The latter were well-named, large green hummingbirds that, when they turned to face me, dazzled with their ruby-red throats. Sr. Jonas chuckled aloud.

"Look at the White-chinned Sapphire! It is a terrible name. Can you see the white chin? It's hardly there at all . . ."

Sure enough, the birds in question had only a faint frosting of white on their Prussian-blue throats. Sr. Jonas continued, "In Portuguese, we call it the *beija flor roxo*—the purple hummingbird. We joke, this is a hummingbird better looked for in Portuguese than in English!"

His laughter was infectious, and behind us was further evidence of his kindly nature. A small, hollow tree stump was placed on the terrace by the open door of the house. In it, sitting upon a carefully arranged lattice of dead twigs, was a female White-chinned Sapphire, one wing hanging limply at her side. Every fifteen minutes Sr. Jonas lifted her, still sitting on her perch, to feed from her own small drinker, his hand cupped protectively beneath her. He explained, "She was fighting with another hummingbird, and her wing was broken. I picked her up from the floor, and I'm caring for her. This drinker has special sugar water in it—she can't catch insects any more, so I sent off for some powdered protein that I add to the water."

She looked bright and alert, despite the obviously damaged wing, and whenever she saw Sr. Jonas she chirped eagerly, clearly recognising him as her saviour.

"They're smart," he said, "for such a small bird. People don't realise how intelligent hummingbirds can be. This isn't the first one I've rescued. A few years ago, there was another, a Reddish Hermit. He wasn't as badly hurt as her, just stunned on the ground when I found him and picked him up.

"I fed him for a while, the same as this little one. And then when he was recovered, he flew off. The following day, he came back, and hovered right in front of my face, chattering loudly. He wanted my protection. They are really small, the Reddish Hermit, and the other hummingbirds drive them away from the feeders.

"So I cupped my hands around a feeder, and he came inside the protective orbit of my hands to feed while I shielded him from the other hummingbirds. From then on, every day for four months, he would find me wherever I was working outside, and the same thing would happen—the hovering in front of me, the loud chattering, until I walked to a feeder and made a shield for him with my hands. You can see video of it, if you search online."

I had only the briefest glimpse of a Reddish Hermit, but other much larger hermits here were unusually confiding for their kind. The fringes of Sr. Jonas' garden were boiling with Saw-billed Hermits—magnificent burnished hummingbirds with heavily streaked underparts, tangerine cheeks and eyebrows, and a weaponised bill hooked at the tip and, on close inspection, sporting minute sharp serrations on the upper mandible. They were impressive hermits, and I was surprised at how fearless they were, feeding brazenly on the waxy pink candelabra blooms of ginger plants mere feet away from us. Sr. Jonas told me, "The gingers aren't native to Brazil, though you see them all over the place. But because they're not native, they don't often get pollinated. Here at Folha Seca, those hermits pollinate the gingers, and they produce fruit. I put the seeds in my salad. They look a little like pomegranates, but they're not sweet. They're good though."

He walked to a nearby ginger plant, pulling off a small, oak apple–sized fruit. Cutting it open with a knife, he scooped out the seeds with the tip of the blade and offered me one. Sure enough, it tasted nutty and slightly bitter—certainly not unpleasant. I suggested to him that he was feeding the hummingbirds and, in return, they were feeding him, eliciting more gales of that irrepressible laughter from him.

"Yes!"

I was similarly enthusiastic about the Festive Coquettes. Sr. Jonas had not been exaggerating when he told me that seeing them in his garden would be a formality, as they were always present there—at least one male bird and sometimes more patrolled one corner of the garden, working his way back and forth between three feeders and a favoured perch. The male was a small, confident hummingbird of immense character, making the best of a muted palette of plumage colours. His upper body was a dark bottle-green bisected, on his rump, by a startling white band that gave way to a bronze tail. His long wings were black, and his underparts mostly a soft dove-grey, with a white breast. What elevated this subtle garb to something extraordinary were his moustaches—elongated green feathers, each tipped with a small white pearl, drooping elegantly from his cheeks.

It was hard to tear myself away from Sr. Jonas' garden. In the hours I had sat chatting with him we had seen ten species of hummingbird, and I was enjoying his good company. A long journey inland lay ahead of me, and I reluctantly said my goodbyes. Sr. Jonas smiled wryly.

"At least you can go," he said. "It's hard for me to get away now, even if I wanted to. The hummingbirds need feeding and looking after every day. They're my responsibility now. With nobody else here to care for them, I need to be here for them."

I sensed that Sr. Jonas was not complaining—he had come here seeking a quiet life, and the hummingbirds had found him in the forest. Their company, when visiting birders were not there, was ample and, in Sr. Jonas, the hummingbirds had found a friend and guardian.

The same could be said of my host for the next few days at Pousada da Fazenda, a working coffee farm hundreds of twisting, turning miles inland from the Atlantic coast. Luis Gonzaga "Zaga" Truzzi greeted me warmly upon my arrival; I was travel-weary and exhausted after battling torrential rain, fog, and erratic Brazilian lorry drivers on my way to his family home. The home in question felt like an oasis of calm after hours on the road—an old, white farmhouse with blue wooden shutters and a heavy terracotta-tiled roof, built in the late nineteenth century around the time Princess Therese of Bavaria visited Brazil and the export of hummingbird fans and feather flowers was at its peak.

"My grandfather came here from Italy as a farm labourer," Zaga told me. "He loved it here, and he ended up buying the farm."

We sat in the small, walled courtyard outside the farmhouse, the soft, worn red-brick paths radiating heat in the early evening. The sun was setting over the large, brick-lined coffee cherry drying area in front of the farmhouse, and we nursed small, strong, sweet coffees while we watched hummingbirds feeding from the heliconias that grew at the back of the garden—yet more confiding hermits, but different species, and more new ones to me. Planalto Hermits frisked their long white tail feathers as they weaved convoluted paths through the bushes, while smaller, duskier Scale-throated Hermits made hit-and-run raids on the flowers.

As I looked into the sun, one of the garden's many Swallow-tailed Hummingbirds was perched nearby, stretching elaborately in silhouette against the rose-streaked sky. The sun bled through the dark primary feathers of his outstretched wings, diffracting to stain them with prismatic rainbow colours.

"Would you like to see the swifts come to roost?" asked Zaga. "The *Cachoeira das Andorinhas* isn't far away. If we go now, we should be there in time to see them."

The "Waterfall of the Swallows" was a misnomer, as the birds that thronged every evening to roost on the dripping rock face behind the cascading water were swifts, not swallows. The two families, while superficially similar insofar as they are fast, sickle-winged aerial insect hunters, are not genetically closely related. The closest genetic relatives of the swifts, belonging to the biological family *Apodidae*, are those birds in the family *Trochilidae*—the hummingbirds. Taxonomists place both families in the biological order *Apodiformes*— distant relatives that branched off from one another in the late Cretaceous or early Tertiary period, some sixty-five to seventy million years ago, but relatives nonetheless.

By the late nineteenth century, on the basis of observed similarities in their morphology, notably the structure of their wings and the relative redundancy of their legs and feet given that members of both families are masters of the air and do not hop or walk in the manner of other passerine birds, the relationship between swifts and hummingbirds was generally accepted as fact. The American ornithologist and artist Robert Ridgway had a particular fascination with taxonomy, and concluded in 1892, "The Humming Birds and Swifts . . . agree in numerous anatomical characters, and there can be no doubt that they are more closely related to each other than are either to any other group of birds."

Curiously, for all that Ridgway's name is linked to some forty species and subspecies of birds, neither a swift nor a hummingbird features amongst them. Nonetheless, he was greatly smitten by hummingbirds in particular, both taxonomically and aesthetically, stating, "Of all the numerous groups into which the birds are divided there is none other so numerous in species, so varied in form, so brilliant in plumage, and so different from all others in their mode of life."

We arrived at the Cachoeira das Andorinhas as light began to fade from the mother-of-pearl sky above. The waterfall itself was not particularly large or spectacular, a short cascade into a large roadside pool. We stood on the edge of the road and looked up above the wooded hillside that loomed in front of us.

"They gather up there just before nightfall," Zaga explained. "Then, all at once, they come in to roost behind the waterfall. Keep watching . . ."

Overhead, we could see a loose flock of some fifty swifts scything back and forth high above the hilltop. They seemed to be getting incrementally lower, and through my binoculars I strained to distinguish any field characteristics that could provide an identification to a species level. An equally frustrating black silhouette buzzed past us, just above our heads, heading across the pool to the trees beyond—a hummingbird, flying with none of the aerial grace of its distant cousins high above, a stuttering and erratic passage through the sky like Woodstock in the *Peanuts* animated films.

It vanished into the trees and, as if it had been a shot across our bows to warn us of the imminent arrival of the swifts, they began to swoop down to the pool below us, skimming low over the surging water before hurling themselves into the very waterfall itself, vanishing into the rushing water at enormous speed. Through binoculars, at the near edge of the waterfall, I could make out their dark torpedo forms clinging to the glistening black rock behind the falling water, clustered together like some mysterious tropical chrysalises. Most of them were Great Dusky Swifts, large, drab powerful forms against the rock face; but one bird had a striking white collar that gleamed brightly in the half-light. Appropriately, this was a White-collared Swift. It was hard to believe these strange, darkly enigmatic birds shared a kinship with the rainbow-hued hummingbirds.

The next day, distracted only by the marmosets that daringly dashed into the garden to steal fruit set out by Zaga for the local tanagers and woodpeckers, I sat in the courtyard hunting humming-birds with my camera. The heliconia-loving hermits were a subtle challenge, while the Swallow-tailed Hummingbirds were made of bolder stuff. Seen in daylight, their navy-blue and green plumage chimed with the greenery of the garden and the nearby farmhouse's blue shutters, though it was their long, deeply forked tails that set them apart from all others. I was hoping for something smaller and more perfectly formed—a pair of Amethyst Woodstars were infrequent visitors to the garden as the day unfolded.

From time to time these tiny hummingbirds appeared, as suddenly as if they had been teleported, at the feeders hung around the courtyard. Their arrival was invariably heard, rather than witnessed—the first warning that one was present being the deep, sonorous buzzing from its wings. The female was shy, but the male habitually perched on a nearby lichen-encrusted twig after he had fed, lord and master of all he surveyed. The other, larger hummingbird species seemed completely oblivious to the woodstars' presence, perhaps perceiving them as insects rather than of their own kind. The Swallow-tailed Hummingbirds fought a running battle with Sapphire-spangled Emeralds, vying for supremacy at the feeders and territorial advantage in the garden as a whole, but the woodstars were left unmolested to come and go as they pleased.

The male was as compact and perfect as a cunningly wrought Fabergé egg, with upperparts of bronze green, a deeply forked tail, and an extensive rich amethyst gorget that seemed to glow from within. I had seen scarcer, more localised woodstars on my travels—Amethyst Woodstars have an extensive range across a large swathe of eastern South America—but the male bird in front of me in Zaga's garden was the most confiding individual I had met, prepared to spend prolonged periods of time perched in the open, oblivious to all around him.

My penultimate day in Brazil was spent further south, at the Espinheiro Negro Lodge, set in the heart of the remaining Atlantic forest. Covering such a large area of the eastern seaboard, the

Atlantic forest comprises a number of different habitat types within the broad brushstroke its name encompasses. The forest surrounding Espinheiro Negro was what I imagined a rainforest to be—tall trees of varying ages, shapes, and sizes, an impenetrable and lush mass of textured vegetation of every conceivable shade of green. In dry technical terms, this was dense ombrophilous forest in different shades of succession; but, viscerally, this was gloriously biodiverse and verdant territory, bursting with life of all kinds, the trees festooned with spiky bromeliads and orchids and the humid air throbbing with the voices of birds and the hum and stridulation of insects.

Some of the bromeliads in Brazil's Atlantic forest are hummingbird specialists, having evolved to be pollinated almost exclusively by them. *Aechmea pectinata* is a typically unassuming bromeliad, with a crown of green leaves that, in the flowering season, becomes flushed with red. Red is a colour that, to a hummingbird, signals a nectar source—hummingbird feeders usually have red plastic apertures for this very reason, and any birder in the neotropics who sports a baseball hat or T-shirt with a red motif is likely to be checked out by a hummingbird at some juncture. When the bromeliad flowers, it produces the largest quantity of the sugariest nectar in the morning between 6 and 10 a.m., the nectar contained in tubular flowers that favour visitors with long, stiff mouthparts—in other words, hummingbirds. Of all visits to the flowers, 90 percent are made by hummingbirds, with Violet-capped Woodnymphs the most frequent visitor, closely followed by Glittering-throated Emeralds and Saw-billed Hermits. The bromeliads are self-incompatible—that is, they cannot pollinate themselves—so they rely heavily upon those hummingbirds to pollinate them, and their flowers are formed in just the right way to deposit pollen on a hummingbird's bill.

The temptation to explore the trails that ran through the bromeliad-laden forest around the lodge was, of course, irresistible, but the hummingbird feeders that hung at the forest edge were where I found myself returning, time and again, drawn back by one species in particular. Other hummingbirds came and went, amongst them a fleeting and elusive Festive Coquette that made me grateful for the superlative views I had enjoyed of his kind in the company of Sr. Jonas some days previously, but it was another inhabitant of the Atlantic forest that dominated, magnificently, the grounds of the lodge.

Black Jacobins thronged here—dynamic, compactly powerful, jet-black hummingbirds with a little white highlight at the rear of their sooty flanks, and snow-white tails tipped with a filigree of further inkiness. Their Victorian mourning garb belied a character that was irrepressibly confident and brassy—theirs was a soap opera existence packed with vociferous fights amongst themselves, and an intolerance of other hummingbirds that bordered on the pathological. It was a brave Black-throated Mango or Violet-capped Woodnymph that dared to attempt to feed in the realm of the Black Jacobins. The interloper would be seen off within moments by one or more enraged jacobins, fleeing into the depths of the surrounding forest, presumably to look for nectar in the time-honoured, if more laborious manner—from flowers rather than man-made hummingbird feeders.

Some birders feel uneasy about seeing hummingbirds at feeders—there's a feeling that it's somehow too easy. Real birding should be difficult and challenging, the sort of activity that involves hardship and infers some sort of superior calibre to the birders in question. Real birders, in the neotropics, suffer for their birds, and see them only fleetingly. For many years antpittas were the ultimate birder's bird in South America—notoriously shy and skulking creatures of dense forest understorey that asked a lot of anyone who wished to catch a glimpse of their kind. Admitting to enjoying hummingbirds could elicit scorn from their disciples. *Hummingbirds? They're just too easy. You just look for them at feeders. They're plastic.*

This condescension had dimmed somewhat in recent years, partly I felt as a consequence of the extensive worldwide use of playback of bird calls to obtain acceptable views of almost every species of bird and, in the neotropics, the burgeoning number of antpitta species that could now be guaranteed at feeding sites where locals scattered earthworms early every morning to the local antpittas' considerable gustatory appreciation. If other, drabber bird families could be readily lured into the open by playback or seen at feeding stations, there was no shame in looking for arguably the most colourful and dynamic family of all at hummingbird feeders.

The monochrome jacobins that whirred and buzzed and jousted around me had a claim to fame that I would have to accept at its word, for it was one that I could neither see nor, in particular, hear for myself. I had come to the Brazilian forest armed with little more equipment than my binoculars and camera. When Claudio Mello, a behavioural neuroscientist from Oregon Health and Science University, visited the forest in 2015 he came armed with a battery of sensitive microphones and recording equipment usually used to record the high-frequency calls of bats, and a hypothesis he was curious to examine. Years previously, when conducting research in the region, he had heard a high-pitched sound on the very edge of hearing—a sound that he concluded, amidst the clamour of life in a Brazilian forest, probably came from a hummingbird rather than an insect or a tree frog. He could not, however, be sure of that—hence the microphones.

What Mello's equipment recorded was nothing short of remarkable. The Black Jacobins were indeed uttering high-frequency calls—but at a level that beggared belief. Most birds hear in the range of two to three kilohertz. The human ear typically hears noises in the range of one to four kilohertz. The Black Jacobins, meanwhile, were repeatedly broadcasting calls above ten kilohertz and up to fourteen kilohertz, way beyond the regular range known for any bird, let alone a small hummingbird.

This was widely reported as Black Jacobins uttering the highest-pitched calls of any bird in the entire world. That was not strictly true, as Mello's paper describing the Black Jacobins' calls was careful to point out—that accolade appeared to belong to another hummingbird, the Blue-throated Hummingbird, whose song included elements that exceeded a mighty twenty kilohertz. However, there was no evidence that the Blue-throated Hummingbirds could hear anything beyond seven kilohertz, while the Black Jacobins' high-pitched calls were not occasional elements in an otherwise normally pitched song—they were vocalizing almost exclusively above ten kilohertz. One has to assume, therefore, that they can hear their own kind, but why have they evolved a call that was so far out of the range of hearing for the remainder of birdkind?

Mello hypothesised that this might be an adaption to their biodiverse surroundings—Black Jacobins are found in a geographic range that includes upwards of forty other hummingbird species and sub-species, not to mention myriad other voices in the forest. Perhaps they evolved to have their own private frequency, one at which there was literally not so much background noise. Some Australian geckos are known to have exceptionally high-frequency calls and hearing, while the Hole-in-the-Head Frog, a species of frog endemic to Borneo, communicates entirely in the ultrasonic range up to thirty-eight kilohertz. If reptiles and amphibians could find evolutionary advantage in communicating in high frequencies, it seems logical to suppose that some birds may have done so too.

While Black Jacobins had elected to shout very loudly to catch one another's attention, another hummingbird species had evolved to let their feathers do the talking. Anna's Hummingbird, the species that, in the United States, is expanding its range north on the coattails of climate change, has a courtship display flight that at first glance is merely visually arresting—the male bird ascends some thirty metres into the air above his prospective partner, tucks his wings into his body, and then plummets in a fast dive towards her. He pulls up at the last possible moment, fanning his tail as he does so, and emitting a loud chirp noise.

Scientists, using high-speed video cameras, have established that the chirp is emitted not from his syrinx, or vocal organ, but instead from his tail. The outer tail feathers of the male Anna's Humming-bird have a trailing van that vibrates as the air passes through it at speed, creating the chirp sound—the birds are singing with their tails. If that were not marvellous enough, further study of the Anna's Hummingbird courtship dive has revealed that during the dive phase, the birds attain an average velocity of 385 body lengths per second, the highest known length-specific velocity attained by any vertebrate.

I had always assumed that Peregrine Falcons were the masters of the skies, but it transpires that a humble hummingbird can justly claim that title. The scientist behind this latter revelation, Christopher Clark of the Museum of Vertebrate Zoology at Berkeley, had a further revelation to make. He observed that at the point at which the hummingbirds pull up from their dive, their chirping tails fanned, they experienced accelerations almost nine times greater than gravitational acceleration. These forces are the highest known for any vertebrate species undergoing a voluntary aerial manoeuvre, with the exception of jet fighter pilots.

Fighter pilots, of course, have the benefit of special G-suits to help them to counteract the considerable physiological effects of pulling 9G. The Anna's Hummingbirds, on the other hand, have only a suit of feathers with a pleasing metallic raspberry-red gorget and head.

While I was struggling to hear the jacobins as they fed and feuded before me, I was hearing only too clearly the news that was coming out of Bolivia with every passing day. My plan was to fly to Bolivia from São Paulo, and spend some time exploring the lowlands before, eventually, making my way to the Madidi National Park in the upper Amazon River Basin, described by the Wildlife Conservation Society as the most biologically diverse place on earth, and renowned amongst biologists for the extent to which its wildlife remains uncatalogued to this day.

I was also eager to follow a little in the footsteps of Yossi Ghinsberg, an Israeli traveller who had visited Bolivia in 1981. Not too closely, however . . . Ghinsberg, trekking in the Bolivian forest with two companions and a German guide who had promised the travellers he could lead them to a lost tribe and, maybe, a river of gold, became separated from the rest of the party. For three weeks, he was alone in the jungle, struggling to survive against all the odds. Subsisting only on what he could forage with his bare hands, he was plagued by insect bites and stings. Forcing his way through the forest on feet that were beginning to rot, he hallucinated and believed he had a female companion at his side. The rainforest was deafeningly loud around him, bursting with life, and Ghinsberg was almost distracted from his overwhelming hunger by the sheer wonder of it all. Fortunately, at the very end of his tether and through his delirium, he heard an engine in the distance and, following the sound to the banks of a nearby river, stumbled across a search party of Tacana-Quechua from the indigenous community of San José de Uchupiamonas. They saved his life. Two of his former lost companions were never seen again.

This was not an episode I was in any hurry to experience for myself, but I hoped instead to visit Chalalan Lodge, in the community of San José de Uchupiamonas in the heart of the Madidi National Park. This was the Madidi National Park's first ecolodge, and Ghinsberg had been a driving force behind it. When, in the early 1990s, the Uchupiamonas community gathered to confront the emigration of their people from the area and the lack of Bolivian government investment or interest in their community, they decided they would build an ecolodge. This would provide local employment, and would bring visitors and welcome income to the community. This plan, though a noble one, was stymied at the outset by the lack of any funds to realise it.

Ghinsberg, upon learning of the community's desire to help itself, and the dire financial straits in which they found themselves, told the people that he would never forget or cease to thank them. He described himself as born in Israel, but reborn on the beaches of Progreso outside San José—he considered it would be an honour to call himself a Josesano.

Ghinsberg matched actions to words, facilitating the involvement of Conservation International and, via them, the Inter-American Development Bank. Three years later, in 1995, the community received the funding that allowed their dream of a community-owned ecolodge to become a reality; at the same time the Madidi National Park was formally created around them. Some twenty-five years later, on the eve of my visit, Madidi was becoming the perfect metaphor for the uncertain future faced by so many of South America's remaining wild, biodiverse places. While climate change threatens the ecology of the entire national park, in particular the fragile, mountainous areas, there are more imminent and tangible threats still—a proposed hydroelectric dam on the Beni River in the Bala Gorge would flood eight hundred square miles of Bolivia, including a significant part of Madidi. If some of my journey through the Americas was to see hummingbirds before they were lost forever, my visit to Madidi National Park might just be to see an entire swathe of internationally famous habitat before it was lost to an avoidable, man-made flood. It would be at the inspiring Chalalan Lodge that I hoped to conclude my exploration of Bolivia—a place that had pioneered an alternative concept of how rural communities could thrive by placing economic value in the very environment in which they were surrounded.

The immediate news emerging from Bolivia as a whole, however, was cause for some concern. During a recent presidential election, the incumbent president, Evo Morales, was narrowly trailing his nearest rival, Carlos Mesa, as the results began to be called. Then, without explanation, the results transmission was paused for a day. When the results transmission resumed, Morales had assumed a clear lead and, with a ten-point lead over Mesa, announced himself the winner. This was not a universally popular announcement within some parts of the country, with accusations flying of electoral fraud and, in some towns and cities, people taking to the streets to protest against Morales. Meanwhile, in Chile, there were protests across the country against the president, Sebastián Piñera, whose resignation was demanded; and civil unrest was boiling in Venezuela too. South America was, suddenly, convulsing.

The day before my departure from São Paulo, with the British government Foreign & Commonwealth Office still not advising against travel to Bolivia, I decided to put my slight misgivings to one side and stick to my plans. I ate breakfast and enjoyed a conversation with Jiri Trnka, the owner of Espinheiro Negro Lodge. We spoke of the unrest across South America. Jiri was in a reflective mood.

"Twenty years ago, when I came here, I thought I'd found my safe place in a crazy world. Here, I have some land to grow food. I have lakes for fish, and my own fresh water source. We can heat water with solar power."

I empathised with him, and told him about my croft back home in Shetland. That had always felt to me as much a safe haven as a home. Jiri considered this, and replied thoughtfully, "The difference, I think, is that here, if the world goes really crazy and breaks down, I will need a gun."

I was reminded of Rick, the lost American I had met when I arrived in Cuba. He too had expressed his fears for the future in an uncertain world where truth was increasingly a casualty and where anarchy might lurk, unseen, just around the corner. I set off for São Paulo wondering what I would find in Bolivia, and hoping for the best. Early that evening, hoping to clear my head, I took myself out for a walk in the streets. In the back of my mind was, as ever, the possibility of some hummingbirds, even in the densely urban surroundings of São Paulo.

Swallow-tailed Hummingbirds, the large, elegant birds I had last seen in Zaga's farmhouse garden, are famously tough and feisty examples of their kind. They brook no argument from other hummingbirds at feeders, but arguably the greatest demonstration of their mettle comes on the sprawling streets of São Paulo. They are found throughout the city, wherever there are some gardens or areas of parkland. The urban surroundings seem not to bother them.

Brazilian researchers studied an active Swallow-tailed Hummingbird nest on the Universidade Estadual Paulista campus, and observed the adult female hummingbird proactively driving other birds of different species away from the vicinity of her nest, including some species larger than herself. One such, Campo Flicker, is a woodpecker that is at least twice the size of the hummingbird; while on another occasion, elsewhere, a Swallow-tailed Hummingbird was said to have attacked a Swainson's Hawk in midair, a predator that is one hundredfold the mass of the hummingbird. Swallow-tailed Hummingbirds are, evidently, not backwards about coming forwards—a trait that would surely stand them in good stead in the cut and thrust of an urban environment.

My walk through São Paulo was a very random transect indeed and, in the event, I did not find any hummingbirds. Or at least, not living, breathing ones. Amongst the graffiti on the city walls, I found several unmistakeable representations of their kind. Their artists had, for the most part, used some artistic licence, and I was unable to assign their artwork to any particular species—though one bird bore a striking resemblance to a Festive Coquette. These were not the first hummingbird graffiti I had seen in South America—they hovered on the walls of the Ecuadorian capital city, Quito, and flew on the gables of buildings on the outskirts of Pereira in Colombia too. They seemed to be a popular motif in the continental graffiti movement—understandably so if some of their kind are such visible, colourful birds even in urban settings.

Some of their champions have crossed borders, their hummingbird work migrating overseas. Luis Martins was born in the outskirts of São Paulo—growing up, he dreamed of becoming a train driver, but changed his mind after winning an art competition at school. Once he picked up a spray can in his early teens, the graffiti artist known as L7M was born. His pieces marry striking, bold geometric forms with elements drawn from the natural world, most notably birds and, amongst them, hummingbirds are a recurrent theme. One such piece appeared on a wall in snow-smothered Innsbruck, a searing neon explosion of hummingbirds in the Austrian winter; in Dortmund, another hummingbird appeared on the wall of an old school sheltering refugees from Syria.

A hummingbird as a symbol of hope, strength, and endurance is a recurrent one in South American folklore. An Ecuadorian folktale tells of a forest on fire—a hummingbird picks up single droplets of water in its beak and lets them fall on the fire. The other animals in the forest laugh, and ask the hummingbird what difference this can possibly make. They say, "Don't bother, it is too much, you are too little, your wings will burn, your beak is too tiny, it's only a drop, you can't put out this fire. What do you think you are doing?"

To which the hummingbird is said to reply, "I'm just doing what I can."

This folktale was the parable chosen by the late Kenyan environmental activist and Nobel Peace Prize winner Wangari Maathai when she addressed an audience of over seven thousand in Montreal in May 2006. It was also the inspiration for a mural painted on the inside of the high walls of the Centro de Rehabilitación Femenino in Quito, a rehabilitation centre for female inmates. The walls, topped with tight coils of razor wire, chain link fence, and still more razor wire, would have been utterly depressing before, but with the assistance of an international Japanese mural project called Over the Wall, the inmates and their children painted a vast forty-metre-long mural of flowers and hummingbirds. Japanese artist Kensuke Miyazaki said,

> Over the Wall created a mural for the children who are being raised here unaware of the outside world. The mural was painted on a wall that can be clearly seen from the daycare facility located at the rehabilitation center.
>
> It is filled with more than sixty types of vivid flowers and hummingbirds hovering among them. We used motifs from the Ecuadorian indigenous story *The Flight of the Hummingbird*, with the hope that it will convey happiness to everyone within this facility.

This mural might not be able to be seen by people around the world, but it has reached the people we most wanted it to reach.

Back in São Paulo, L7M cites John James Audubon as one of his artistic influences, an understandable homage to the outstanding bird artistry of Audubon. Walking the streets of the city, now looking for hummingbirds on walls rather than in flight overhead, I wondered if Martins was aware of another American bird artist, lesser known, who came to Brazil in the 1860s and was so enamoured of the country's hummingbirds that he began to paint a series of pictures of them for a book, provisionally entitled *The Gems of Brazil*. American naturalist and artist Martin Johnson Heade's life overlapped with that of Audubon during the early nineteenth century, and he was a contemporary of the great English hummingbird fanatic John Gould. Heade was every bit as openly obsessed by these enigmatic birds. He said, "From early boyhood, I have been almost a monomaniac on hummingbirds."

His first visit to Brazil was in 1863, and was followed by two further trips to the country he had fallen so in love with. At least forty-five canvases were created, many incorporating hummingbirds in lifelike poses in natural settings, alongside orchids and other tropical vegetation. Heade's hummingbird paintings combine biological accuracy with an intensity of light rarely found in depictions of nature—he brought an artist's eye to bear on his subject without compromising detail. Whilst living in New York he shared a studio with landscape artist Frederic Edwin Church, and it is thought that the intensely coloured realism of Church's style influenced the developing artistry of Heade.

We cannot be sure just how many hummingbird paintings he created—though we know *The Gems of Brazil* never came to fruition. In his lifetime, Heade was never recognised as an artist of any note. Whatever local reputation he enjoyed was said to have evaporated when he moved from New York in 1881. At the time, he was the only landscape artist in New York never to become even an associate member of the National Academy of Design; and after his death in 1904, he was soon forgotten.

It was only decades later that Heade's hummingbirds began to see the light of day, often propped up against table legs in yard sales. To this day, Heade's paintings continue to emerge from dusty basements, cobwebby attics, and house clearances—stories of their rediscovery and enormous profits for their finders abound. A painting bought for $18 in California sold at auction for $425,000. A garage sale in Wisconsin yielded a painting, *Two Magnolias on Blue Plush*, for $29 that sold at Christies for $882,500 a decade later. *Magnolias on Gold Velvet Cloth*, acquired by the Museum of Fine Arts in Houston for a cool $1.25 million in 1999, had been used for years by its owner, a worker at a tool and die company, to cover a hole in the wall of his Indiana home.

Heade's underappreciated reputation has grown, posthumously, and he is now recognised as a major artist of his era. His hummingbird paintings, in addition to possessing Heade's characteristic luminosity, also have the lustre of rarity—with only a few dozen known to have been painted, they are outnumbered by his botanical creations. For his admirers, the emergence of a lost hummingbird painting will have all the serendipitous thrill of rounding a city street corner and finding an L7M hummingbird graffiti piece blazing with life and movement on a wall or, for the birder, the sudden arrival of a rare species at a flower.

My arrival in Santa Cruz had none of that spontaneity, but my slight misgivings about travelling to Bolivia under the current political circumstances were immediately reinforced by the sight of a roadblock formed of worn car tyres and tree branches as we left the airport. A dozen men stood idly around it, waiting for traffic to intercept. I had been collected from the airport by the owner of a small hotel on the outskirts of the city. He hooted the horn of his car as we passed the roadblock, eliciting friendly waves from the bystanders.

"The roads are blocked all across the city," he confided. "The people of Santa Cruz are angry with Morales. The police have all stopped working—they say they don't want to stand in the way of democracy.

"No vehicles are coming or going from the city, so food is starting to become scarce, and it's hard to move around inside. I gave these guys a chicken this morning, so we're okay."

At the hotel that evening I met my companions for this first leg of my Bolivian adventure—two Swedes, Lars and Bjørn—and our guide for the coming week, Jose Antonio Padilla, an affable Peruvian birder. We sat around a table in a windowless dining room, eating fried chicken and rice from polystyrene boxes, discussing the situation outside in the city. Our plans remained the same, to look for birds just outside the city limits for a day and then, roadblocks allowing, to leave the city and head deeper into the country. Jose Antonio was cheerful about the birding prospects that lay ahead of us, but a serious note underpinned the conversation.

"I've been talking to our driver," he said. "He's not sure the situation is completely safe. It's hard to move around the city, but he's got a permit from the people to display in the window of his car. It says he's allowed to pass through the roadblocks because he's moving patients and medical supplies around.

"So we should be okay tomorrow, but I don't know if we'll be able to easily leave Santa Cruz the following day. We'll just have to wait and see."

Early the next morning we gathered outside the hotel. Our driver, Ivan, had arrived in a small cherry-red Fiat Uno. A muscular man in his early thirties with his hair shaved short at the back and sides, Ivan was at pains to reassure us.

"I've got the permit in the windscreen," he said, indicating a photocopied piece of paper that proclaimed he was carrying a patient in need of dialysis, "and the flag here. We're ready."

Tied to the back of the car was a green and white flag—the flag of the state of Santa Cruz. This was, we were to learn, a symbol of resistance and a statement of defiance for the people of Bolivia's largest city who opposed the reelection of Evo Morales. As we drove through the largely deserted streets of the suburbs, other cars, upon seeing the flag streaming behind us, would sound their horns in solidarity. We passed through a number of unmanned roadblocks, scattered piles of tyres and debris strewn across even residential streets, and made our way along an unmade road out into the fields on the outskirts of town.

The day passed uneventfully. Predictably, this close to the city, and in an area of largely agricultural land use, the range of birds we found was not particularly large. I felt sanguine about that, knowing that the days to come should hold the hummingbirds I hoped to find in Bolivia. It was only as we made our way back into the city that the first signs of a deteriorating situation became evident. We found our first rural roadblock, a dirt track blocked by a chain slung between two trees, the Santa Cruz flag hanging limply from it. Two men stood at a pickup truck parked behind it, and waved as we passed by—Ivan's flag seemingly ensuring smooth passage. Our evening meal was more basic than that of the previous day—with food becoming scarcer, we visited a general store where we bought large packets of greasy crisps and some beer.

The following morning brought bad news. We woke to a pall of acrid smoke hanging low in the sky over the city—the protestors had been burning tyres at the barricades overnight. The roads in and out of the city were still blocked, and impassable for all traffic. We tentatively laid plans to attempt to leave in the small hours of the following morning and, for now, would make our way into the city to the botanic gardens. Covering almost two hundred hectares, and containing a mixture of habitats, the gardens promised some birding variety to while away the day. Actually getting to them would prove a different matter entirely.

Leaving the outlying district of the city in which our hotel sat was difficult enough—Ivan avoided two local roadblocks by detouring along rough tracks through fields and then, once we found ourselves on a wide straight road heading into the city, picked up speed. We drove through the smouldering, unmanned remains of overnight barricades, the little Fiat slaloming around shattered lumps of concrete in the road. In the front of the car, Ivan and Jose chatted quietly between themselves whilst, crammed together on the backseat, my Swedish companions and I watched the city gradually becoming more built-up and less rural as we moved towards the centre. Sitting by an open window, feeling increasingly emboldened by our unhindered passage, I did something that, with hindsight, was foolish.

I began filming, on my phone, our rapid progress down the road, bursting through the debris of first one unmanned roadblock and then another. Ivan was driving so quickly, the next roadblock came upon us before I had time to realise it was manned. Before I knew it, we were braking hard and, in my phone's screen, I could see a boy at the line of tyres stretching across the road looking at us, his face freezing and his eyes widening as he noticed my phone. I hastily pulled it back into the car and wound up my window, as the boy walked urgently to one of the men standing nearby—a powerfully built man in black shorts and a black vest, with a green bandana tied around his head, carrying a large wooden stave in his hands. The boy conferred animatedly with him. With two armed companions, and trailed by his smug young informer, he walked towards us.

We were in trouble.

Ivan and Jose lowered their windows a little, and an animated conversation in machine-gun-fast Spanish ensued. Green Bandana was angry, and was gesturing towards me. I could follow the general thrust of the conversation—they knew I'd been filming and wanted me and the phone out of the car, immediately.

"Jon, they say you were filming them," said Jose. "Is that true?"

The lie came easily, while I tried to discreetly delete the footage from the phone.

"No, of course not. I was just trying to get a mobile signal. I wanted to check my emails, that's all."

Our interrogator, one shiny cheek distended and swollen with a wad of coca leaves inside his mouth, clearly did not believe Jose when my reply was relayed to him. One of the other men, a machete hanging from his belt, tried the door handle beside me. To my immense relief, Ivan had locked the car. Ivan called to Green Bandana, and he walked around the front of the car to Ivan's window, which was ajar. Ivan spoke quietly but firmly, punctuating his words with emphatic gestures. Green Bandana's bloodshot eyes flickered, once or twice, to look at the three of us in the back of the car and then, with a disgusted snort, he walked away from the window and gestured to his colleagues to pull the tyres and branches from in front of us, allowing us to proceed unhindered. Ivan pulled smoothly away, laughing now, but Jose was in an understandably more sober mood.

"Jon, that wasn't good. That was really stupid. Please, don't do that again."

I needed no telling. An innocent, if ill-judged action had created an ugly situation that could easily have spiralled out of control. I looked with fresh eyes at Ivan—I now understood the closely cropped hair, and the air of calm authority. Ivan was an off-duty policeman, like all of his colleagues on unpaid leave whilst Bolivia's turbulent domestic politics played out. His services as a driver were simply an initiative to earn a little cash in the meantime. We had been lucky to have him under the circumstances at the roadblock. Whatever quiet threat he had issued to Green Bandana had come with sufficient weight to carry the moment in our favour.

It took a further half hour to reach the botanic gardens, and here we found a much larger and angrier roadblock altogether. The mood in the city was heating up faster than the morning air in the rising sun. Dozens of men milled on the roadside, armed with staves and machetes. Ivan, gesturing at the permit on the windscreen, talked us through and drove a short way down the road before pulling over. We had passed the gates of the botanic garden, chained shut. There was nothing for it but to head back to the hotel and regroup.

Ivan left us there, promising to return later in the afternoon. We saw nothing of him until the evening, when he returned after dark. After hastily conferring with Jose, he left us once more. Jose relayed the bad news.

"Evo has been on the television this afternoon. He said he's going to teach the people of Santa Cruz how to protest."

I asked what that could mean. Jose shrugged.

"Maybe he means he's going to send in the military to crush the rebels. Nobody knows. But Ivan told me something else he's heard. It's really worrying. He says that he's heard the rebels are saying they're going to take foreign hostages. To get the world media's attention, but also as human shields.

"It's up to you, but I think we need to call off the trip altogether. The driver, he says we can't drive out of the city, even at night. Some of the roads in the countryside are still open, but to get to them we'd need to walk maybe eighteen kilometres tonight, carrying all of our gear. And even then, if we can organise another car, we don't know what we're going to find outside of the city. The protests are happening all over Bolivia."

Our decision was swift, and unanimous—we'd leave Bolivia at the earliest opportunity. Bjørn decided to head to Panama, and was able to find a seat on a plane leaving later that night. For Lars and I, the earliest flight we could catch was a day later. That night, Santa Cruz descended further into anarchy. My room in the hotel had a narrow window set well above head height. Standing on a chair, I was able to look out across the low rooftops. Fires were visible scattered across the city beyond. The people were taking to the streets. Walking down to the hotel lobby, I found the doors locked, and a young man with a machete asleep on the chairs in the reception area. The hotel owner had installed some security.

Later, after I had left the country, I learned that five people were shot, though happily none fatally, that night in Santa Cruz, while in La Paz tear gas was fired at protestors.

I was glad to leave, even though I had not set eyes on a single hummingbird.

Chapter Nine

ROBINSON CRUSOE

~

Chile, Isla Robinson Crusoe. 33° S

*O*NE WOULD THINK THAT MAROONING ONESELF ON THE ARCHE-
typal desert island, to search for a hummingbird found nowhere
else on Earth, and one that precious few birders have ever seen, would
be a relatively straightforward business. Desert islands are, after all,
better known for being difficult to leave, rather than to arrive upon.
No island has a stronger claim in this regard than Isla Robinson Crusoe, formerly known to the Spanish in the seventeenth century as
Más a Tierra, or Closer to Land—a name that is technically accurate,
insofar as the island is closer to South America than any others in the
scattered Juan Fernández Archipelago, but remains somewhat ironic
as more than four hundred miles of the Pacific Ocean lie between it
and the nearest point of the Chilean coast.

First discovered by the Spanish sea captain and explorer Juan
Fernández in 1574, the ten-mile-long island was uninhabited by
man at the time, but home to a small variety of land and seabirds

and, around the shores, a burgeoning population of fur and elephant seals. The Spanish came to regard Más a Tierra as a moderately useful stopover—somewhere to find a safe place in which to anchor, stock up on fresh water, maybe kill some fur seals for their pelts and, once they had established a feral population of goats on the island, to hunt for some fresh meat. Inevitably, they also inadvertently introduced cats and rats.

Those rats were to prove bothersome for the island's first long-term European resident. The island must have been a welcome sight in September 1704 for the Scottish sailor Alexander Selkirk. He had been a crew member on an expedition initially led by the swashbuckling English polymath and privateer Captain William Dampier and, latterly, serving on board the vessel *Cinque Ports* under Captain Thomas Stradling. The previous year had been spent preying upon Spanish shipping and settlements along the Atlantic and Pacific coasts of South America but, by the time Más a Tierra hove into view on the horizon, Selkirk was harbouring some grave reservations. They were twofold, though not unrelated—he was extremely concerned about the seaworthiness of the worm-eaten vessel on which he was serving under Stradling's command; and he considered Stradling himself to be an arrogant, privileged young fool oblivious to the suffering of his men and unseaworthiness of his vessel.

Morale on board, by this point, was at an extremely low ebb. Privateers were legally sanctioned pirates, and theirs was, by definition, a brutal and cruel life. In order to crew captured ships, the privateers would put to sea with many more men—usually desperate and degenerate men—than their boats ought to be carrying. Inevitably, providing adequate provisions for that many men was a perennial problem, and disease would spread rapidly in such a confined and unhygienic space. A privateer vessel was the perfect incubator for slow starvation, typhus, and dissent.

By October 1704, having been harboured in the shelter of Más a Tierra's Cumberland Bay for a month, the crew were better fed and the *Cinque Ports* was restocked with goats, crayfish, and some vegetables. To Selkirk's immense dismay, Stradling had made no effort to repair the vessel itself, despite the fact that it was leaking so badly that the crew were forced to pump water from within the hull day and night.

Stradling ordered his men to set sail from Cumberland Bay. It was time to return to some active harassment of the Spanish and enrichment of the crew. Selkirk, the *Cinque Ports'* navigator, flatly refused. An argument erupted between Selkirk and Stradling and, in the heat of the moment, Selkirk requested that he and any other men who shared his reservations should leave the vessel and remain on Más a Tierra until such time as a seaworthy vessel should put in for provisions and they could obtain safe onward passage.

Selkirk was put ashore with some basic provisions—his bedding and navigation instruments, a musket and some gunpowder, a hatchet, a knife, a cooking pot, a little cheese and jam, two pounds of tobacco, a small flask of rum, and his Bible. What he did not have, however, were any companions. The rest of the crew, perhaps driven by greed and the prospect of stolen wealth, or perhaps not relishing the prospect of abandonment on a remote Pacific island well-known to the Spanish, elected to remain on board the *Cinque Ports*. The Spanish did not treat captured British privateers kindly, routinely torturing them to a slow and agonising death. This may have preyed upon Selkirk's mind when he found himself alone on the shore of Cumberland Bay. He pleaded with Stradling to allow him to return to the vessel.

Stradling, evidently enjoying the moment and wishing to set an example to his crew, refused. He ordered his men once more to set sail, and the *Cinque Ports* slowly made her waterlogged way to the horizon, leaving Selkirk alone on the island.

He was to remain there for the next four years and four months, waiting for a British vessel to chance upon the island and provide him with a means to escape. He would, perhaps, have enjoyed some small frisson of satisfaction to learn that the *Cinque Ports* had foundered off the coast of Peru, with just Stradling and a handful of his men surviving—only to be captured by the Spanish. Another privateer, Captain Woodes Rogers, writing of the incident in 1712, recounted, "They had been four Years Prisoners at Lima, where they liv'd much worse than our Governour Selkirk, whom they left on the island."

In his early days on the island, Selkirk would not have shared that sentiment. The sound of bellowing fur seals and elephant seals on the coast was so incessant that he was driven inland. An initial diet of fish did not agree with him, as they "occasion'd a Looseness" in his bowels. At night, he was set upon by hordes of starving rats that gnawed at his clothes and his feet whilst he was asleep. Understandably, he grew depressed and then suicidal at the immediate hopelessness of his situation. The essayist Richard Steele interviewed Selkirk in 1713, and said of these early days, "He grew dejected, languid, and melancholy, scarce able to refrain from doing himself Violence, till by Degrees, by the Force of Reason, and frequent reading of the Scriptures, after the Space of eighteen Months, he grew thoroughly reconciled to his Condition."

By the time he was rescued, in February 1709, by the British privateer vessel *Duke*, captained by Woodes Rogers and piloted by none other than William Dampier, the original leader of the expedition he had signed up to in 1703, Selkirk had adapted to his environment. He had learned to hunt the feral goats, at first shooting them but later chasing them down on foot after his gunpowder had run out. He had domesticated some of the feral cats, alleviating his problems with ravenous rats. He had built a hut for shelter, and had learned which native plants he could eat—amongst them the leaves of the cabbage tree and, according to Rogers, "A black Pepper call'd Malagita, which was very good to expel Wind, and against Griping of the Guts."

Importantly, he had hidden from the crews of two Spanish vessels who had visited the island in the meantime—on one occasion he was seen, shot at, and pursued. He escaped by hiding up a tree under which, at one point, two of his pursuers paused to urinate.

Selkirk's story only came to light three years later, when Rogers wrote his account of his discovery of Selkirk in his broader account of his privateering exploits, *A Cruising Voyage Round the World: First to the South-Sea, Thence to the East-Indies, and Homewards by the Cape of Good Hope.* During the intervening years Selkirk had been the navigator on the *Duke*—a profitable time, as the *Duke* had enjoyed considerable success preying upon Spanish interests. Selkirk returned to England and, in due course, found himself something of a celebrity in the port cities of Bristol and London—happy to tell his tale of survival to anyone for the price of a meal and a pint or two of beer.

Rogers and Steele's published accounts, inevitably, came to the attention of the author and political activist Daniel Defoe. Defoe certainly met with Rogers, if not Selkirk himself and, in 1719, inspired by Selkirk's story, he anonymously published *The Life and Strange Surprizing Adventures of Robinson Crusoe*, a story set in the Caribbean but rooted firmly in Selkirk's Pacific experiences. The decision to remain anonymous was a prudent one—*Robinson Crusoe*, while on the face of it a thrilling account of a tenacious and resourceful shipwrecked sailor, was also the vehicle for barely disguised social and political critique—Defoe was a religious Dissenter whose family was persecuted by the Stuarts and their supporters for his belief that the Church of England remained too closely allied to the Catholic model of belief and worship, and as such he spent a lifetime raging against the Restoration of the Stuart kings. Aspects of Defoe's Nonconformism permeate the book, and it is surely not coincidental that the eponymous hero's story is approximately contemporaneous with the Restoration—Defoe seems to suggest that the true spirit of England resides, in this period, in exile many miles away from home. At a time when expressing such views could get an author hanged, it was sensible for Defoe to distance himself from his popular creation. And popular it certainly was—it went to multiple reprints, and was quickly translated into Dutch, French, German, Russian, and Spanish.

The story proved to be an enduring one. In 1966 the Chilean government even took the step of renaming the island Isla Robinson Crusoe, dropping the former Más a Tierra in favour of the island's most famous literary forebear. Another island in the Juan Fernández archipelago, *Más Afuera* or Further Out, was renamed Alejandro Selkirk, commemorating the nonfictional inspiration for Defoe's literary hero.

As a young boy reading Robinson Crusoe, I was blissfully unaware of any of the book's subtexts, but I was definitely taken with the story of a man forging a new life on a remote island. Defoe's book was at least part of the genesis of my yearning to do just that for myself one day in my future. In time, I came to hear about a hummingbird that lived on the island upon which Alexander Selkirk had been marooned for four years—the Juan Fernández Firecrown, a magnificent, isolated castaway that had evolved to look quite unlike any others of its kind. Indeed, as lately as the 1980s scientists believed there were not one, but two species of hummingbird endemic to the island, so different and strongly marked were the plumages of the male and the female birds of what, in time, we came to recognise as just one species after all.

The male birds are clad entirely in rich, rufous chestnut plumage, with a gold and crimson forehead. Unusually for a hummingbird, where females are normally dressed in muted shades of green and off-white, suitable for camouflaging them during the critical nesting period, the female Juan Fernández Firecrowns have plumage that is as beautiful, if not more so, than that of their mates. Their upperparts are the clear blues and greens of the surrounding ocean waters, their underparts snow-white and ermine-spotted with spangles of metallic emerald. The absence of significant predators in their isolated island home would have allowed this exuberant hummingbird fashion statement to evolve; but the arrival of rats, cats, and, with the eventual colonisation of the island by mankind, more alien species besides, all made for a new and unwelcome chapter in the Juan Fernández Firecrown's history.

My journey into the Pacific began with me standing, alongside a small group of other passengers, outside a small aircraft hangar on the periphery of the airport in Chile's capital, Santiago, nervously eying an elderly Dornier Do 228. We were waiting for news from Isla Robinson Crusoe—the weather there had delayed our flight by over an hour already.

The alternative, a passage by sea, had appealed to the romantic in me. Selkirk arrived on the island by boat, and I would have liked to do so too. Isla Robinson Crusoe is served, however, by a Chilean naval vessel whose irregular timetable, try as I might, I could not be entirely sure was even remotely accurate. My attempts to book passage were met with maddeningly vague responses. On the last leg of my hummingbird travels, I needed certainty—I had a flight to catch to Argentina's southernmost city, Ushuaia, in a little over a week's time, and I could not afford to find myself stranded, like Selkirk, for an indefinite period of time on an island. It would have to be the plane—if the weather relented.

Abruptly, and with no great ceremony, we were invited to board our aircraft.

"The weather is clear there," the captain announced. "We must leave, now."

Three hours later we landed, back where we started, in Santiago. We had got halfway to Robinson Crusoe before the island radioed the captain to inform him they were smothered once again in a thick bank of fog. The decision was made for him, in that moment—we had to return to a clear runway. The air of gloom on board the plane was pervasive.

"We'll not get there today," prophesied one of the local passengers. "We'll be here for days now."

We filed back into the small terminal building, informed that our luggage would be unloaded shortly. We could help ourselves to coffee if we were thirsty. My coffee was not cool enough to drink before the captain repeated his previous exhortation. "The weather is clear. We must leave, now."

While I, by now, had little grounds for optimism that we would actually land on Robinson Crusoe, I was at least relieved that we were trying again. My relief blossomed, some three hours later, as the boxy plane banked around the end of Robinson Crusoe to make its approach to the cracked and potholed short runway that serves the island. The changeable maritime climate might mean that I would struggle to leave Robinson Crusoe on schedule at the end of my stay, but at least when I did leave I ought now to do so having spent some time with the Juan Fernández Firecrowns.

Robinson Crusoe's airstrip is at the extreme western end of the island, set on a rare flat area of land amidst a rocky, arid moonscape of red and ochre rocks. A ridge of volcanic mountains runs up the spine of the island towards the greener, more verdant and fertile eastern side, where, fringed by high peaks, the island's only settlement, San Juan Bautista, nestles on the shore of the same Cumberland Bay where Alexander Selkirk was abandoned in 1704. It is possible to walk from the airstrip to San Juan Bautista, but the hike is an arduous and time-consuming one. While two German tourists elected to make the effort, I joined the locals walking down a track from the airstrip to a nearby pier in a rocky bay fringed with clamorous fur seals. The air smelled dry and the only signs of life on the side of the track were the dead stems and large rattling seedheads of poppies. I absentmindedly picked one as I walked by, slipping it into my pocket—I did not realise I had done this until I returned home, weeks later, and found the seeds like grains of sand in the lining of the pocket. At the time, it was hard to imagine how anything, let alone a hummingbird, would find food to eat or a place to rest in such a barren landscape.

A fast launch carried us, at speed, the length of the island's north coast, past vast, sheer cliffs that dropped straight down into the water. For miles there was no clue that the landscape above had changed at all. I was barely paying attention, however, as the archipelago is famous amongst birdwatchers for, in addition to the Juan Fernández Firecrowns, being home to a range of rare petrels. The waters around it are rich fishing grounds for them, and for albatrosses too. I was in something approaching a sea-birder's nirvana although, frustratingly, all I could find over the water were a handful of scything Pink-footed Shearwaters—new birds for me, but not the rarities I longed to see.

Nearing San Juan Bautista, the landscape began to open up above the cliffs, revealing large areas of deforested grasslands and, above them, heavily wooded peaks and steep slopes. Habitat loss is considered one of the significant pressures that have led to the decline of the San Fernández Firecrown—BirdLife has deemed it Critically Endangered, estimating there are a mere one thousand birds left on the island. It breeds in native forests at high elevations and, after breeding, comes down to low elevations almost at sea level. Unfortunately for the birds, many of those high elevation forests have either been lost altogether, or replaced with introduced eucalyptus.

We passed Puerto Inglés, a wide-open cove with a small wooden cabin set near the shore. Our boatman, Rodrigo, pointed out holes dug into the adjacent cliff base and land around it. "There's a foreigner, he's been coming here for the past twenty years to dig for buried pirate treasure," he explained, with a wry shake of his head. "He's not found any treasure. Just some old pieces of iron, some bullets . . . It's archaeology, really. But it's enough to make him think he's digging in the right place."

It seemed like Isla Robinson Crusoe was a lodestone for remarkable stories, for it transpired that the subject of Rodrigo's mild derision was, in fact, not necessarily the deluded fantasist he at first seemed. Bernard Keiser, a Dutch-born nationalised American businessman, has been searching for a hoard reputed to contain eight hundred barrels of gold and silver coins, ancient gold Peruvian statues, and a necklace that belonged to the wife of Atahualpa, the last Incan emperor.

The treasure was accumulated by the Spanish captain Juan Esteban Ubilla y Echeverria, and was buried on the island in 1714 before his vessel could be intercepted by the British, also still in the area at the time. British captain Cornelius Webb was sent to retrieve the treasure in 1761—he found the hoard, but was forced to reinter it after bad weather damaged his boat. Webb then drew two maps with coded instructions to lead to the treasure. One of these he sent back to England; the other, passing through various hands down the centuries, was acquired in 1998 by Keiser.

From that point onwards, Keiser had been following the instructions he perceived from a real-life, eighteenth-century treasure map and, in September 2019, he was granted permission by the Chilean authorities to excavate a four-hundred-square-metre area of land at Puerto Ingles, where he was sure the treasure trove was buried, in a man-made tunnel deep beneath a large, heavy slab of rock. The value of the combined hoard was estimated to exceed $10 billion.

When I set foot on the pier at Cumberland Bay, I had treasure of a different kind on my mind. Not for me looted Incan gold. I wanted to see my first Juan Fernández Firecrowns. I had been told that they were relatively common in the gardens of the village, and all I need do was look for the endemic cabbage trees. The hummingbirds could not resist their clusters of large, orange flowers.

By this stage I knew all too well that hummingbirds rarely played by the rules, so I was not entirely surprised to find that there were no Juan Fernández Firecrowns to be seen. I stopped to ask a local man if he knew where I might find them. Marcelo paused from sweeping the path to his house.

"El picaflor rojo?" he asked. The red hummingbird? "You should try the gardens above the library, around the offices of CONAF."

CONAF (Corporación Nacional Forestal), the Chilean National Forest Corporation, is a private nonprofit organisation that, overseen and funded by the Chilean government, is charged to sustainably manage and develop Chile's forestry interests. As I was to discover, they had their work cut out for them on Robinson Crusoe, but, in the late afternoon of my first day on the island, it was what they had lurking in their office garden that was of the most pressing interest to me. A prominent sign on the office wall did not seem like a good omen—a large photo of a male and female Juan Fernández Firecrown bore the legend *"Me EXTINGO . . . Ayudame. Tu identidad de isleno/a se EXTINGOS con ellos"*—I am dying out . . . help me. Your islander identity dies out with them.

The sign bore silhouettes of rats and cats, some sort of fruiting vegetation, and a long-tailed animal that looked very much like the overconfident coatimundi I had met in Peru, and an exhortation to islanders to control these *amenazas*, or threats.

I need not have worried. Deep inside a flowering bush beside the office was a familiar form—the unmistakeable silhouette of a perched, watchful hummingbird. By this point in my journey my eyes had a search image for this shape, and I was finding myself able to pick out a hidden hummingbird on the merest glimpse of a distinctive elongated wing or needle-fine bill. I shifted my position slightly around the bush, moving slowly and cautiously. The Juan Fernández Firecrowns share their island home with another hummingbird, the considerably commoner Green-backed Firecrown—I did not want to startle my first hummingbird on the island, let alone before I had had a chance to see if this really was the rojo that Marcelo had assured me I would find here. Another window in the dense vegetation presented itself, and now, with the low sun at my back, I could see more than a backlit, black hummingbird profile.

The setting sun rendered this, my first Juan Fernández Firecrown, ablaze with fiery colour. He seemed to glow from within, like a hot ember, a rich burning umber. I could feel the hairs rising on the back of my neck, and realised I was holding my breath. I exhaled slowly. He was simply magnificent and utterly unconcerned by my proximity to his low roost. He stared evenly back at me, his head slightly cocked. Discerning no threat, he shuffled slightly on his perch and fluffed his feathers, shook slightly, and looked away from me. For a fleeting instant his forehead caught the sunlight and went supernova, an intense dazzle of searing orange. His eyes slowly closed, and I chose to walk softly away from him. I had a week stretching ahead of me—plenty of time to share more moments with him and his kind.

My home for the coming week was down on the very edge of the shore, a room in the home of Ilka Paulentz. Another guest was sharing Ilka's home—a young Chilean documentary filmmaker, García Bloj. Over a bottle of Archipelago, the local beer, that evening at Maren Strum, a bar on the seafront that seemed to double as a community hub, García told me Ilka's story.

Ilka was famous on the island for surviving the devastating tsunami that struck Robinson Crusoe early in the morning of February 27, 2010. The tsunami early warning system had failed, and the people of San Juan Bautista were unaware of the imminent arrival of a three-metre-high wave sent toward them by a magnitude 8.8 earthquake off the coast of mainland Chile. A twelve-year-old girl, Martina Maturana, happened to notice the sea withdrawing and the fishing boats in the harbour starting to strain violently at their moorings and, realising something untoward was happening, she ran across the village to ring the emergency bell and rouse her community from their sleep. As a consequence of her prompt, decisive actions, many islanders managed to retreat to higher ground and safety—but the wave, when it hit the island, destroyed much of San Juan Bautista, and sixteen people lost their lives. This would be a tragedy under any circumstances, but in a fishing community just a few hundred people strong, the loss was all the more profound.

Ilka had been awake before the emergency bell rang. When she heard the bell and came outside her seafront home on the outskirts of the village, it was to see the tidal wave rushing towards her. She knew she did not have enough time to retreat to higher ground—her home was almost at sea level. Instead she ran towards the advancing wave and dived into the sea as it broke over her. García told me, "Ilka is a very strong swimmer, even though she is an old lady. Her actions undoubtedly saved her life. But her home was destroyed and, with it, all of her possessions and furniture were lost. She was left with nothing but her life.

"She's originally from Germany, and she loves to play the accordion. After the tsunami, the villagers found her accordion on the other side of the bay from where her house had stood. It was full of sand, and broken. When Ilka's house was rebuilt, she went to the Continent to buy furniture, as everything had been destroyed. She came back, instead, with a new accordion! Playing it helps her to conquer her fear of still living beside the sea after such a profound tragedy."

Later I fell into conversation with the bar's owner, and explained that I was on the island to spend some time watching the endemic hummingbirds.

"You want to know all about the hummingbirds? You need to meet Pablo Manríquez. He's the head of OIKONOS, the conservation people on here. He's in charge of saving the bird. Pablo! Come here! There's a man who wants to meet you . . ."

With that, I was swiftly introduced to Pablo, an affable man who looked disconcertingly like sculptures of Aristotle, replete with curly black hair and beard. I told Pablo that I had seen my first male Juan Fernández Firecrown, and was looking forward to seeing more of them, and the females too. Pablo grimaced. "The males, they're down in the village now. You'll see them easily. But *la hembra*, the female . . . it's harder to see at this point in the year. They're mostly still hiding up in the forest. You would need to hike up to El Yunque, and look for them there."

El Yunque was one of the mountains that overshadowed the village, a steep looming presence clad with trees. I decided that this would be my destination the following day, and promised to let Pablo know if I was successful in my search for la hembra. I asked Pablo about the sign I had seen earlier in the day. I recognised the rats and cats, but what were the other threats the firecrown faced? He laughed, humourlessly.

"Well. There are rats—both kinds, black and brown. There are mice too. And then there are the cats—every house has them, and they are wild, also all over the island. Of course, many people have a dog too. Many years ago, in the 1930s, someone brought coatimundi here—they say, though I don't know if this is true, that this was to make the island "more interesting" when it became a national park.

"Then there are all the animals that destroy the native plants—rabbits, goats, sheep, cows, horses . . . Much of the forest was felled, and replaced with nonnative eucalyptus and pines. And then there is the problem of the brambles. They are smothering and outcompeting the native vegetation, but nothing wants to eat them . . ."

Legend had it that an islander introduced the brambles thinking they would make a useful, blackberry-bearing livestock-proof hedge. The resident Austral Thrushes on the island certainly approved of the new fruit-bearing plants, avidly consuming the blackberries and, via their droppings, spreading them far and wide across Robinson Crusoe. The thrushes, a colonising species in their own right, are also implicated in the decline of one of the island's other endemic bird species, the Juan Fernández Tit-tyrant—blood parasites carried by the thrush have been found, by researchers, in the blood of the tit-tyrants.

This plethora of introduced species, and their combined impact upon the native vegetation of Robinson Crusoe and the birds that depended upon it, was an unpleasant revelation. I knew the Juan Fernández Firecrowns were red-listed by the International Union for Conservation of Nature (IUCN), but I had not realised quite how much pressure they were under. Naively, I asked Pablo if their one thousand–strong population was still falling, or if the decline had plateaued. He shook his head sadly.

"One thousand? You've been reading the IUCN statistics. They know nothing. We count the nests, every year. We know almost exactly how many adult birds there are at that point. There are no more than four hundred birds remaining now. We're trying to eradicate the brambles, to replant native species, but . . ."

Pablo shrugged, expressively and hopelessly, "It is hopeless. We do not have enough resources. And no matter what we do up there, in the forest, the birds still come down here to the village, and the cats catch the young, inexperienced birds every year. We can try to control the numbers of feral cats, but the people still keep cats in their houses, and they are not neutered. So the cat population remains healthy, and the firecrowns—their numbers are still declining. In maybe twenty years . . ."

He left the implication of extinction hanging, in silence. My worries about whether I would easily see a female bird suddenly felt shameful. I knew that, no matter how beautiful the birds might be, for the first time in my journey through the Americas I would be looking at a species that was almost certainly doomed to be extinct within my lifetime. It was a sobering and terrible thought. Extinction, from a distance, is an abstract concept—an awful one, but still different when one step removed. Extinction is, when one has, just a few hours beforehand, enjoyed close eye contact with the creature in question, a very different prospect indeed. I felt like I could cry at the hopelessness of it all. I walked back to Ilka's house, a very chastened birder. The calls of Pink-footed Shearwaters, carrying through the darkness from their hillside nest burrows above me, mirrored my mood. They sounded mournful and sad—as well they might be, for their numbers too are impacted by the predatory activities of cats, rats, and coatimundis.

The following morning, I began the long hike up to El Yunque. The village's main road runs parallel to the shore of Cumberland Bay and, from it, a number of narrow concrete roads lead uphill, serving houses built on higher ground, and each bearing signs pointing uphill—"Via de Evacuacion Tsunami." One such tsunami evacuation route turns into a winding, stony two-mile-long track that climbs some three hundred metres through swathes of invasive brambles to its conclusion in a large, flat clearing at the edge of the native forest with, rather incongruously, picnic tables and barbecue facilities. The Plazoleta El Yunque is, apparently, a popular picnic site for the island's residents.

Historically, it was home to another shipwrecked waif, following in the illustrious footsteps of Alexander Selkirk—Hugo Weber, a survivor of the sinking of the German warship SMS *Dresden* in Cumberland Bay on March 14, 1915, returned after the war to settle, in self-imposed isolation, at the Plazoleta El Yunque. He was known in his native Germany as the German Robinson Crusoe and only left the island in 1943 when he was accused of being a Nazi spy. His story had, by that point, certainly found favour with the Third Reich—in 1938, Joseph Goebbels, the Reich minister for propaganda, commissioned director Arnold Fanck to create a propaganda film that would loosely tell Weber's story—concluding with the character based upon him, inspired by the wonders of National Socialism, rejoining his former comrades on a new battleship bearing the name *Dresden*. The opening scenes of *A German Robinson Crusoe* were filmed on what was still then known as Más a Tierra. Fanck was not impressed. He described his first impressions of the island as incredibly disappointing, and felt the island lacked visual appeal. He went even further, describing the decision to go to Más a Tierra as a disastrous mistake, and wishing he had followed Defoe's lead in basing the story in the Caribbean.

Walking into the native forest, I had to wholeheartedly disagree with Fanck. The location in which Weber had chosen to make his home had a primeval, *Lost World* quality to it. It felt like stepping back into a more ancient time—I passed by immense tree-sized ferns and underneath the enormous circular, palmate leaves of the endemic gunnera. Early settlers were said to have used the leaves, each with a diameter of a metre, as umbrellas.

Living here for many years, Weber would have known the forest's birdlife intimately. The Juan Fernández Firecrowns, breeding in the trees that surrounded his mountain home, would have been his companions and familiars. This was scant consolation for me, as I still could not find any, let alone the beautiful, elusive female birds I hoped so desperately to see. Small birds were moving through the gunnera, but not the hummingbirds I sought—these were the endemic tit-tyrants, known on the island as *cachuditos*, or little horned ones, owing to the spiky, punky feathers on their heads.

I tried to imagine what it would have been like to live in this environment, less than a century ago. Presumably it would not have been greatly different from the present day, though perhaps the vicissitudes wrought by the various invasive species upon the island's native flora and fauna would not have been as apparent as they now were. I also wondered how Weber would have felt to leave his home. He would, surely, have been sorry to go. He was said to have been wrongly accused of being a Nazi spy, but given Hitler's ambitions in South America generally, and in Chile in particular, one wonders whether it was such an outrageous claim after all.

As an aside, it is curious that Hitler should have used the word *kolibri* as the codename for one of the earliest demonstrations of his growing power—*Unternehmen Kolibri*, or Operation Hummingbird, was the codename for what came to be known as the "Night of the Long Knives," when Hitler unleashed the Schutzstaffel (SS) and the Gestapo to round up prominent members of the paramilitary Sturmabteilung (SA), or Brownshirts. Almost one hundred German officials, and some of their wives, were executed as part of a brutal political purge that was named after one of the most inoffensive bird families of all.

Their name had already been appropriated by another Austrian earlier in the twentieth century—Franz Pfannl, a watchmaker, created the world's smallest ever handgun in 1910. The Kolibri was chambered for a bespoke 2.7mm centerfire cartridge that fired a miniscule 3-grain bullet with less muzzle velocity than most airguns. The gun was semiautomatic and, as such, was an impressive piece of miniaturised engineering as befitted its watchmaker genesis. It was not, however, taken seriously as an offensive weapon. Advertised as a self-defence weapon suitable for women, it was not a runaway commercial success—less than a thousand were made before production ceased in 1914, when the First World War gave the Austro-Hungarian Empire more pressing munitions issues to address.

If the firecrowns had been more numerous during Weber's time on the island, they certainly were not present in appreciable numbers in the course of the morning I spent wandering the paths that threaded their way around the flanks of El Yunque. Dispirited and hungry, I made my way back down to the village on the shore, foraging on ripe blackberries as I went. I had arranged to join one of the local men, Marcelo Rossi, for a few hours that afternoon in his boat, looking for seabirds a little way offshore. The islands of the Juan Fernández archipelago—Robinson Crusoe, Alejandro Selkirk, and Santa Clara—are hotbeds of endemism. The forest I had been exploring in the morning features dozens of plants found nowhere else on earth and, besides the Juan Fernández Firecrown and the cachudito, the islands also have other endemic bird species I dearly hoped to see whilst I was there. In particular, I hoped to see a trio of petrels—seabirds that usually spend their entire lives far out in the deepest reaches of the Pacific Ocean, only returning to these scraps of land to breed.

The world population of both Juan Fernández and Stejneger's Petrels breeds on Selkirk; whilst Masatierra Petrel, despite being named after Más a Tierra, breeds on a handful of Chilean islands, Santa Clara amongst them. All have populations classified as Vulnerable. All three are graceful birds in flight, with an effortless soaring and gliding action skimming the waves that makes a mockery of man's clumsy passage in their realm. A lazy, twisting swell that afternoon made me glad of my Shetland sea legs, though it helped to focus on the steady immensity of Robinson Crusoe on the near horizon. From a distance the island appeared black against the sky, a monolithic presence that was at once reassuring and faintly threatening.

The previous evening I had spent a while chatting with a Spanish volcanologist, Laura Becerril Carretero, who was staying on the island to study the geology of Robinson Crusoe and Selkirk. The archipelago was, apparently, as compelling for determined volcanologists as it was for birdwatchers, having never been connected to the South American mainland, and being formed entirely of volcanic material ejected from a number of volcanoes over the course of several million years. The islands' venerable age and permanent isolation explained why so many species had evolved to be unique to the archipelago. I wondered what, in time, would become of the introduced alien species if they were not eradicated and were left to their own devices for many thousands of years. I had heard apocryphal tales of the hungry rats on the island being more arboreal than their mainland counterparts. Perhaps evolution was already changing them, favouring the agile rats that could forage for food in the trees. Rats like that would, of course, find hummingbird nests.

These thoughts were soon pushed from my mind by the arrival of the first seabirds around our small boat. Marcelo cut the engine when the first of several immense Black-browed Albatrosses wheeled around us and then pitched down onto the water beside us, curious to see if an easy meal would be forthcoming. They were in luck, as Marcelo had a bucket of fish for this very purpose and, before too long, I found myself gazing into the bottomless dark wells that are the eyes of a Black-browed Albatross. Our small boat was low on the water, and from my position sitting near the stern I was at eye level with the bird, bobbing on the water just a couple of feet away from me. It was difficult not to succumb to a very human sentimentality face to face with such a majestic creature. I wanted to assign it some sort of Coleridgean significance and wisdom. The bounds of its sagacity appeared, however, to extend to swiftly realising I was not the purveyor of fish pieces—it paddled to the prow where Marcelo sat, deftly slicing fish with a sharp knife and tossing pieces onto the water, where a trio of albatrosses set about swallowing them as quickly as he served their dinner.

This activity, and the smell of fish oil on the water, soon wrought a remarkable transformation in the immediate area of the boat. The air above the seemingly empty, roiling sea was suddenly filled with birds. Petrels came from nowhere, cutting parabolas over the waves. Most of them were Juan Fernández Petrels but, amongst their number were some smaller birds—pale dove-grey Masatierra Petrels, and one strikingly different bird with wings that looked as if they had been dipped in black tar. This was my Stejneger's Petrel—a bird that I had particularly longed to see, as it enjoys a reputation for being one of the most enigmatic, difficult seabirds in the world for a birder to catch a glimpse of. Here I was, watching one fly around me, trying to steady my camera against the rocking of the boat in which I stood. I felt dangerously top-heavy, and decided to sit down and abandon my attempts to take photos. I knew the moment was what I should immerse myself in, rather than the ocean, involuntarily.

Our return to the harbour as the sun dropped below the horizon was a triumphant one. Marcelo was delighted with the variety of species we had found offshore—more than he had expected, and certainly more than I had dared hope for. He opened up the boat's throttle and, with music playing at a volume where the boat's speakers began to distort, carved his way between fishermen's boats and the buoys that marked the wreck of the SMS *Dresden*. As an expression of exuberant machismo our approach felt like the helicopter assault scenes of *Apocalypse Now*, though the affable Marcelo made for an unlikely Lieutenant Colonel Kilgore and the Monkees' "I'm a Believer" a surreal substitute for Wagner's "Ride of the Valkyries."

Another day had passed, but I was no nearer to seeing a female Juan Fernández Firecrown. The following morning I joined Pablo and six workers from the Chilean Ministry of Agriculture, and we returned to El Yunque—on this occasion arriving just after first light. We hoped that the hummingbirds, if they were there, ought to be more active in the early morning. The logic was impeccable, for we had gone no more than a few yards into the enveloping canopy of the gunnera before a flash of white, whirring past us, revealed itself to be a female firecrown. She landed, briefly, on the underside of a gunnera leaf, hanging upside down in the green aqueous light filtering through the leaf above, before the noise of the exuberant workmen in the clearing behind us startled her. With a small, indignant squeak she took to the air again, and vanished as quickly as she had come, into the dense vegetation that surrounded us. The entire encounter had lasted a matter of seconds, barely time to register her for what she was.

For the next few hours we walked the same paths I had followed the previous day. Pablo showed me the previous breeding season's nests, tiny woven cups of green moss and brown fibrous material built around branches that looked too thin to support them. In one nest lay a white egg, an impossibly tiny unrealised life. Hummingbirds usually lay just two eggs—the difference between breeding success and failure then rests on a knife-edge until those eggs have hatched and the nestlings have flown the nest.

"They abandoned the nest. We don't know why. One day la hembra was sitting on it, the next . . . she was gone, and she didn't come back. Perhaps something happened to her."

The noise of the workmen, now eating their lunch at the plazoleta—the small clearing at the end of the trail that led up from the village below—followed us through the trees, and I began to realise the disturbance would make my chances of getting better views of another female bird extremely slim. Pablo, sensing my despondency, tried to cheer me up.

"Maybe they're starting to come down to the village now. You should try looking for them down there this afternoon, and tomorrow. Maybe in the early morning and late afternoon, when they are all more active. But Jon—they can be hard to see at this time of year. Sometimes days go by without a sighting. They are secretive. And, of course, there are not so many birds in the first place, nowadays."

We returned to San Juan Bautista and, following Pablo's advice, I returned to where I had seen my first male Juan Fernández Firecrown some days previously. If there had been one there, perhaps the area was a favoured one generally for his kind. The afternoon that followed was, on the one hand, extremely pleasant—I found at least three male birds holding feeding territories in the area. Each seemed to have a favoured flowering bush he defended, driving away any other male that had the temerity to attempt to poach some of his nectar resource with a typically voluble, chattering, high-speed attack. The interloper invariably fled into the safe heights of one of the surrounding trees. However, what was conspicuously absent were any female birds. It was hard to resist the pessimistic conclusion that I might leave the island in a few short days' time without having encountered one for more than the most fleeting of moments.

I walked back towards Ilka's house, and bumped into the original Marcelo who had first pointed me in the direction of CONAF's garden. He was accompanied, on this occasion, by his brother, and I spent a while in conversation with both old men. Marcelo asked, "How is your hummingbird hunt going? Did you find the rojo?"

I told him I had, and thanked him for his kind assistance. I explained that I was struggling to find la hembra, hoping that he would be able to weave similar magic and point me in the right direction of a garden renowned for them. He shook his head.

"Ah, la hembra. She is shy. Not like the rojo. He is like this . . ."

He puffed out his chest.

". . . So confident! He is not hard to find."

His brother laughed, and agreed with him. "Yes, the macho is brave. When we were boys, fifty years ago, we used to hunt them too. With slingshots."

He paused to mime firing a catapult at an imaginary bird hovering in front of us.

"All the children used to do it. We would compete to see how many rojos we could kill. Of course, we know better now. The children don't do that any more."

I had heard for myself the pride that the younger generation of islanders felt about their hummingbirds. One of the young men I had met at the airfield on the day of my arrival on the island, Germán Recabarren, had told me how important they were to him. He showed me photos of the birds he had taken and posted on his Instagram feed.

"They are the most beautiful and endangered birds in the world," he said. "For me, they are part of my identity. They are the soul of this place."

However, I wondered how far this sense of pride extended. Pablo's resignation and sadness at the extent and cost of the task facing anyone wishing to address the myriad alien species that threatened the island's biome as a whole, let alone the hummingbirds in isolation, haunted me. The island's younger generation might now value their endemic hummingbirds in a way that their forebears had not, but a sense of pride was not going to save a species. For that, there needed to be radical action—eradication of rodents on the isle seemed feasible, as this was now happening on other remote islands, albeit at significant financial cost. The removal of invasive brambles would be a much more costly and painfully time-consuming exercise— technically feasible, but probably prohibitively expensive if it was to encompass the entire island. The removal of domestic cats, though, seemed more unlikely—nobody likes to be told they can't have pets, after all. In Britain, conversations were starting to be had in earnest about the carbon footprint attached to taking flights for holidays or work; while Sir David Attenborough had breached the hitherto unspeakable topic of the environmental damage inherent in the burgeoning human population of the planet. Nobody yet had dared to publicly suggest that domestic cats and dogs were a carbon-emitting luxury we should consider giving up for the sake of the environment. I wondered when, if at all, that Rubicon would be crossed. Back here, on an island riddled with mice and rats, it did not seem like a topic that could be usefully raised, no matter how much damage those cats annually wrought on the reproductive success of what was left of the entire world population of Juan Fernández Firecrowns.

I sensed the regret that Marcelo's brother felt about killing them for fun when he was a boy, but did not feel it was my place to speak about the other, present dangers the hummingbirds faced. I could only speak of problems, but could offer no solutions. I understood Pablo's hopelessness about the task in hand.

The following morning, my luck finally took a turn for the better, and almost on the very doorstep of Ilka's house. A few hundred yards away, and a little uphill, there was a small playpark for the island's children, replete with the usual swings and suchlike, and benches for parents to sit and pass the time upon. Dotted around the playpark were some large flowering examples of the endemic cabbage tree and, that morning, I found a male Juan Fernández Firecrown busily feeding from the pendulous, tasselled orange flowers at the crown of one tree. This, in itself, was unusual, as I had not yet seen any firecrowns at such a low elevation in the village, almost at sea level. I decided to linger a while on the benches, taking some photos of the male when the opportunity presented itself. If I was honest with myself, I was postponing the long walk back up to El Yunque—despite Pablo's advice, I felt I had to return to the one place I had been able to catch even a glimpse of a female. It was the only lead I had to follow, after all.

Half an hour later I was girding myself to make a fresh assault on the heights of El Yunque when the male hummingbird, perched nearby, uttered a sound quite unlike any I'd heard his counterparts make in the previous days. Hitherto their utterances had been limited to angry denunciations as they sped into battle with one another in brief, intense territorial disputes. This sounded very different as he leapt into flight—a disyllabic call that, when I saw where he was heading, made sense. This was the Juan Fernández Firecrown equivalent of actor Leslie Phillips' lecherous catchphrase uttered upon meeting an attractive woman: "Well, *hello* . . ."

The firecrown dashed towards a nearby bush, proceeding to hover in front of the veil of leaves that shrouded the bush's interior, swaying back and forth like a pendulum, before darting inside and out of sight. I shifted a little on the bench, and found myself now able to see him perched on a branch, extravagantly spreading his wings and tail wide open, and gazing intently at the object of his desire—a female firecrown, sitting a few inches away from him. She was playing it cool, under the circumstances, showing no sign whatsoever of being aware of him, let alone interested in his advances. She flew to an adjacent, more exposed branch. The male repeated his delighted call, launching himself after her. This time I could see more clearly

his swaying display flight. It had to be said he was intruding somewhat into her personal space, for his bill was almost touching her
face. She remained completely unmoved by him, at first leaning back
on her perch away from him, and then, with crushing nonchalance,
launching into flight to feed from some nearby purple morning glory
flowers. The spurned male landed where she had been perched, the
picture of dejection.

I spent the morning with them in the playpark, watching them
feeding, preening themselves and, in the case of the male, fruitlessly
displaying to the disinterested female. Finally seeing one of her kind
for myself, I could understand his ardour. She was utterly beguiling,
her plumage more sophisticated than that of the male. Her forehead,
a shimmering blaze of heliotrope, merged into aquamarine on her
crown, with spangled ultramarine jewels cascading from her throat
down her white breast and flanks. She was resplendent in her own
right, and I finally understood why, until so very recently, it had been
believed the two sexes were entirely different species.

I wondered how many people had ever been fortunate enough to
witness the courtship display of the Juan Fernández Firecrown and,
with an unwelcome pang of realism, how long the birds would endure and allow others to enjoy that rare honour. In the course of
the few hours I had watched these two birds, a number of cats had
slunk through the bushes in the playpark. One scrawny tortoiseshell
had seen the female hovering at the low-flowering morning glory,
and began to stalk towards her glacially slowly, belly brushing the
ground and tail tip twitching with anticipation. The hummingbird
continued to feed, oblivious to the imminent threat. I removed the
lid of my metal water bottle and threw the contents over the approaching cat, eliciting a satisfying direct hit and a mortified retreat.
The victory was a small but significant one—0.25 percent of the
estimated world population of Juan Fernández Firecrowns lived to
feed and, hopefully, breed another day.

It was with considerable reluctance that I left Robinson Crusoe,
my passage by light aircraft as uneventful and timely as Alexander

Selkirk's eventual departure from the island had been fraught and protracted. I had immediately liked the warm, friendly islanders—they reminded me of my island neighbours at home in Shetland, even down to the linguistic peculiarity of a double repetition greeting. In Shetland they say *hi-aye*, a contemporary adaptation of the older *aye-aye*; in Robinson Crusoe, *hola-hola*. Of all the places I had visited in South America, Robinson Crusoe was the place that felt most like home. I would, in the months to come, find myself daydreaming about what it might be like to live there. This was, I knew, nothing more than a daydream.

My visit would be, like that of William Dampier, the pilot of the *Duke*, the boat involved in the rescue of Selkirk in 1709, a fleeting one at best. When not rescuing castaway sailors like Selkirk from remote islands, Dampier had enjoyed a chequered career—the first man to circumnavigate the globe three times, despite often being drunk on duty, he was a prodigiously successful privateer, yet on one occasion narrowly escaped being eaten by his own men whilst adrift in the Pacific. Less well known are his achievements as a naturalist—he combined a career of legally sanctioned piracy with a sideline in botany and anthropology. He was the first man to describe the flora and fauna of the Galápagos Islands, a century before Charles Darwin set foot there. He collected botanical specimens from around the coasts of the West Indies and South America, and was the first not only to describe, in 1697, the *avogato* or avocado, but also what sounds like a sweet precursor of guacamole:

> The Fruit as big as a large Lemon. It is of a green colour . . . The substance in the inside is green, or a little yellowish, and as soft as Butter. This Fruit hath no taste of its self, and therefore 'tis usually mixt with Sugar and Lime-juice, and beaten together in a Plate, and this is an excellent dish.
>
> It is reported that this Fruit provokes to lust . . .

If Dampier's unsung legacy was the introduction to the English-speaking world of the aphrodisiac avocado, Alexander Selkirk's legacy had been a literary one—immortalised by Daniel Defoe as Robinson Crusoe, but also in his own right by other subsequent writers. Charles Dickens used him as a simile in *The Pickwick Papers*: "Colonel Builder and Sir Thomas Clubbe exchanged snuff-boxes, and looked very much like a pair of Alexander Selkirks—'Monarchs of all they surveyed.'"

This itself was a reference to an earlier work, *The Solitude of Alexander Selkirk*, by poet William Cowper. Cowper concluded,

> *I am the monarch of all I survey*
> *My right there is none to dispute;*
> *From the centre all round to the sea,*
> *I am lord of the fowl and the brute.*

The irony of that verse was not lost on me as the small plane that carried me off Robinson Crusoe swept along the towering cliffs before heading away over the sea towards mainland Chile. I looked down at the green areas of the island, now understanding that the people who lived there were far from in control of the fate of the native birds they shared their island home with, nor those of the invasive mammals and plants their forebears had brought to the island. Like so many of us, they were well-intentioned and decent people, but found themselves helpless to deal with environmental forces beyond their ability and resources to control.

CHAPTER TEN

THE END OF THE WORLD

~

Argentina, Tierra del Fuego. 54° S

*W*HILST BEST KNOWN FOR HIS STUDIES OF THE FLORA AND fauna of the Galapagos Islands, Charles Darwin's account of his voyages around South America on board HMS *Beagle* reveals that his keen eye for detail was seldom closed. To the modern reader, his observations about the native peoples he met can be jarring—of his first encounters with the native people in the immense archipelago of Tierra del Fuego, he concluded they were, "Like wild beasts . . . abject and miserable creatures [that] closely resembled the devils which come on the stage in plays like *Der Freischütz.*"

Yet his natural history insights were unfailingly astute and, at times, his personal observations make the great scientist endearingly human.

The *Beagle* set sail from Britain in December 1831 on what was intended to be a two-year expedition. In the event, almost five years had elapsed before she returned to her home port in Falmouth. Whilst Darwin spent a shade over three years of that time exploring South America on land, eighteen months of the intervening period was spent at sea—a time Darwin found incredibly trying, for he suffered badly from seasickness. He considered life at sea to be vastly overrated.

> And what are the boasted glories of the ocean? A tedious waste, a desert of water . . .
>
> If a person suffer much from sea-sickness, let him weigh it heavily in the balance. I speak from experience: it is no trifling evil which may be cured in a week.

On January 29, 1833, passing from the turbulent waters of the South Atlantic into the relative shelter of the Beagle Channel that bisects Tierra del Fuego, Darwin found some relief from his affliction. That day marked his first sight of the glaciers that pour down from the mountains to the shore of the channel, and he felt sufficiently moved to record, "It is scarcely possible to imagine anything more beautiful than the beryl-like blue of these glaciers, and especially as contrasted with the dead white of the upper expanse of snow."

Running on an east/west axis, the Beagle Channel lies at a latitude of some 55° south. To put just how far south this is into perspective, Prime Head, the northernmost point of the Antarctic continental mainland, is at a latitude of 63° south, approximately 550 miles south in total, and the forests of the most southerly point of New Zealand are found way further north, at 47° south. Tierra del Fuego would, then, seem to be an unlikely location in which to find a hummingbird, not least because of the climatic extremes the region can suffer, particularly during the winter months. These led the *Beagle*'s former captain, Pringle Stokes, to record in his journal in the height of the southern winter in 1828,

Nothing could be more dreary than the scene around us. The lofty, bleak, and barren heights that surround the inhospitable shores of this inlet, were covered, even low down their sides, with dense clouds, upon which the fierce squalls that assailed us beat, without causing any change . . . Around us, and some of them distant no more than two-thirds of a cable's length, were rocky inlets, lashed by a tremendous surf; and, as if to complete the dreariness and utter desolation of the scene, even the birds seemed to shun its neighbourhood. The weather was that in which . . . the soul of man dies in him.

A few weeks later, Stokes shot himself in the head—an initially unsuccessful suicide attempt, as he remained conscious and coherent, a painful irony for a man who was already suffering from depression. He finally died eleven days later after gangrene had set into the wound. A short while later, when the *Beagle* arrived in Montevideo for maintenance work, Robert FitzRoy was given command of the vessel, and it was he who led the expedition to which Darwin had committed himself.

Darwin would have known about the renowned bleakness of Tierra del Fuego, and the effect it had wrought on the unfortunate former captain of the ship on which he sailed. He would, however, also have had cause for some optimism about the natural history that he would find on those supposedly bird-shunned "inhospitable shores," for the previous expedition's overall commander, Phillip Parker King, had been a keen observer of the fauna he encountered during his time in the area, and had described to Darwin an occasion on which he had encountered Green-backed Firecrown hummingbirds "flitting about in a snowstorm." If hummingbirds could weather the conditions of Tierra del Fuego, Darwin would have been quietly confident he would find other remarkable life there besides.

Commander King's hummingbird connections do not end here for, two years later, in 1832 his name was immortalised in the scientific name for the Long-tailed Sylph, *Aglaiocercus kingii*, by the French naturalist René Primevère Lesson. Lesson had spent a career serving as a surgeon and pharmacist in the French navy, including during the Napoleonic Wars. Bad blood clearly did not exist between these two naval men of formerly bitter enemy states.

In fact, with the benefit of a voyage that extended so far up the Pacific coast of South America, Darwin was able in time to observe that Green-backed Firecrown was a particularly tenacious and adaptable species, with a range of over 2,500 miles "from the hot dry country of Lima to the forests of Tierra del Fuego." In the cool, rain-lashed forests of Chiloé Island, hundreds of miles north of Tierra del Fuego, he found the hummingbirds to be numerous, and their nests frequently encountered.

This was not the case in Tierra del Fuego, for here the hummingbirds existed at the very limit of their range. On Chiloé Island, Darwin had noted that, in the absence of any flowering plants, the hummingbirds were feeding not on "honey," or nectar, but instead on small flies and insects. We now know that many hummingbirds supplement their largely nectarivorous diets with the protein hit of insects, but at the time the observation was novel.

Commander King's sighting of hummingbirds on the wing during a snowstorm was very much on my mind as I stood, braced against driving sleet, on a black pebbly beach on the northern shores of the Beagle Channel, hoping to see a Green-backed Firecrown for myself at this southerly extremity of the hummingbird tribe's global range. The skyline was framed by the snow-topped heights of the Martial Mountains and, in the near distance, the marbled white snout of the Martial Glacier reared over the city of Ushuaia. Ushuaia, described by the Argentine marketers as "the most southerly city in the world," also has the dubious distinction of being known locally as *Fin del Mundo*, or the End of the World.

Emanating from somewhere deep in the nearby dripping bushes I could hear a litany of subdued Spanish curses. When he visited Patagonia in 1959, naturalist and animal collector Gerald Durrell was accompanied by auburn-haired Josefina and blonde Mercedes. Instead of two elegant female travel companions, my birding companion was Federico Ezequiel Moyano, a young ski instructor during the winter who, in what passed for summer in the cool, maritime surroundings of Ushuaia, enjoyed birding. We had become firm friends in the short time we had known one another, but the conditions today were proving too much even for one as implacable as Federico. We had caught a glimpse of what I thought might have been a hummingbird feeding at one of the few remaining flowers on a Chilean Firetree, but the bird, if indeed there had been one in the first place, was nowhere to be seen. While I maintained a vigil of the greater area from the shore, Federico was making heavy weather of clambering through chest-deep vegetation in the immediate vicinity of the small evergreen tree in question.

The timing of my visit was not ideal. The first snow of winter had fallen on the surrounding mountains the night before my arrival in Ushuaia and, to my mounting alarm, the preceding days had been cold too, frost blackening many of the remaining scarlet-red flowers on the firetrees that dotted the forests along the shores on either side of the city. The firetrees are the favoured food source for the Green-backed Firecrowns that call the southern edge of Tierra del Fuego home during the damp, cool months of summer. When they finish flowering, the hummingbirds' departure is imminent.

Darwin had noted that Green-backed Firecrowns were migratory, fleeing the cooler extremities of the Chilean coast for the warmer central part of the country during the autumn, and only returning to breed in the spring.

"Some," he observed, "however, remain during the whole year in Tierra del Fuego."

Tierra del Fuego, its ownership divided between Argentina and Chile, encompasses a vast area at the southern tip of South America with the main island, Isla Grande, alone covering an area of 18,500 square miles. While Green-backed Firecrowns might sit out the southern winter in a warm microclimate of a sheltered corner of the islands, Federico had been matter-of-fact about the habits of those found along the shores of the Beagle Channel. We had no sooner met in Ushuaia than he issued a stark disclaimer: "They migrate from here once it gets colder, and when the food is gone . . . Well, I can't guarantee we will find the hummingbird. It isn't the ideal situation, the timing of your visit."

The timing of my visit had been somewhat beyond my control. Having come as far as Santiago, the Chilean capital, it made sense to combine searching for the world's most southerly hummingbirds with my expedition to Isla Robinson Crusoe. That I had seen Green-backed Firecrowns on that remote island was not really the point—having seen Rufous Hummingbirds in the Alaskan north, I wanted to see their southern counterparts on the cusp of Tierra del Fuego. Federico had continued with one further fillip of advice:

"Jon . . . if anyone here in Ushuaia asks you where you are from, it's probably best not to say you're British. Most people would be okay with that, but here in the city . . . memories of La Guerra de las Malvinas are still fresh and sore, for some people. It is perhaps not so bad in the rest of Argentina, but here maybe you should not tell the truth about where you are from."

I had already inadvertently touched upon the raw nerve the Falklands War of 1982 still aroused in some Argentinians, for my hitherto taciturn taxi driver in Buenos Aires the previous day had, as we passed the floodlit Museo Malvinas, shouted over his shoulder to me, "Malvinas! Las Malvinas son Argentinas!"

The Falklands are Argentinian. I had come to Argentina to do something as innocent as looking for a hummingbird, and had no wish to reopen political wounds best left well alone. With my Shetland island home enjoying a Viking heritage that extended to centuries of Scandinavian ownership, I felt I could tenuously claim to be Norwegian if put on the spot. I hoped, however, that out in the countryside searching for hummingbirds, I would be unlikely to be questioned about my nationality, let alone expected to make conversation in Norwegian. In the event, nobody had so far discovered I was British, but nor had we found a definite hummingbird.

Behind me, over the lead-grey waters of the Beagle Channel, Southern Giant Petrels patrolled, as ugly as xenophobia. Their flight over the sleet-stippled water was graceful, but their appearance was brutish—their thick, pale bills the perfect tools for both killing other seabirds and butchering carrion. Larger than some albatrosses, their presence was commanding. A more benign note was struck nearer to the shore where, just a few metres offshore, a pair of Flightless Steamer Ducks paddled grimly into the stiff offshore breeze. Each large, stout duck was as grey as the water it forged through, with a head that appeared way too big for its body, and a large, comical, tangerine beak. Federico, joining me back on the shore, dispelled any notions I might have entertained about their harmless appearance.

"They can be very aggressive. They'll chase off the petrels if they land on the water near them, and they fight amongst themselves. They can even kill other birds sometimes."

It seemed that every bird I had seen so far in Tierra del Fuego needed to be tough to survive this challenging place—from the predatory hook-billed Southern Caracaras that hunted over the roadsides outside the airport and the giant petrels patrolling the length of the Beagle Channel, to the sinister, outwardly innocuous steamer ducks. I wondered anew at the tenacity of the Green-backed Firecrowns, eking out an existence in such an extreme environment. They did not have to be there—yet they had found a niche they could exploit, and here they were.

Or rather, they weren't. We could find no further sign of the bird we had seen earlier, and continued to walk along the shore to where Federico hoped we might find a firetree with a few surviving flowers and, hence, maybe a hummingbird. As we walked, ducking beneath fibrous glaucous clots of Southern Mistletoe growing on the low-hanging branches of the Southern Beech trees we passed, Federico told me about the indigenous Yámana people who lived along the shores of Tierra del Fuego at the time the first Europeans arrived there. It was the fires lit by the Yámana along those shores that gave the archipelago its name—Tierra del Fuego means Land of Fire. Darwin saw those fires from the decks of the Beagle, recording in his journal as they entered the Beagle Channel, "Fires were lighted on every point, both to attract our attention and to spread far and wide the news [of our arrival]."

In the early twentieth century, the Austrian anthropologist Martin Gusinde followed in Darwin's footsteps, and spent time with the Yámana. He likened them to restless migratory birds, saying they were only happy and inwardly calm when they were on the move. Decades before Gusinde, Darwin made a number of more prosaic observations about the lives of the Yámana, not least of their semi-nomadic habits: "The inhabitants, living chiefly upon shellfish, are obliged constantly to change their place of residence; but they return at intervals to the same spots, as is evident from the piles of old shells, which must often amount to many tons in weight. These heaps can be distinguished at a long distance by the bright green colour of certain plants, which invariably grow on them."

Crossing small areas of short grass that extended down to the shore, we came upon several such midden heaps, just as Darwin had described them, with more verdant plant growth upon them. One such heap had been bisected by a cattle path, and where the cows' hooves had worn through the turf I could see the dark-indigo debris of countless thousands of fragments of mussel shells and charred pieces of bone. Federico paused to look carefully at the exposed debris.

"You never know what you might find in these mounds," he said. "I once found a bone harpoon."

In that moment I wanted nothing more than to find a centuries-old Yámana artefact, a carved bone harpoon or knapped flint arrowhead, but, inevitably, our cursory search of the exposed mound revealed no such token of the past. I remained keen to keep searching for the real treasure I hoped Tierra del Fuego still held—a Green-backed Firecrown. The Yámana knew the hummingbirds and, like so many of the indigenous people throughout the Americas who shared their land with them, the hummingbirds featured in their folklore in the form of Omora, a brave hummingbird to whom the people appealed in times of trouble. One such story, typical of the qualities of selflessness and bravery the people saw in the hummingbirds, involves a time of great drought, during which the people of the region came close to dying of thirst.

A sly fox, Cilawaia, found a small lake of fresh, sweet water. He built a fence around it, and allowed only his close family to drink from it. In time, the people learned of the lake, and came to seek water for themselves, but found themselves confronted by Cilawaia and the barrier he had erected. They begged him for water, but he was unmoved by their pleas.

"If I allow you to drink, there will soon not be enough water for me and my family," he said. "Why should I help you?"

The people, desperate by now, appealed to Omora for help. The hummingbird, a summer visitor to their lands, was tiny but braver than anyone else they knew of. If anyone could help them, Omora would. Omora listened to their story and, indignant, flew at once to the lake to confront Cilawaia. He found the selfish fox bathing in the lake's water. Hovering out of reach of the fox's jaws, he confronted him, demanding that Cilawaia share the water with the drought-stricken people. Cilawaia poured scorn on Omora.

"Why would I help them? There's barely enough water here for me and my family. If I let the people drink from the lake too, soon there won't be any water left, and then my family will be thirsty. This water is mine, and I'm not going to share it."

This enraged Omora, and he flew from the lake to gather some sharp stones. Returning to within earshot of Cilawaia, he gave the fox one last chance:

"Share the water, Cilawaia, with the people, for now and forever. If you don't, your selfishness will cost them their lives."

Cilawaia was indifferent to the hummingbird's entreaties. He shrugged.

"They can die, for all I care. It's not my problem. If I share the water, in time I will die of thirst, and my family too."

Omora flung one of the sharp stones at Cilawaia, striking him and killing him instantly. The people, who had been watching from a safe distance, rushed forwards, breaking down the fence and dropping to their knees to drink deeply from the lake. Sure enough, Cilawaia had been right, for the water level dropped rapidly and soon there was just wet mud where once there had been a pool of clear water. The people looked at one another—had this just been a temporary reprieve? They had slaked their thirst today, but tomorrow there would be nothing to drink.

Omora's grandmother Sirra, the wise owl, instructed all the other birds to gather mud in their beaks, and to fly to the slopes of the surrounding mountains, where they should drop the mud. They did as they were bid, and where they dropped the wet mud small springs erupted from the ground. The rivulets of water, trickling downhill from them, joined to form streams, and these fed into rivers that flowed down into the valleys below. From that time forwards, the Yámana always had fresh, sweet water that flowed from the mountains.

I had heard so many folklore stories involving hummingbirds throughout the Americas. The hummingbirds in those stories were usually benevolent, but always brave. The quality of bravery made immediate sense to me, as anyone who watched hummingbirds defending a nectar source would soon appreciate their spirit. They were demonstrably pugnacious and never shied away from a challenge. The benevolence the native peoples ascribed to them was a more elusive quality, at least in the wild. Hummingbirds were no more selfless than any other bird. Why had so many people attributed kindness and generosity to them?

I wondered if—in the same way I had encountered so many people in my travels who, to this day, related to hummingbirds in a manner to which they did not to other birds, giving them names and personalities—perhaps people had always felt that hummingbirds touched them in some indefinable but positive way. Maybe it was that very fearlessness in the face of man that some species of hummingbird display, even now after centuries of mankind doing its worst, that had always appealed to us. Perhaps, knowing innately that human nature was not always a beautiful and benevolent thing, the hummingbirds' fearlessness in our presence has always helped to make us feel better about ourselves, and diminished any residual sense of guilt we may feel about our impact on the world around us.

Federico and I continued to make our way along the shore of the Beagle Channel, the Chilean island of Isla Navarino visible across the water. The Omora Ethnobotanical Park on its northern shore commemorates the legend of Omora, named not so much after the hummingbird than what his legend represents—a time when humans and other animals lived in the same society, with little Omora helping to resolve disputes within the community, maintaining a dialogue between society and nature.

The morning's icy squalls gave way to thin, watery sunshine. We paused while Federico prepared *maté*, a caffeine-rich infusion made from Yerba Maté leaves. A hot drink would be welcome and would set us up for an afternoon of concerted hummingbird hunting. Behind us were signs of beaver activity, a phantom forest—the white spars of dead beech trees pointing skywards from a flooded area and, beyond that, the jumbled mass of a dam. I had not expected to find beavers here, and asked Federico about them. He looked up through the steam rising from his maté.

"They're not native here. The government brought them to Tierra del Fuego in the 1950s, and released them into the countryside. They wanted to create a fur industry. That never happened, but the beavers liked it here. There weren't any natural predators, there were lots of trees and rivers and streams. It was like a kind of beaver heaven. Now they're a real problem. They're changing the landscape, and they've spread all over the place.

"The Chileans, they blame us for giving them beavers. We say that's only fair—they gave us rabbits . . ."

In 1936 four European Rabbits were released into the wild on the Chilean side of Tierra del Fuego. They bred like, well, rabbits and by 1953 their population on the island was estimated to number a staggering thirty million animals.

Federico's lighthearted quip may have had the virtue of truth, but it was making light of the scale of the problem of alien organisms in the environment. The beavers crossed into mainland Chile in the 1990s, and their overall population is now estimated to be in the region of one hundred thousand animals, a colossal population explosion from the initial fifty animals that were released in 1946 by the Argentinian government, and one which, despite some efforts to control their numbers, continues to grow with every passing year. Scientists estimate that the beavers have already destroyed some 120 square miles of pristine Patagonian habitat, an area larger than the English city of Birmingham. The law of unintended consequences was starkly playing out at the southernmost tip of South America.

If the beavers' impact was at a landscape scale, another invasive species was having a more insidious effect across South America. While we drank our maté, one of its kind was flying around us. What could be more benign than a bumblebee?

South America has twenty-four known species of bumblebee native to it, but the Buff-tailed Bumblebee is not one of them. Federico may have bemoaned the historic Chilean release of rabbits on Tierra del Fuego, but his Chilean neighbours on the mainland had inadvertently blotted their copybook more recently still. In 1998 the first Buff-tailed Bumblebees were introduced from Europe to Chile—nobody seems particularly sure why they were brought to the country, but one must assume that agriculture of one kind or another lay behind the decision. Buff-tailed Bumblebees are bred in vast numbers in Europe to be sold as fledgling colonies for seeding around commercial crops—for example, tomatoes—to assist with pollination. Inevitably, some bees have escaped into the wild and, provided they can find a source of nectar and a reasonably conducive climate, they go native, and spread. Chile is far from unique in this regard, as at least thirty countries worldwide now have Buff-tailed Bumblebees at large where they ought not to be.

One might think that having something as inoffensive as a pollinating insect introduced into an ecosystem would pose no significant risks, but it appears as if this is far from the case. Dave Goulson, professor of biology at the University of Sussex and preeminent bumblebee scientist, has suggested that the invaders may be contributing to the decline of native bumblebee species, through competition and, perhaps, through diseases they carry to which native bumblebees have little or no resistance.

Chilean scientists from the Universidad de los Lagos in Osorno have also been studying the invaders and quickly realised that the European bumblebees, in the temperate forests of Chile, were proficient and widespread nectar thieves. The bumblebees have learned to hack the usual pollinator and plant relationship, whereby a plant provides a pollinator—whether it's an insect or a hummingbird—with nectar in return for pollination services rendered by the inadvertent transmission of pollen from one flower to another. Instead, the bumblebees bite the walls of a flower's nectary and suck the nectar from within, bypassing entirely the effort involved in entering the flower via the petals in the usual manner evolution had intended.

The flowers examined in the study in question were those borne by bushes of Hardy Fuchsia—a plant that has evolved to be pollinated by Green-backed Firecrowns, hence its alternative English colloquial name, hummingbird fuchsia. Considering the possible impact of this nectar theft on the plants and their hummingbird pollinators, the scientists suggest that nectar robbing may trigger reductions in plant populations due to lowered reproductive success, and this in turn may impact upon the hummingbird populations associated with those plants. The very shape of the flowers may change in time as the bumblebees exert new evolutionary pressures upon the plants, with unforeseeable implications for the hummingbirds.

The study in question was only examining the incidence of nectar robbing in fuchsias, but, of course, there is no reason to suppose that

Buff-tailed Bumblebees will not be robbing other species of flowering plant wherever they are found in the Americas as a whole. Given that hummingbirds are found throughout the Americas, it is not unfair to suppose that other species of hummingbird far rarer than the widespread and adaptable Green-backed Firecrown may, in time, find themselves the unwitting victims of nectar crime performed by an invasive species of bumblebee.

Meanwhile, the fates of bees and hummingbirds alike are colliding across the Americas with the continuing widespread use of neonicotinoid (neonic) pesticides. These pesticides are widely used in agriculture, persist in water and soil for months or even years, and in plants are systemic—permeating everything from the tips of the roots to a plant's pollen and nectar. They are highly toxic to insects—and to birds too. The American Bird Conservancy has discovered that one seed coated with imidacloprid, a popular neonic, is enough to kill a songbird. Researchers are concerned that repeated ingestion of nectar laced with neonics will have the same effect it does on bees—a disruption of their brain function and, specifically, their short-term memory and their ability to navigate.

For many hummingbirds, both of those brain functions are critical. On a day-to-day basis hummingbirds, like bees, return to favoured and remembered nectar sources time and again. Birders sometimes refer to this as "working a trapline," a reference to the activities of fur-hunters in Alaska and Canada. Moreover, some hummingbirds, like the Rufous Hummingbirds I had searched for in Alaska, are long-distance migrants, and will rely on their brain function to navigate distances that seem unfeasibly long for such a small creature. The loss of this ability, in what is known as migratory disorientation, could lead to significant mortality.

Rufous Hummingbirds have been in long-term decline since the late 1960s—a cumulative decline that represents a staggering 62 percent of their population lost between 1966 and 2014. Researchers are concerned that neonics may have played a part in that decline—Dr. Christine Bishop, of Environment and Climate Change Canada, has been studying the prevalence of pesticides in Rufous Hummingbirds in British Columbia, in the heart of their core breeding area, though it should be noted that the historic range and migration routes of the birds overlaps some of the most intensive agricultural areas of North America. Other factors may be playing a part in the hummingbirds' decline—habitat loss and climate change being implicated too—but Bishop's findings give ample cause for concern. By collecting Rufous and Anna's Hummingbird urine and faeces for testing in the vicinity of commercial blueberry fields in British Columbia, she has been able to establish that the birds, either directly from nectar imbibed or from insects eaten that have been visiting toxic plants, are themselves contaminated with neonics—a contamination mirrored in native bumblebees in her study areas. She discovered that the birds' urine contained pesticides at a rate of almost four parts per billion—a concentration that, to a lay person, does not sound particularly high, but to a scientist it rings alarm bells.

This was one study, in one corner of North America. When I thought of how widespread the use of neonics was, and how much of South America was being turned into agricultural land, and at such a pace, the implications for hummingbirds seemed bleaker than ever.

That this entire train of thought ran through my mind whilst sipping maté on the shores of the Beagle Channel felt like an unwelcome intrusion. The guileless Buff-tailed Bumblebees nectaring on yellow wildflowers at my feet had started a chain reaction. They would themselves, in time, make a very tiny contribution to science—I was contacted by a Chilean bee researcher, José Montalva, working at East Central University in Oklahoma, asking where I had seen them. They turned out to be some of the most southerly Buff-tailed Bumblebees ever recorded in South America; an unwelcome accolade, I felt. Professor Dave Goulson, writing in 2017, hypothesised that the climate of Tierra del Fuego might be too cold for Buff-tailed Bumblebees, though he rather doubted that this would prove to be the case. Just a couple of years later, at the southernmost extremity of the island, with snow visible on the landscape around us and the hum of foraging bees in my ears, I was unhappy to confirm that his fears had been abundantly realised.

It was time to move on, and to listen for the hum I really wanted to hear—that of a Green-backed Firecrown in flight. The bumblebees on the wing were, perhaps, a good omen of a kind. If the temperature was still warm enough to sustain the fast metabolisms of bumblebees, perhaps one or two hardy examples of their avian counterparts might not have migrated north just yet. I told myself that as we trudged along the shore of the Beagle Channel, but I was not sure if I really believed it.

I could draw a little more solace from Darwin's observations about the climate in late December 1832. He noted, "The climate is certainly wretched: the summer solstice was now passed, yet every day snow fell on the hills, and in the valleys there was rain, accompanied by sleet. From the damp and boisterous state of the atmosphere, not cheered by a gleam of sunshine, one fancied the climate even worse than it really was."

While Federico seemed pessimistic about our chances of finding a hummingbird, the present weather did not seem so very different from what Darwin had recorded at the height of summer. I preferred to remain optimistic.

Perhaps I should not have been surprised to find a penguin—I was, after all, only a few miles away from their nearest breeding colony. All the same, breasting a rocky bluff to find a sleeping Magellanic Penguin basking in the weak sun on the shore at my feet was, nonetheless, startling. Quite unconcerned by our presence, it cracked open an eye to look at us before drifting back to sleep once more. It brought home just how hardy the hummingbirds were to exist at such a frontier for their kind. This was a cool climate more suited to birds clad in a thick layer of insulating blubber. A well-fed penguin could afford to spend some time dozing in the sun. A hummingbird, on the other hand, needed to feed at regular intervals throughout the course of the day: if a bird remained at this southerly latitude, it ought to be feeding voraciously.

Early European visitors to Tierra del Fuego placed great emphasis on sheltered bays in which they could find respite from the turbulent waters of the Atlantic and Pacific Oceans. The names they gave some of those safe anchorages reflect the sanctuary they found, such as the Bay of Good Success. The German cruiser SMS *Dresden* found respite in one such secluded bay when fleeing from the British towards her eventual final resting place at Isla Robinson Crusoe—the sole German survivor of the Battle of the Falkland Islands in the First World War, she hid for a while in the Beagle Channel in early 1915, provisioned by sympathetic Germans from the Chilean port city of Punta Arenas on the north coast of Isla Grande. British residents in Punta Arenas, aware that the *Dresden* was rumoured to still be in the area, were said to have noticed dogs vanishing from the city streets, and to have joked about the doggy flavour of the sausages served to the *Dresden's* crew.

In the late afternoon, with steady rain now falling, it was at another small, secluded bay that we finally found what I hoped so fervently to see here at the End of the World. The bay itself was tiny, too small to hide a fugitive battleship, and barely large enough to provide shelter to a pair of shy Kelp Geese, the male as white as the snow that topped the surrounding mountains. Between the shore and the steep lower slopes of those mountains was a flatter area of scattered trees and lush, chest-deep vegetation, a sheltered bowl almost completely enclosed and protected from the elements. From the narrow, black stony strip of beach on which we stood we could see three firetrees, all of which still had scarlet blossoms scattered amongst their branches. Federico perked up at the sight of them.

"This, this is our best chance, Jon. If the hummingbird has not left for the winter, it is here we will find it . . ."

The rain fell in curtains, intensifying to the point where we could barely see the trees some fifty metres away from us. We sheltered as best we could beneath the branches of a Southern Beech tree. Our breath steamed and hung in the cold air, clouds of our own making. I drew the hood of my jacket tighter around my face. Water was dripping from the peak of my cap, and I was beginning to feel uncomfortably chilled. My optimism was hard to maintain, under the circumstances.

A caesura in the rain's drumbeat was the moment an unseen Green-backed Firecrown had been waiting for. Other hummingbirds might wait for falling rain to stop entirely, but these hardy hummingbirds had learned to make the best of a bad lot—a short period of persistent drizzle was nothing to him. Federico and I saw him at the same time, both exclaiming aloud as he appeared at the largest firetree, working his way along the seaward side of the tree, darting in and out from the dripping red flowers, attending each blossom for a split second, just long enough to drink whatever chilly nectar he could find within.

In these watery, dull conditions his crown gave only the merest hint of the fiery orange that lent him his name, fleeting flashes visible only in the moment he turned his body to precisely the right angle to allow the feathers to flare for us, gone as quickly as it came, like a spark sent flying from a flint and steel that extinguished and failed to catch fire. The rest of his plumage, his green upperparts and white underparts, was readily lost in the background noise of wet, shining green leaves through which he threaded his path. It was easy to lose him altogether for a while before, miraculously, a glint of light from his crown would betray him once more.

For the next hour I watched the hummingbird feeding, marvelling at his tenacity in the face of the conditions. It seemed like he was finding slim pickings this late in the season, and I wondered how long he would remain in the area before heading north to warmer, easier surroundings for the winter. It would, surely, be only a matter of days before he was gone. I would almost certainly outstay him, though my return to Shetland would scarcely see me migrating in search of better weather conditions.

In the event, he turned out to be the first and the last humming-bird I would see in Tierra del Fuego. Like his counterpart nine thousand miles away in Alaska, the Rufous Hummingbird that had fleetingly visited the feeder hanging beneath the eaves of the Eyak Lake Compound lodge outside Cordova, he existed at the very limits of what was possible for his kind. I would leave the Americas having seen hummingbirds that persisted just a few hundred miles from the Arctic and Antarctic Circles and, in between, in habitats that varied from arid deserts to saturated cloudforests, from sea level amongst mangroves to high in the Andean páramo, within sight of the At-lantic Ocean and in splendid island isolation deep in the Pacific.

EPILOGUE

Those who glitter with the glory of the hummingbird, meaning
Death
Those who sit in the stye of contentment, meaning
Death
Those who suffer the ecstasy of the animals, meaning
Death
Are become unsubstantial, reduced by a wind

—From *"Marina," by T. S. Eliot, 1930*

I HAD SEEN A GREAT MANY OTHER BIRDS BESIDE THE HUMMING-birds I found between Alaska and Tierra del Fuego, but my passion for them remained undimmed—their myriad, iridescent colours were simply without compare anywhere in the bird world. Having spent weeks of my life in their company, and years searching for them wherever they were to be found, I came away with a fresh appreciation for their adaptability—an ability to exploit almost every habitat the Americas afforded them, despite what at first glance seemed like the obvious constraint of relying on such a high-energy diet. With hindsight, I had come to realise that, far from being a hindrance, the consumption of nectar was like ingesting high-octane fuel—it allowed them to perform at the outer limits of what was biomechanically possible for a bird. At every turn, the hummingbirds had astounded me.

I knew I was immensely fortunate to have had this opportunity. What rested uneasily within me was the dawning realisation that, wherever I went, I had seen evidence that their world was changing irrevocably. Habitat loss alone would have been bad enough, let alone at the scale and pace that was taking place in Brazil during the latter stages of my journey. Economic development, lauded as the catalyst of social change and improvement by governments the world over, applied pressures to land that had, for millennia, been relatively untouched by the agencies of mankind. A legacy of invasive species introduced by man in years past placed other hummingbirds in imminent peril of extinction. Climate change appeared to be wreaking more profound changes still, altering the suitability of entire ecosystems for some species, and contributing to the disruption of migratory habits that had gone unaltered for millennia beforehand.

Here and there I had encountered examples of where human intervention had come just in time and, locally at least, had pulled a hummingbird back from the brink. The otherworldly Marvellous Spatuletail in Peru was thriving in habitat that, just a few years previously, had been a working coffee farm. In Ecuador, local women were growing native flowering plants that just might help to sustain what was left of the entire world population of Black-breasted Pufflegs. Yet I could not escape the feeling that these efforts were papering over the cracks that were appearing across the continents in which the hummingbirds were found. They were indeed, I realised now, the most beautiful canary in the coalmine.

The irony of that metaphor was, itself, black as carbon. All of the pressures the hummingbirds were enduring were, ultimately, caused by us—our expanding population was placing the habitats they relied upon under untenable stress. Our use of fossil fuels was a convenient scapegoat for the ills of the world and, yes, I was feeling increasingly uneasy about the flights I had taken in the course of my travels, but I felt this avoided a more uncomfortable, unpalatable truth. There were simply too many of us, living in a global society that ceaselessly and carelessly consumed resources of all kinds—a society that venerated economic development as the engine that powered the supply of our needs, and to which sustainability was simply a cost to be factored in, if at all. Our carbon emissions were a symptom of a deeper, more profound problem, of which I was far from uniquely a contributing part. I feared that our epiphanies about our effect on the planet came too late in the day, and either could not or would not resonate amongst enough of us to effect meaningful change. Alexander von Humboldt recognised that an informed and empowered minority was not enough—writing in 1799, he noted sadly, "Ideas can only be of use if they start living in many minds."

Maybe too much had gone before for us to do any more than locally assuage our guilt here and there whilst, inexorably, on the global stage things would only get worse. It seemed we may yet be a very selfish ape indeed.

I had, in recent weeks, been corresponding with novelist Jeff VanderMeer. Jeff's writing has an unsettling and compelling quality, and a recurrent theme is a dystopian near future, where humanity reaps what it has sown in what remains of the natural world. Hummingbirds, meanwhile, have a special resonance for him. He recalled,

When I was eight, very ill with asthma and allergies, on oxygen at altitude in Cuzco [Peru], I had a kind of vision involving hummingbirds. I have to tell you, I felt extremely old at eight years old. My body felt decrepit and malfunctioning back then. And I was lying in bed, staring out the hotel window, which was right up against a hillside, with a kind of little biosphere of moss and lichen and ferns in front. And just then as I was looking out the window, two amazing iridescent hummingbirds appeared, courting. And they just hovered there for several seconds, but by the time anyone else came into the room they were gone. I just was so moved by their presence, existing in such an altered state. Their beauty was so at odds with what I was feeling physically, it was a kind of miracle. So every time I see a hummingbird, I think of that amazing moment, that drew me so out of myself.

His next novel, *Hummingbird Salamander*, takes that youthful introduction to hummingbirds and inflects it with the concerns for the future that Jeff and so many more of us were now harbouring. Jeff told me, "In the novel the protagonist is given a taxidermied hummingbird that proves to be of an extinct species. The taxidermy is illegal contraband, and figuring out where it came from and why she was given it sends her into a downward spiral and a maze of wildlife traffickers, eco-terrorists, and more . . ."

The hummingbird as a fragile symbol of nature's vulnerability was playing on my mind when, with a day to kill in London on my way home, I found myself walking through the underpass that led me towards the Victoria & Albert (V&A) Museum. I was not paying attention to my surroundings and, when the hummingbird appeared beside me, the moment had a dreamlike quality. A billboard, metres long and high, advertised the imminent arrival of the Cirque de Soleil at the Royal Albert Hall. The show in question was *Luzia*, a "poetic and acrobatic ode to the rich, vibrant culture of Mexico." Larger than life, a man's torso in a white tuxedo was surmounted by a vibrantly colourful hummingbird's head, with one hummingbird wing extended behind his shoulder. Without my trying, another hummingbird had found me.

In the museum, it took some time to find the exhibit I was looking for. Even the helpful museum staff struggled, at first, to uncover the sixteenth-century carved boxwood and silver-gilt triptych of scenes from the Crucifixion that I hoped to see. Neither I nor the V&A gallery assistant were expecting it to be quite as small as it was—small enough that it was hidden away from the public in a dimly lit metal drawer in, rather counterintuitively, the Europe 1600–1800 Gallery. What had drawn me to see this was not the intricate carving of the eight-centimetre-tall piece itself, but the lining of the triptych's tableaux—a delicate filigree of hummingbird feathers. The triptych dates from the time when the amanteca Aztec featherworkers' skills were being turned to produce Christian iconography for export to Europe—the first examples of a commercial trade in hummingbirds that was to continue, unabated, into the early twentieth century. Under a white LED, those four-hundred-year-old feathers flared into emerald and sapphire life again, a faded but still potent shining shadow of the shimmering feathers that once graced living, breathing birds.

From our first recorded encounters with hummingbirds, it seems we have been consumers of their beauty, using them to gild our religions, our homes, and our haute couture. Even when trade in their skins finally petered out, the assault on their kind had simply changed its approach to become something more insidious. Our consumption of all things was now so wanton it threatened the very places that the hummingbirds, and myriad other life besides, depended upon.

This account of my travels begins, and ends, with wildfires. That should just be a terrible, statistically unlikely coincidence, but I'm not so sure it really is, these days. I began my journey beneath a pall of smoke from a wildfire on the edge of the Alaskan Arctic. Smoke from wildfires that burned, out of control, in Australia in 2019 had been recorded in South America whilst I was looking for firecrowns in Tierra del Fuego, the Land of Fire. In Colombia, I watched grown men reduced to tears in a café whilst footage of kangaroos racing, helplessly, into the flames in the Australian outback played on the television.

The ripples of the stones we had thrown into the pond in recent centuries were now being felt worldwide. For the hummingbirds' sakes, and for that of all global biodiversity, I returned from the hummingbirds' world fearing the waves to follow.

ACKNOWLEDGMENTS

My journey through the hummingbirds' world would have been quite impossible without the assistance, cooperation, encouragement, and generous guidance of a host of kind people that spanned continents. Many of them were already friends, and many of those I met on my travels were set to become close friends. Adrian Cobas Arenciba; Dr. Richard Bate; Matt Berry; García Bloj; Tessa Boase; Diego Calderón-Franco; John "Killer" Carnegie; Laura Becerril Carretero; Guto Carvalho; Elizabeth Cory-Pearce; Adrianne Covino; Sarah Cuttle; Jonas D'Abronzo; Esteban Daniels; Victor Manuel Martos Davila; Teresa, Sue, and Earl DeKoker; Duverney Ospina Diaz; Brian Egan; Victor Emanuel; David Fairhurst; Valda Farmer; Dick Filby; Ivan Flores; Jonathan Franzen; Richard Garrigues; Caroline Gibson; Courtney Gillette; Mark Golley; Wendy and Colin Grant; Paul Greenfield; David Lynn Grimes; Jair Serna Guardabosque; Gleison Fernando Guarin; Nicola Halcrow; Joe Harkness; Maurice Henderson; Juana and Bernabé Hernández; Rachael Hume; Judd Hunt; Lorna Hunt; Leah Irvine; Kenn Kaufman; Mitch Kochanski; Dr. Alex Lees; Dr. Sara Lodge; James Lowen; Pablo Manríquez; Beezy Marsh; Angel Martinez; Orestes "Chino" Martinez; Kate McLaughlin; Andy Mitchell; Kensuke Miyazaki; José Montalva; Federico Ezequiel Moyano; Nils Navarro; Pat O'Donnell; Lars Olavsson; Milton Oldman;

Ilka Paulentz; Henry Gonzáles Pinedo; Germán Recabarren; Pam Reid; Jose Antonio Padilla Reyes; Marcelo Rossi; Forrest Rowland; Arnulfo Sanchez Salazar; Chris Sharpe; Richard Smyth; Andrew Stafford; Dr. Helen Steward; John Thomas; Brydon Thomason; Pepper Trail; Jiri Trnka; Luis Gonzaga "Zaga" Truzzi; Jeff VanderMeer; Nikki Waldron; Rebecca Wheeler; Rob Williams; Dr. Jonathan Wills; Stuart Winter.

To you all, and to anyone I have carelessly omitted, my sincere thanks. I couldn't have done the tale of the hummingbirds of the Americas justice without you.

As I found on my travels, there are myriad local initiatives throughout the Americas where folk are trying to protect, conserve, and restore the habitats upon which hummingbirds, and countless other birds and wildlife depend. They all need all the help and support they can get. As I know all too well, for anyone contemplating diving into the hummingbirds' world, to learn more about them and their conservation, it's hard to know where to begin. I wholeheartedly recommend joining the Neotropical Bird Club (www.neotropicalbirdclub.org), the American Bird Conservancy (www.abcbirds.org), and Audubon (www.audubon.org)—for starters . . .

Once more, I must thank Tim Bates, my agent at Peters, Fraser & Dunlop, for setting the ball rolling. At Bloomsbury, I must thank my editor Michael Fishwick for his peerless support; and at Basic Books, I must thank my editor Lara Heimert for her support and for introducing me at just the right time to Roger Labrie, to whom I owe a particular debt of gratitude for his light, assured touch; Katie Lambright for her good-humoured patience; as well as Brynn Warriner; Shazia Amin; and Liz Wetzel.

Closer to home, I have Ethan Dunn to thank for hummingbird notebooks and calendars that gave my travels structure and form, and for his understanding when I was away for so long. We'll get to Chile one day, I promise.

Above all, my heartfelt thanks go, once again, to Roberta—her patience and support were boundless during the many months I was away from home. I really could not have contemplated this journey, let alone embarked upon it, without her.

Jon
www.jondunn.com
@dunnjons

PERMISSIONS

Page 43: Excerpt from *Kingbird Highway* reproduced by kind permission of the author, Kenn Kaufman.

Page 92: Excerpt from *Endemic Birds of Cuba* reproduced by kind permission of the author, Nils Navarro.

Page 192: Excerpt from "Humming-Bird" from *The Cambridge Edition of The Works of DH Lawrence: The Poems* by D. H. Lawrence (Cambridge University Press, 2013). © Cambridge University Press 2013. Reproduced by permission of Paper Lion Ltd, The Estate of Frieda Lawrence Ravagli and Cambridge University Press.

Page 220: Excerpt from "The Hummingbird Whisperer," from *Mama Amazonica* by Pascale Petit (Bloodaxe Books, 2017). Reproduced with permission of Bloodaxe Books.

Page 307: Excerpt from "Marina" from *Collected Poems 1909–1962* by T.S. Eliot. Copyright © 1952 by Houghton Mifflin Harcourt Publishing Company, renewed 1980 by Esme Valerie Eliot. Reprinted by permission of Houghton Mifflin Harcourt. All rights reserved.

INDEX